r calls for a radical change in our view of religion, rejecting
deas both for and against as provincial, out of touch with the
lacking in explanatory power, and argues that no view of faith
to acknowledge its power as well as its weaknesses can survive
crutiny.

phasizes the prominence of the desire for and experience of
n the world's religions — something mostly ignored by philosophers
ion — and recognizes the conditioning effect of the social and
l environment on all religious beliefs and customs — something
most believers deny or concede only partially. This opens the way
ntifying the core of religion as an experience of the sustaining,
orming power of a transcendental orientation coming to different
rns of expression in the earth's family of spiritual traditions.

uilding on this global picture of religion and using methods adapted
a the natural and social sciences, the author develops an explanatory
ory of religion as the result of humanity's resourceful finitude in
ding ways to overcome the problems of vulnerability and pain in a
sterious, threatening yet also sustaining cosmos, depicting the questing
irit as an adventure of nature and an affirmation of the earth, as well as a
eler held out for signals of transcendence. His theory also shows why
ligion exists in a variety of forms all over the world.

The book ends by applying the theory to give a provocative view of the
uture of religion in a world wary of promises but as hungry as ever for
guidance and well-being.

Dr. Martin Prozesky is Associate Professor in the Department of Religious
Studies at the University of Natal in Pietermaritzburg, South Africa,
specializing in the philosophy of religion. He lectured previously at Rhodes
University and the University in what is now Zimbabwe, working between
those two appointments as an editor in the field of academic publishing.
He studied at Rhodes University, Trinity College, Oxford, and at the
Episcopal Divinity School in Cambridge, Massachusetts. Dr. Prozesky has
published articles in theological journals in Britain and South Africa and is
editor of a new journal called *Religion in Southern Africa*. In 1982 he was
visiting scholar at the School of Theology in Claremont, California.

RELIGION AND ULTIMATE WELL-BEING

An Explanatory Theory

Martin Prozesky

Associate Professor in the Department of Religious Studies, University of Natal, Pietermaritzburg

St. Martin's Press   New York

ISBN 0–312–67057–5

Library of Congress Cataloging in Publication Data
Prozesky, Martin.
Religion and ultimate well-being.
Bibliography: p.
Includes index.
1. Religion.   I. Title
BL48.P76   1984   200′.1   84–3340
ISBN 0–312–67057–5

Why don't you examine the religious life itself? Examine especially those highest reaches of the spirit in which all other activities are held back or even suspended, and the whole soul is dissolved in an immediate sense of the infinite and the eternal. . . . Only those who have observed and truly come to know people in these stirrings can rediscover religion in its external manifestations (Friedrich Schleiermacher 1806: 21).

There is a verge of the mind which these things haunt; and whispers therefrom mingle with the operations of our understanding, even as the waters of the infinite ocean send their waves to break among the pebbles that lie upon our shores (William James 1902: 421).

Contents

Acknowledgements

A work like this, drawing on all that the author has experienced and learnt concerning religion and several other spheres of interest, naturally carries with it an indebtedness much too extensive to be fully apparent even to the recipient, and certainly too extensive for complete, individual identification. That general assistance is none the less gratefully acknowledged, and will be apparent in the following pages to family members, mentors, colleagues, writers, students and friends, and also to a few respected intellectual adversaries. Touching many personal matters, these debts are perhaps best left unpublicised anyway.

That the ideas provoked in part by these benefactors should now be appearing in print is, on the other hand, a matter for which specific thanks are due to a number of people and organisations. Professor John Hick gave indispensable encouragement for initiating and conducting the project and much practical advice; my departmental colleague Mr Patrick Maxwell has throughout been a fertile source of information, criticism and support, while academic friends elsewhere proved invaluable in providing me with detailed criticisms of a draft paper from which the present work has grown. In addition to Professor Hick they are Dr James Moulder, now at the University of Cape Town but then also at the University of Natal, who also commented helpfully on chapter three; Dr David Novitz of the Department of Philosophy and Religious Studies at the University of Canterbury in Christchurch, New Zealand; Mr Iain Boal, presently working in Cambridge, Massachusetts; and Professor T. A. Burkill, formerly head of the Department of Theology and Philosophy at the University in what is now Harare, Zimbabwe.

Completion of the book was made possible by a year's sabbatical leave generously granted and partly financed by the Council of the University of Natal; by a University Travelling Fellowship awarded by The Ernest Oppenheimer Memorial Trust, and by a

Senior Research Grant from the Human Sciences Research
Council in Pretoria. Opinions expressed and conclusions reached
in this book are not, of course, to be regarded as those of any of
the parties to whom I am indebted for assistance. I must also
thank the President, Dean and Faculty of the Southern California
School of Theology in Claremont, and especially the senior staff
of its Center for Process Studies, for giving me the status of
Visiting Scholar for the spring semester in 1982; and the governing body of Trinity College, Oxford, for generous and helpful
arrangements in the latter part of that year. During the course of
my visits to these and other centres several scholars kindly
provided verbal comments and suggestions about particular
aspects of the present work, and I am bound to thank them by
name also: Dr Bruce Long, Professors Carl Ernst, Frederick
Sontag, John Hutchison, David Griffin, Dean Freudenberger and
John B. Cobb Jr, all of Claremont, California; Professor Roy
Fairchild of the San Franscisco Theological Seminary; the Revd.
Dr Peter Hinchliff of Balliol College, Oxford, and Mr Edward
Robinson of the Religious Experience Research Unit in Oxford,
as well as Professors Ninian Smart, Wilfred Cantwell Smith,
Maurice Wiles and Basil Mitchell. Along the way there were
many others whose informal reactions and interest are greatly
appreciated but who are too numerous for me to mention
individually. I am also grateful to colleagues at the University of
Natal who have helped me with their expertise in various connections. The encouragement of Professors Victor Bredenkamp and
Gordon Hunnings is particularly valued. My wife, Mrs Doreen
Johnston and Mrs Joy Randall provided typing skills of a high
order, while the editorial and production staff of The Macmillan
Press have been models of assistance to me in preparing the book
for publication. I only wish I could have made superior use of
such exceptional helpers and friends.

Lastly, I must record especial gratitude for patience, support
and companionship to my immediate family, particularly my
wife, for whom the following pages are by now an oft-heard tale.
But in them their voices are also present, and I, for one, am
thankful.

University of Natal   M.P.
Pietermaritzburg
South Africa

1 Rethinking the Meaning of Religion

This book adds its voice to the growing call for a radically new understanding of religion, because the ones we have inherited cannot do justice to the global phenomenon of faith in all its basic forms and characteristics. And since this phenomenon has been a dominant concern of people in virtually every society for thousands of years, until we improve our understanding of it we are unlikely to develop reliable concepts of what it means to be human either.

There is as yet no standard conception of religion even among believers, which is itself a sign of the problem before us. Seeking insight into the spiritual life, enquirers who consult the writings of famous experts will find there as many views of the subject as there are authors. Friedrich Schleiermacher wrote that faith is a well-founded sense of absolute dependence, while Freud thought of it as an obsessional neurosis. William James on the other hand declared that religion comprises a relationship with what he called friendly, higher powers. Emile Durkheim pronounced it to be the result of social causes, whereas A. N. Whitehead defined it as what people do with their own solitariness. For his part Rudolf Otto saw the basis of religion as a sense of the holy, but Paul Tillich, a younger contemporary of Otto also from Protestant Germany, described it as ultimate concern. When influential writers dealing with a common subject come to such diverse conclusions we have every reason to suspect that much rethinking still needs to be done.

In particular there are seven problems that seriously undermine most existing views of religion. Seen in isolation each one is disturbing; taken together they imply an urgent need for sweeping conceptual improvement. Let us consider them in turn. The first one relates to our revolutionary modern understanding of the

1

nature and discovery of knowledge itself, in any field of enquiry. We ourselves create not only the concepts that express our findings but also the world-views that coordinate them into meaningful patterns. As human creations they reflect and share humanity's cognitive characteristics: fallible, evolving, experimental, incomplete, provisional and tinged with local colour. We have learnt that the search for knowledge is always affected by these factors and that within the limits they impose the most fertile method is rigorous logical and observational testing of surmises about the problems we try to solve. Above all we have come to recognise that although immense progress is possible our understanding of things is never complete and that in this respect there are no such things for us as prefect accuracy, absolute certainty or immunity to supersession by better ideas. Finite mental equipment like ours means that there will necessarily be limits to what we can grasp or produce with it.

Religions generate concepts and world-views. Therefore our understanding of them must be changed by the new insights we now have into the nature of human cognition. In particular we now recognise that world-views are especially provisional because they say so much more than any of us or even all of us could presently verify. Among them the greatest reliability attaches to ones that are consistent with and can be supported by the largest number of tested observations. All world-views have what we could call a built-in expansion factor. This is the extent to which they go beyond the observations and experiences which support them. Some rest on few, others on many. The less there are, the more speculative the world-view and the more tenuous its account of things, though many people, especially those who are unaware of this limitation, may none the less find immense personal satisfaction from it. We must of course take great care not to confuse psychological considerations of this kind with logical and cognitive ones. In any event, the point at issue has momentous consequences for religion. All the existing faiths involve world-views which formed when relatively or even extremely meagre amounts of rigorous, observational support was available. Therefore their cognitive status is correspondingly tenuous. Yet they are among the most influential ideas ever propounded. The great ages of religious creativity and the modern mind are on opposite sides of a mental revolution with far-reaching, relativising implications not only for the way modern scholars should perceive the spiritual life they study but also for the spiritual life itself. Prevailing views of religion like the ones referred to above mostly pay insufficient attention to this revolution, and in the ranks of believers the majority appears to be oblivious of it. To that extent they are unable to help us understand religion. In this book by contrast, the modern conception of knowledge plays a decisive part.

The next problem is conceptual parochialism. Inherited ideas about religion usually have their origins in a time when there was little or even no accurate, extensive knowledge of other spiritual cultures. In the present century and especially in the past few decades that situation has changed dramatically. It has been possible to investigate the religions of humanity on a planetary scale and for believers to get seriously to grips with the fact that not only are there mature faiths other than their own but also that there are major similarities as well as differences in the ways the various strands of the human family have lived and thought religiously. Within each branch religious ideas have emerged and developed largely in isolation from most of the other branches, though the work of Wilfred Cantwell Smith has shown that there were some important mutual links among several of the great faiths in ages past (1981). The problem that results is as follows: how can concepts that formed in isolation in one among many different traditions of religious existence be applied to others, let alone to all of them, without serious distortion? Now that we are at last able to investigate religion globally we find ourselves hampered by parochial concepts of the phenomenon we are investigating. This is a problem that always occurs when old isolations end and the world is found to be bigger, richer and more diverse than our own backyards, mental and otherwise. The ancient Egyptians with their rainless climate spoke of rain as Nile-in-the-sky, and used the same words for northwards and down-stream on the one hand, and for southwards and upstream on the other, once more basing things on the great river that sustains their land. The Euphrates, which flows southward in part of its course, taxed the Egyptians' conception of things to breaking point, drawing from them the wonderfully instructive but hope-lessly inept assertion that the Euphrates goes downstream upstream (Frankfort 1971: 45f). Like climates, cultures and religious traditions vary, and ideas that make perfect sense in one can cause conceptual havoc when imposed on another or on them all. And that, precisely, is the second problem about most of our inherited notions of religion. They belong too much to the provinces and the past to do justice to the planetary present and whatever global future awaits us, if any.

The next reason for criticising inherited ideas about religion is closely related to the one just identified. It is a matter of severely incomplete information. A set of ideas based, however accurately, on the spiritual habits of Anglican bishops is obviously not going to suffice for an investigation into divination among the Zulus or Zen meditation on Mount Baldy. The other side of the coin of parochial concepts is parochial information, and it means that a good many of us still carry in our minds a severely incomplete mental map of religion, rather like those mediaeval charts which are tolerably accurate around the Mediterranean and western Europe but deteriorate steadily into sheer guesswork for other regions. The religious world therefore needs new and better maps, as a few pioneering thinkers have forcefully argued. We all know that defective ones lead to frustrating and even fruitless travels because of the inaccuracies they contain about parts of the landscape.

The fourth criticism is that even on their own ground most of our received notions about religion are at fault because they so seldom give due prominence, not to say pride of place, to the enormous importance of salvation and related matters in actual religious experience. As will be shown in later chapters and as is implied in the title of this book, the concern people have with salvation, or whatever else we should call the desire to be delivered from the deepest and most enduring of our predicaments, is centrally important in the religious life. This is not speculation but demonstrable fact. Yet the astonishing truth is that prevailing notions usually gloss over it or even fail to register it at all as a defining characteristic of religion. This is especially so with most of the classical academic views; only one in the list above even hints at it, namely James, and the list is typical. Ironically, the major thinker who comes closest to focussing attention on it is Marx; his dismissal of religion as a fake cure for a grimly real ailment may cause indignation among the devout but at least it recognises what religion is all about: the need for healing. In this respect Marx is ironically closer to the great spiritual leaders of the past than many latter day religious thinkers. In any case the problem caused by neglecting topics like salvation is severe. To revert to the metaphor used previously about mediaeval maps, the position turns out to be worse than just a matter of inaccuracy concerning religious territories beyond one's own, caused by poor information. Even on home ground where the maps had seemed tolerably reliable they turn out to omit an exceedingly important, not to say supremely important feature of the very landscape on which the cartographers lived. As later chapters will show, a concept of religion that fails to deal with salvation and its equivalent concepts fails to deal with religion, for, as John Hick says, salvation is what religion is all about (1981: 5).

The fifth criticism to be levelled at inherited ideas about the spiritual life concerns those that come to us from believing scholars. They seldom explain their subject or even try to explain it in any rigorous sense of the word. But explanation, in which we turn from description and interpretation, which tell us what a phenomenon is, to saying why it exists, is surely the supreme goal to which academic investigation should work. Therefore an account of religion which provides no element of explanation must be incomplete even if it deals splendidly with the pre-paratory tasks of describing, characterising and interpreting the subject, indispensable though these are in their own right. It is not enough to be told that religion is faith in the grace of God or veneration for one's ancestral spirits, or even a path to salvation. We also need to know why such beliefs are held, why people spend large sums of money building economically unproductive structures like cathedrals or mosques or meditation centres, why they suffer (and inflict) martyrdom, why doctrines and rituals differ, why faiths persist and sometimes die. A worthwhile view of religion should help us to find the answers to questions like these. To do so it must have an explanatory function (Smart 1978: 183).

The sixth criticism concerns popular views of religion held by many believers and comprises a cluster of related complaints. For one thing these views seldom, if ever, give a satisfactory account of the rejection of religion. Sometimes this is even dismissed by means of rank caricature, sceptics being portrayed as immoral or shallow-minded. Why decent, brilliant and highly educated people should reject religion is not a question to which most of the devout have a convincing answer. Another failure is unwillingness to recognise the amount of human creativity which religion, even if valid, necessarily involves, a failure often revealed by the refusal to take seriously some very telling proposals from thinkers like

Feuerbach and Freud about the formation of the concept of God. Our forebears invented religious concepts themselves just as surely as they made flint knives or discovered how to make fire. Of this the inferential evidence is conclusive, as will be shown later in the present book. But nobody invented the experience-able powers to which those concepts often refer. Next there is a frequently unconvincing account of other faiths. Some valuable anthologies of these accounts have been published, (Hick and Hebblethwaite 1980; Thomas 1969) so no more need be said here except that it stretches credibility to breaking point for a person in one religion to portray as confused or wrong the members of other faiths whom personal contact shows to be models of good-ness, learning and mental sophistication. This is especially so when the beliefs that are rejected show some striking resem-blances to those held by the person who declares them to be confused or mistaken.

The seventh and last criticism is levelled at concepts of religion propounded by authoritative sceptics, despite much that is instructive and valuable in their work. Freud's idea that faith is a species of obsessional neurosis is hard to credit when one thinks of the mental qualities of a Buddha or Thomas Aquinas. Believers may be wrong but it is asking too much to brand them all as even mildly insane, though religion naturally also has its quota of behavioural oddities and deviations (Küng 1979; Freud 1943). Ludwig Feuerbach's theory that religion is a projection of human ideals, like Freud's use of the same cognitive principle in order to explain belief in God, is in itself a valuable disclosure of part of the complex process by which theistic religion works, but tells us nothing about Taoism, or Shankara, or Zen, or religious natural-ism in the west. It helps us understand the formation of the concept of a personal deity, but this is merely to account for one populous region on the religious landscape, leaving the rest entirely untouched. And the materialistic tenet that faith can be no more than illusion is itself unproven by these thinkers. By what criteria can it be shown that even the most incisive materialist is a better guide to the nature of reality as a whole than a Plato, a Muhammed or a Galilean? In Freud, Feuerbach and *Das Kapital* we are not told. And if faith is merely the delusory refuge of the oppressed, why does it flourish in the world's richest and least down-trodden nation? Another problem about these theorists is their subjective reductionism, the doctrine that religion involves no more than human factors. The evidence of actual religious phenomena, carefully examined, simply refutes this assumption. Those who have so theorised have correctly drawn attention to the importance of human factors in the genesis of faith, but there is no way of successfully avoiding the conclusion that more is involved than just projective thinking, wish-fulfilment or any other merely subjective process. Interpreting the objective side of religion in the terms used by believers may be a mistake. But to say that it is merely subjective is to advertise a misunderstanding of faith and indeed also of human existence, as will be shown in Chapters 4 and 5.

It would be difficult to demonstrate that there is a single cause for all these problems. But prominent among whatever central factors can be diagnosed as responsible for the lack of a satisfactory account of religion is the absence, in the work of the people we have considered, of sufficient attention to the problems of method in dealing with this subject. It is a shortcoming which the present book tries to help remedy. With difficulties of this magnitude to overcome it is surely clear that we really do need a radically new understanding of religion, and some extremely important contributions to the process of rethinking its meaning have already been made by thinkers like John Hick, Ninian Smart, Wilfred Cantwell Smith and others. They have proposed important solutions to the problems of parochial concepts and perspectives, patchy information and inadequate method, so initiating and conducting a vitally important process of reconceiving the meaning of religion. Their value can hardly be exaggerated, both intrinsically and because they enable others to continue the process, confronting the rest of the problems described above.

Fortunately, these are remarkably fruitful times for such a project. For the first time in history modern investigators can explore human existence and its religious expressions on a global scale and piece together from some extraordinarily fertile historical scholarship a comprehensive picture of the nature and development of the various religious traditions. Then there is the waning – still incomplete but sufficient – of that academic hostility to religion that hampered the emergence of religious studies, or whatever else we should call it, as an academic discipline in the west, inclining some people to underestimate the importance of religion as a personal and social force. Religious beliefs may be false and they may strike critics as naive remnants from a previous, superseded phase of human existence. This they may be. But it does not therefore follow that religion is void of personal and communal importance. On the contrary, at the very least we need to know why some people are gripped for life by certain beliefs while others relinquish or decline them, why popes wield power without panzers or how mullahs orchestrate mass social energies. Religion clearly is an extremely widespread and longlasting phenomenon with all sorts of unexplained characteristics, and it absorbs too many resources to be exempted or excluded from the utmost effort to understand. Fortunately, this is increasingly recognised even by critics of religion. And it is greatly facilitated in many centres where religion is studied by the adoption of a phenomenological method that neither advocates nor opposes faith and which can be practised by anyone, irrespective of personal conviction. This policy has created a particularly favourable situation for the task of rethinking the meaning of religion in any and all of its expressions, because it is much more likely to escape the problem of conceptual distortion which frequently besets those who, publicly or otherwise, regard one particular religion as true or normative or who assume that all religion is false. So we have on one side a mass of information about the subject from all over the world covering many centuries and on the other a favourable academic atmosphere together with a scholarly method that is neither evangelistic or militantly secular, but simply tries to understand religion and portray it faithfully.

There is a third beneficial factor, the progress made by philosophers towards specifying what would constitute an adequate explanation of something. This is a matter that religious theorists have mostly taken for granted but it is in fact far from obvious. In any case, as was mentioned previously, prevailing views of religion seldom even attempt to provide rigorous explanations. So it is a great benefit to be able to draw on the progress thinkers have made on this question at a time when sufficient information is available for us to ask anew what religion is and to ask additionally why it exists.

This brings us to the purpose of the present book. Its aim is to contribute to a rethinking of the meaning of religion by proposing a causal theory of the subject, an explanatory account of the landscapes of faith wherever they have supported human existence, in a manner that will be free of the difficulties that so gravely reduce the value of our inherited ideas. To achieve this the present theory advocates a set of concepts that are planetary in scope, based on data from the whole family of faiths, with due prominence being given to topics like salvation, and constructed in such a way that those concepts can function as an explanatory theory of religion while at the same time incorporating our modern view of knowledge itself. Naturally such a wide-ranging project, covering a dauntingly broad spectrum of disciplines, runs the risk of inadvertent naivities, while its experimental nature involves additional difficulties, especially the problems of sustained conceptual reorientation and bringing the proposed perspective into crisp focus. It would perhaps be presumptuous even to try were it not for the urgency of the issue and the fertility of the times. After all, even a pebble can contribute to a landslide. In any event, the explanations offered in this book are limited to the basic religious characteristics set out in chapter two. If the experiment with these proves worthwhile it can always be extended to more specific problems later.

A brief summary of the theory will help prepare the way for the detailed discussions of subsequent chapters. The heart of the proposal is the phrase 'the quest for ultimate well-being', and evidence will be produced to show that what we call religion mostly involves the search for a supreme, imperishable blessing in a transcendental realm of existence, through contact with or through the agency of powers in, around, and beyond the believer which are held to yield that well-being, a search embodied in various traditions of contextually conditioned ideas, actions, artifacts and associations, often decisively shaped by highly influential founding or modifying figures, by events and by sacred writings. In other words, religion will be portrayed as the instrument humanity has fashioned in relation to certain objective forces to heal forever its deepest maladies. The story of its fashioning is a journey into the very nerve-centre of human existence. Contrary to the opinion of many secular-minded people who think of it as an optional activity on the fringes of the real business of life, religion will be shown to be typically human. And contrary also to those conventionally devout people who foster the idea that faith is in essence a channel to the supernatural, it will be shown that religion is an adventure of nature and an affirmation of being human, even at its most other-worldly.

To think of religion in this way is simultaneously to think about what it means to be a person. Human existence is here seen in terms of a drive to maximise well-being whose fruits are our systems of commerce, agriculture, government, education, technology, social organisation, music, literature, art and leisure activity; in short all that we generate. What we nowadays call religion results when the drive to maximise well-being encounters, among others, the problem of finding a perfect and permanent cure for all that distresses us, and answers it with the vision of a transcendent level of reality closed to our physical senses but none the less available and accessible by other means. In the following chapters a picture will be drawn of religion as having its source in our natural human hunger for relief from the miseries to which we are prone, in our natural human creativity as we find such relief as we can in our ignorance and fallibility, and in our natural engagement with the invisible forces that indwell and encompass us and which we discover have such great effect on the cycles of distress and relief which mark our experience. To be religious is to wrestle with the acutest infirmities, seeking for them a cure in a realm of liberating, edifying, sustaining forces beyond the visible. Seen in this light, religion is an expression of our basic, human drive to find the greatest possible well-being. This drive will be presented as the operative force in all our achievements. It will be shown that in certain critical experiences it encounters a supremely formidable enemy, namely our own strictly limited ability to deal with the problems and miseries we inevitably undergo. At that critical frontier of human limitation the drive to maximise well-being finds and marshals fresh resources and experiences their benefits. There it becomes religious.

If the various religions indeed have a common source in our shared humanity, why do they differ so much? The theory expounded in this book has an answer whose details appear in chapters four and five. But in a nutshell the answer is given by pointing to the facts of environmental variation, cultural isolation, historical change and to differences of mental advancement and personal variation. All people want relief from distress and security for the things they cherish. But depending on where and when they live, and on some other conditioning variables, what distresses them, what they cherish, how they think about these things and what ameliorating resources are open to them will vary, which gives ample grounds for explaining why religion exists in such a diversity of forms.

By using the words ultimate well-being, which do not come from any of the religions but which none the less embrace them (as will be shown in chapter two), the present theory is built on a concept that avoids being conceptually parochial and restricted in its coverage to merely a part of the family of cultures and faiths, while at the same time capturing the all-important concern with salvation and equivalent concepts without which no view of religion can be adequate. But in what way does the theory explain religion? It does so by identifying what appear to be the causes of this desire for ultimate well-being within the individual person and in reality at large with its interacting forces, together with an identification of the conditioning factors which are responsible for the variations that we find from religion to religion. These causes and factors are described in such a way that religion is their natural and logical effect. The full account is a good deal more complicated than this but the point is the same: the theory has an explanatory function because it specifies necessary and sufficient conditions for the rise and persistence of faith, so advancing from an account of what religion is to saying why it exists and why it exhibits the particular forms that it does.

The structure of the book derives from the logical requirements of an explanatory theory. To start with there is the phenomenon that requires explication, namely religion. So the next chapter is devoted to a presentation of the subject as a planetary reality whose various constituent traditions reveal a common concern, among other characteristics, with what we have been calling, for introductory purposes, salvation. Being Latin-based, this is a word that belongs mainly to Christianity, so it is not suitable for a theory that aspires to deal with all of the religions. But in the absence of an established, all-embracing equivalent there is no real alternative to its use in this opening chapter. As we proceed, other, less sectional terms will be used, especially benefit and well-being.

With a global picture of religion in mind the next step will be to consider in some detail what the process of explaining it would involve. Therefore chapter three deals with the art of explanation, relating recent philosophical treatments of this matter to religion and modifying them as necessary. It will be shown that the art of rigorously explaining or explicating a problem hinges on an identification of the set of factors whose presence would necessitate the occurrence of the problem, or at least make its appearance extremely likely. So, to explain religion we must look beyond it for those necessitating or predisposing factors. Identifying them is the purpose of chapter four, in the form of a general treatment of human existence coupled with a general account of the kind of world, in the broadest sense, of which human existence is part. We will then have the main ingredients of an explanatory theory of religion. Chapter 5 expounds it in detail. It will therefore be clear that each chapter prepares for the ones that follow, with the last one incapable of being properly understood on its own.

The subject matter dealt with in this book is in one sense all the phenomena to which we commonly apply the word religion – Judaism, Christianity, Islam, Hinduism, Buddhism, Taoism, Confucianism and Zoroastrianism; the ancient polytheisms of Egypt, Mesopotamia, Greece and Rome, and the traditional faiths of Africa, the Americas and Oceania – but in a deeper sense it is human existence itself. The book is not limited to beliefs, rituals and doctrines or to any other externally observable dimension of religion, but extends also to those who form, accept and live by them. The reason for this policy is simple: religion is not just a set of beliefs or rituals. It is a human phenomenon, a very special preoccupation of the people who hold those beliefs and perform those activities. Not to include this basic, human element is to leave out a most important part of the subject. So the project of developing a theory of religion turns out to be in considerable measure what we might call religious and philo-sophical anthropology. But in so far as human existence cannot be understood apart from its setting in the world, there must also be due consideration for the context in which people live in the form of a general cosmology.

This raises the question of the method used in the book. The best labels for it are experiential, phenomenological and philo-sophical. It is experiential because primary importance is attached to information about the religious life that comes from participation and observation. It is phenomenological in the sense of allowing that information to speak for itself so far as possible. This also means setting aside or bracketing any verdict on the debate about the existence of a transcendental spiritual order. The phenomenological method requires that we faithfully record and report what believers think, say and do, and when any of their assertions are denied by others, this must also be reported. It is not up to the investigator who uses this method to affirm or reject the claims people make about a transcendental realm, but to record that they do make such claims, and, where appropriate, that their claims are denied by others. The book is philosophical in a dual sense: analytic and constructive. The information gathered empirically and recorded phenomenologically is analysed in order to find its constituent elements, patterns and causes, and it is constructed into an explanatory theory to illuminate the religious dimension of human existence. Exactly how this is done is set out in Chapter 3, where most of the methodological issues pertinent to the present project are handled. But there too the appeal to ordinary experience will be prominent. In general, the chapters that follow may be said to involve a sustained exercise in synthesising and developing a series of important contributions made by others: data about religion from all over the world, brave new religious philosophies relevant to spiritual pluralism, principles of explanation in the natural and human sciences, discoveries about the way people think, learn and behave, and insights into the nature of theory-building stemming especially from the work of Sir Karl Popper. Whatever is novel has been made possible by these earlier achievements, which are gratefully acknowledged.

To end this introductory chapter there are a few further clarifications that must be made. Expressions like 'mankind' which the women's liberation movement has valuably helped us to see as contributing to a sexist bias in society have been avoided wherever this was possible without falsifying primary sources, and any that have none the less found their way in the text must be seen as entirely unintended. Secondly, the convention of preferring the abbreviations BCE and CE to the more familiar but quite unphenomenological BC and AD has been followed throughout, as is surely desirable in a non-sectarian work like this one. Thirdly, the uncapitalised word 'god' is used whenever the reference is generally to the divine being or beings in which theists believe, while the capitalised form is used only as the proper name of the deity worshipped by monotheists. And lastly, every effort has been made to cast the following chapters in a readable style, as free as possible from the technicalities and obscurities so often relished by some academic writers. A wide-ranging subject like this should be stylistically accessible to people who claim no special expertise in religious studies or philosophy and their respective jargons, or for that matter in any other academic field, and not just to specialists. To make the present theory available to these readers the appropriate stylistic policy of favouring simplicity over complexity has mostly been followed, even in chapter three where abstractness and technicality can easily get out of hand. The price to be paid is that some adepts in given fields will here and there find themselves reading clarifications they may not need, but which others could find helpful. These clarifications should be understood in that light.

2 Religion in Global Perspective

Before a phenomenon can be explained there must be an accurate and thorough familiarity with it, so that the enquirer can be quite clear what it is that needs explaining. Given this requirement, it follows that the present chapter should provide a general description of religion to serve as a factual foundation for the ones that follow. Bearing in mind the conceptual narrowness of inherited ideas, it is essential that all the main spiritual traditions of the earth be covered, and because those ideas pay too little attention to salvation and related matters like redemption, liberation or enlightenment, it is also essential to present in some detail the evidence for their importance in the religious life wherever it is lived. And while all this is being done it will also be necessary to introduce several key terms as expressions for the dominant, global characteristics of religion which this chapter identifies.

How can we meet this vital requirement of paying careful attention to the spiritual life itself? One way might be to reproduce in summary form some of the portrayals of the world's faiths contained, for instance, in text books on the subject. Many of these are highly respected works by specialists, so this could seem a promising tactic. But on methodological grounds it would undermine rather than promote the investigation. We need to work from information coming directly from the religious life and not from presentations of that information, which would be an undesirably indirect procedure. To revert to the cartographic metaphor: the present project must be based on the spiritual countryside itself and not on previously drawn maps of it whose reliability we have, in any case, reason to suspect. This is what sound, empirical method demands. Existing presentations of religion which lack this grounding in primary data, as opposed to

15

source material from the religions themselves, run the risk of being too much coloured by preconceptions about the subject to be fully reliable guides to the spiritual life itself. The way the faiths are introduced and described, the principles governing what the author thought worth including and what was deemed unimportant, all these factors affect the writing of a history of religion, and all of them are influenced, consciously or otherwise, by the author's views about the subject. None of this is reprehensible because it is inevitable. That is how histories of religion are written. But it does mean that too pronounced a theoretical or interpretive element could be present, unduly affecting the way the material is handled. For our purposes this is a crucial disadvantage because it moves the portrayal of religion away from direct contact with the religious life itself.

Another problem about relying for our data on existing histories of religion is of course their treatment of salvation and related matters as merely one aspect, and perhaps even a relatively secondary one, of the subject and in any case to subordinate them to belief in a spiritual realm as the paramount characteristic of religion. This misrepresents the subject, as the evidence given later in the present chapter shows. Clearly, then, any picture of religion that depends only on existing maps cannot possibly be in sufficient, direct contact with the landscapes of faith. We need something more basic than that.

In theory the proper method is straightforward, namely to use primary evidence from the various religions supplemented by reports of first-hand, observational research containing a maximum of descriptive, observational terms and a minimum of interpretive expressions, giving priority to whatever comes immediately from the religious life and ensuring a wide coverage from tradition to tradition and over the centuries. But while this approach is indispensable for achieving secure foundations for a theory of religion and has in fact been followed in the preparation of this book, it involves an insurmountable problem so far as presentation is concerned. This is the sheer bulk of the material, whose encyclopaedic compass is quite incapable of being reproduced in the space available. So we find that a methodological imperative clashes with sheer practicality.

The solution is to distinguish between preparation and presentation. In attending to the former there is no alternative to the procedures just described. The religious life must be explored at

first hand. There is no other way to do justice to it or be in a position to test the reliability of existing descriptions and where necessary improve them. In short, the religious countryside – terra
religiosa, as I shall sometimes call it – must be described on the
basis of first-hand exploration and the resulting descriptions must
be given priority over any previous map of it, no matter how
widely accepted. Presenting the knowledge so obtained is a different matter, with the need to ensure effective communication in
a limited number of pages being a legitimate consideration, provided that the account is always based fairly and squarely on a
foundation of primary source material. The picture of religion
that follows is based on personal observations and research, documentary evidence and the reports of trained observers, some of
them anthropologists. To reduce the mass of evidence that was
examined to manageable proportions, most of the detail has had
to be left out, and to ensure that the omissions did not alter the
character of the original material a policy of descriptive generalisation has been followed (Crosby 1981: 8f). This means that a
picture of religion was formed on the basis of the full range of the
evidence that was examined by detecting the dominant, recurring
features in that evidence; then, with the picture already in mind,
a selection was made from the evidence such as would yield the
same picture, though in less detail. A good analogy can once
again be taken from cartography. An ordnance survey map of a
particular area based on field work and aerial photography will
show vastly more detail than a small-scale map of the same
region, but the latter can include dominant characteristics just as
clearly, and perhaps even better. It will not show every hedge and
duck pond but it will show the same rivers, hills, towns and
forests. Certainly there will be less detail than on the large-scale
map, but with regard to the main features of the region it will be
no less accurate or representative.

Obviously the crucial step in the exercise is to detect the
dominant characteristics. So far as religion is concerned this
means establishing two things. Within an individual tradition it
means establishing what receives greatest attention from the
believers themselves, pervading, governing or underlying other
aspects of their faith; and it means finding out whether the
various traditions so analysed follow a pattern by giving
prominence to the same sort of thing, and if so, what that pattern
is. When these two steps are taken the investigator is in a position

to identify the leading characteristics of religion as a whole, at least sufficiently to formulate a hypothesis about the subject. Thereafter it is simply a matter of scaling down the resultant maps of terra religiosa to fit the available space. Equipped with such a picture the enquirer can then assess earlier accounts, adopting from them whatever is sound and changing or adding whatever is inaccurate or incomplete. The presentation of the religious life of humanity that follows has been constructed just like this, except that it has sometimes been necessary to find fresh ways of formulating the adopted information. Religion will be portrayed by means of eight defining characteristics, and it should be remembered throughout that the picture so painted is a broad one, designed to indicate only the dominant, recurring features of the subject when seen in planetary perspective. To do this it is not necessary to paint every blade of grass on the spiritual landscape.

RELIGION AND BENEFIT

Whatever else religion may be, it is certainly a matter of seeking to diminish or overcome evil, misery or whatever else may threaten people, and of conserving or increasing whatever they value. It fulfils these functions in many ways, for example by giving believers a sense of hope, meaning or certainty, by assuring them that the grave is but the threshold of eternity, by enlightenment, fellowship and forgiveness, or by supplying an authoritative scripture in terms of which to handle life's riddles. In the absence of a better word, let us simply call these the benefits involved in religion as judged by believers themselves. The evidence for this set of statements is quite unambiguous because it occurs prominently in every one of the world's faiths. However, because it is so poorly reflected in prevailing conceptions of religion, much more space will be given to documenting and describing this characteristic than to any of the other seven that follow.

The evidence in question is of four kinds: personal accounts of religious experience, testimony from the scriptures of the various spiritual traditions that have them, including material from or about the great founding or guiding figures of religious history, observers' reports and finally the views of relevant experts, cited purely to support what the first three kinds of evidence reveal. As we shall see, there are historians of religion and other investigators who are well aware that religion is substantially a concern with the attainment of some kind of benefit. It is helpful to refer to their conclusions to support the present portrayal and correct the common view which pays such scant attention to this characteristic concern on the part of believers all over the world.

Personal testimony about religious experience

Let us begin with the most fundamental kind of evidence, personal accounts of religious experience in which those who know the life of faith at first hand describe what it involves. The published evidence is unevenly available, coming almost entirely from the pioneering research of Edwin Starbuck and William James in America at the turn of the century and more recently from Sir Alister Hardy's Religious Experience Research Unit at Oxford. As such it naturally refers to the theistic faiths of the west, a limitation recognised by the researchers in question and by the present writer, but which does not deprive it of importance as far as it goes because it is so direct a revelation of the religious life. Here are some typical examples of this evidence:

> now, when I think of the holy Trinity, or hear It spoken of, I understand how the three adorable Persons form only one God and I experience an unspeakable happiness (James 1902: 412).

> After this, things cleared up within me and about me better than ever, and the light has never wholly died away. I was saved from suicide (James 1902: 185).

> I now recognise that I used to fall back for support upon this curious relation I felt myself to be in to this fundamental cosmical *It*. It was on my side, or I was on Its side... and it always strengthened me and seemed to give me endless vitality to feel its underlying and supporting presence (James 1902: 64f).

> I saw that the universe is not composed of dead matter, but is, on the contrary, a living Presence; I became conscious in myself of eternal life. It was not a conviction that I would have eternal life, but a consciousness that I possessed eternal life then; I saw that all men are immortal; that the cosmic order is

such that without any peradventure all things work together for the good of each and all; that the foundation principle of the world, of all the worlds, is what we call love, and that the happiness of each and all is in the long run absolutely certain (James 1902: 399).

It cannot be sufficiently emphasised that these reports come from the very heartland of the religious landscape, not from some second-level theory thought up by an investigator. They take us as directly into our subject as it is possible for the enquirer to go. As such their value is immense; and if we would rightly understand the humanness involved in religion we must be guided above all by evidence like this, for, as Ninian Smart has said, '...one cannot adequately explain religious developments by external factors alone' (Smart 1973: 152). Personal reports like the ones just quoted disclose the important inner dimension of faith in the experience of believers themselves. William James was uniquely empirical among formulators of the classical conceptions of religion, so his own conclusions about its character are of great relevance to this book. We shall consider them later in the present chapter.

The systematic recording of first-hand evidence of religious experience at the Unit founded in Oxford by Sir Alister Hardy gives us a more recent source of published information. Like the work done by William James, it reflects the beliefs of a culture whose faiths are theistic and therefore exemplifies only one of the world's main types of religion. This affects the kind of inference we can safely draw about the object of religious faith, for, as we shall see, this object is not always thought of as a deity. But the material is every bit as explicit as James' so far as the effects of religious experience are concerned. In most of the reports that were published in Hardy's book *The Spiritual Nature of Man* there is precisely the same reference to finding some kind of significant benefit that a careful study of William James' material reveals. Here are some typical examples:

About 20 odd years ago I was rather poorly and one evening felt so ill that I decided to go to bed. While in my room preparing I suddenly felt all round me a beautiful warm Presence so comforting that I said out loud 'Well Father if I have to be ill to feel *you* like that – I will be ill'. Then the room filled with triumphant music – so beautiful it conveyed to me that I had chosen aright....

The most important part is that ever since then I have a sense of Peace – sometimes more, sometimes less, but I feel cared for and led (Hardy 1979: 41).

The next example refers to a teenage baptism experience:

I tried praying, and did so for about two minutes. The result was an encompassing sense of peace, security and well-being (Hardy 1979: 75).

The third example from Hardy's book reports a comparably beneficial outcome after an experience of illumination. The words used are extremely relevant to a central thesis of this book, namely that religion is a means of seeking ultimate well-being:

The barriers began to fall and one veil after another parted in my mind. From a self-centred happiness I now wanted to share it with others, first those near me, then wider, until *everyone and everything was included.... I knew* that all was well, that the basis of everything was goodness, that all religions and sciences were paths to this ultimate reality (Hardy 1979: 78).

For the kind of benefit sought and reportedly found in the religious life the following extract, referring to a recent commitment to Jesus Christ by the person who submitted the report, could hardly be bettered:

This has resulted in the most wonderful feeling of freedom and a flow of love and compassion for others – a much more complete understanding of their needs and feelings. I also have loads more energy and a courage to stand up for my ideals and enter into difficult relationships with people I have hitherto avoided. Far from chaining me into a narrow religious outlook on life I can now understand what Christ means that he has come that we may have life more abundantly (Hardy 1979: 102).

The examples just quoted are not untypical of the wider collections of published material from which they were taken, which are redolent with references to problems overcome and benefits obtained. Exactly the same was found in 1980 in an unpublished pilot study conducted by the author and a colleague at the University of Natal, following the example of Hardy and his fellow workers, in an area of exceptional suitability because it has large Hindu, Muslim, Christian and traditional African communities, besides other smaller ones. Taken together, the evidence of this kind leaves no doubt that the faiths involved are strongly characterised by experiences of significant benefit, whatever other characteristics may be present. The benefits are significant in two ways: firstly, they matter a good deal to those involved, and in the second place the benefits are often ones that most people would regard as important in themselves, like health and happiness. It would of course be desirable to have similar studies about religions elsewhere in the world but in the mean time there are alternative ways of investigating them, mainly through scriptures and other central texts. As items that have long been read and cherished by enormous numbers of people, it is reasonable to infer that what they say has struck an extremely responsive chord in the people concerned. If they contain strong indications of the well-being reported above, it would surely be very likely that people in those cultures have also experienced the kind of benefit reported by their theistic counterparts in the west. Such evidence will of course be inferential but the chain of inference is strong. In any case the first-hand reports that are available point quite unambiguously to religion being a source of profound benefit in all sorts of ways: happiness, increased energy, a new zest for life, improved relationships with others, healing, a sense of peace, courage to face adversity, strength to resist temptation, the expectation of a happy existence beyond death, and much else besides.

Scriptural evidence

We now turn to the next category of primary religious source material, namely the scriptures possessed by some of the world's spiritual traditions. These often report the teachings and actions of great religious leaders, besides reflecting long-lasting interests on the part of the people whom they have nourished over the centuries. Being classics from the realm of faith their relevance to our enquiry is clearly very great indeed.

Deliverance and benefit in the Hebrew scriptures

As presented in the sacred texts of the Jewish people, ancient Israelite religion involves a particularly graphic process of this-worldly deliverance which gives much food for thought to any who think that faith only touches the spiritual side of human life. Here physical existence is very much involved, so much so that a respected older reference work in biblical studies can say that in most of the Old Testament 'salvation is a conception which has meaning only for this life' (Adams Brown 1902: 360).

It is not clear to what extent the narratives about Abraham were intended as historical records, but taking them as though they are they tell of transformation from wandering Mesopotamian origins to a home in the land of Canaan and from childlessness to the fathering of nations, a transformation anchored in a steadfast faith in God. We would probably not want to call the patriarchal narratives which give the details of this transformation a story of deliverance or salvation, but the material is none the less of great importance because Abraham is seen as initiating a history which frequently is salvational, as we shall shortly see. Nor is it irrelevant to the theme of this book that his story involves the providing of great benefit – faith, a family, posterity, a homeland and thus an increase of well-being. Under the influence of a concept of religion that one-sidedly emphasises only the believer's contact with the transcendent, we have tended to see Abraham as a model of trusting faith in and obedience to his god. It is truer to the scriptural evidence to see him also as being at the forefront of a history of deliverance, a man whose faith, for all the hardships he encountered, went hand in hand with blessing in the sense of substantial good, including 'health, long life, many and enduring progeny, wealth, honour, and victory' (*Encyclopaedia Judaica* 1972: vol. 4, 1084).

The pattern of faith, hardship overcome and blessing is even clearer in the life of Moses. He is usually described as a prophet and a divinely appointed law-giver. But it appears from the relevant Hebrew scriptures, again taken as historical records, that his main contribution was as a leader in the exodus and in transforming the Israelites from slavery into a new existence as a people in covenant with Yahweh their god, guided for their own good by the laws he gave them. It may of course be objected that social and economic liberation are not the same as religious salvation, but this is to adopt an unduly narrow view, constricting the investigation to the outlook of those who interpret religion in purely spiritual terms and, worse still, contradicting the biblical view of the matter. Therefore it is necessary to define salvation more broadly as meaning deliverance from a significant problem, usually with the aid of some or other spiritual agency or technique and promoting a beneficial goal, often but not necessarily of a transcendental kind. Seen in the light of this definition, Moses obviously was a figure of outstanding salvational importance. Powerful confirmation for this verdict comes from the famous biblical account of his decisive encounter with the god of Israel at the burning bush. Yahweh tells Moses 'I have indeed seen the misery of my people in Egypt. I have heard their outcry against their slave-masters. I have taken heed of their sufferings, and have come down to rescue them...' (Exodus 3: 7–8). Fired by this experience, he returned to Egypt and there became the catalyst in a drama of salvation that has influenced a sizable part of the human race. If this does not establish him as a person of the greatest saving significance, it is difficult to know what would.

The picture of Moses just drawn is fully consistent with relevant linguistic considerations. Discussing the Semitic origins of the concept of salvation, Willard G. Oxtoby relates it to a root meaning 'breadth and or spaciousness, hence ease or lack of constraint' (Oxtoby 1973: 18). This links easily with experiences in which hardship is removed, as with the exodus, and also with the definition of redemption given by the *Encyclopaedia Judaica*, namely 'salvation from the states or circumstances that destroy the value of human existence or human existence itself' (vol. 14, col. 1). The word redemption appears more frequently in English translations of the Hebrew scriptures than salvation and has its own associations with legal and commercial matters, not shared by words like deliverance, liberation and salvation, but all of them are logically related ways of expressing the removal of hardship in one or other form. Interestingly, the first Christian martyr, Stephen, is reported in the New Testament as calling Moses a redeemer (Acts 7: 35). It is thus with good scriptural backing that Alan Richardson has commented as follows on the events associated with Moses: '...the evidence of the Old Testament leaves no room at all for doubt that the determinative experience of Yahweh's salvation was the deliverance from Egyptian bondage, the miracle of the Red Sea and the subsquent experience of God's fatherly care in the wilderness (Richardson 1962: 171). The provision of benefit is quite clear.

Moses was of course not the only person to lead Israel towards an enriched future. His successor Joshua is noteworthy too, giving successful military, political and devotional leadership in taking the Israelites from the fringes of their land of promise and plenty to conquest and occupancy, and renewing at Shechem the covenant of loyalty with their god. As such Joshua too was a figure around whom Israel's fortunes turned, and although not referred to as a saviour or deliverer, he definitely was a source or at least an instrument of benefit. At this point in the discussion it is helpful to pause and reflect on the fact that we do not usually speak of Joshua or Abraham as deliverers or think of the events associated with them as instances of salvation, despite the fact that the name Joshua actually means 'God's salvation'. The words deliverance and salvation have too narrow a meaning for that. Yet there is a vital logical link between them and those men's deeds. To save is to rescue from peril or other misfortune, so that its connotations are often negative. But logically the word is both positive and negative because rescue from peril is as much a movement towards relief as it is a movement away from distress. To be freed from evil would be regarded by everybody as in itself good. So the word is indeed also positive. Analysed like this, salvation and liberation or deliverance logically imply a beneficial transformation. The contributions of a Joshua, so enormously favourable to the Israelities, clearly involved precisely this kind of transformation. Therefore what he did and what the words we are discussing logically involve are one and the same. This enables us to recognise an extremely important fact: the word salvation may be the best known term for the kind of deeply significant benefit that the history of ancient Israel so repeatedly reveals, but its usual sense is too narrow to express that benefit satisfactorily. It points to but falls short of expressing adequately the sort of ameliorating development which religion reportedly makes possible, and illustrates perfectly the problem of conceptual narrowness that was mentioned at the beginning of this book. Salvation is a word most often used in Christian theology; its prevalence there and the prevalence of logically or linguistically related terms like redemption or liberation in other faiths alerts us to a centrally important feature of religion. But those words are incapable of expressing that feature satisfactorily. This obliges us to find an alternative expression that will retain the implication of benefit without the impediment of narrowness. Later in the chapter we shall return to this issue.

The next relevant figure in Israel's history is David because his military and political exploits freed the people from the threat posed by hostile neighbours and gave them the national unity and power on which Solomon his son built the cultural and commercial achievements for which he is so well known. Here too we find the provision of important benefits for which the word salvation is unlikely to be used, though it would be acceptable to speak of David as saving ancient Israel from its Philistine enemies by defeating them in battle. But it is surely also for those military, political, commercial and cultural attainments that David and his son are remembered in the Hebrew scriptures, not only for devotional and cultic measures like patronising the clergy, promoting the music of worship and building the first of Jerusalem's temples. Thus the evidence itself cautions us against imposing on our subject a separation between this-worldly and other-worldly blessings that is alien to the outlook of ancient Israel. Nor should we overlook the connection between Moses who liberated the Hebrew slaves by the power of Yahweh and led them towards their promised land, and David, whose gifts as a soldier made that land secure for them, or Solomon who helped it prosper and beautified its capital. It was all one complex process of deliverance and blessing, seen by the scriptures as taking place under the saving power of the same deity, with Moses, Joshua, David and Solomon all instrumental in bringing it about, though not by identical contributions.

One, complex saving process the experience of the ancient Israelites may well have been, but none the less it involved distinguishable facets, military measures being a case in point. Another was the righteousness called for in the laws of Yahweh, so that those laws can be seen as promoting the moral and spiritual improvement of a people whom the bible says were to become 'a holy nation and a kingdom of priests' (Exodus 19: 6). This facet of the process was continued and developed by the great prophets from Nathan at the time of David to the second Isaiah, or whoever else wrote the material preserved in chapters 40 to 55 of the book of that name over four hundred years later. They applied the moral demands of Yahwism to unacceptable parts of public life and personal behaviour in the form of judgement, condemnation, and warnings about imminent divine punishment through the agency of enemy invasion. The link here between ethics and politics is very telling for its implication that the welfare of the people depended on morality and loyalty to the nation's god. This alone should caution the investigator against confining religion to spiritual matters or against excluding the prophets from the concept of salvation. Their warnings in the name of Yahweh that wickedness was leading to national disaster fall within the meaning of salvation as defined above. Certainly they relate to the good of the people.

Further evidence of the beneficial ministry of the prophets is available in specific parts of the literature they created. There is, for example, the foretelling of a messiah who would bring great blessing (Isaiah 9: 6f); or the way the author of Isaiah 40–55 turned the fall of Jerusalem to the Babylonians in 586 BCE into an opportunity to salvage, reinterpret and greatly strengthen Israel's confidence in her god, repeatedly referring to him as a redeemer; or in Ezekiel's vision of a valley of dry bones to which life would return (Isaiah 41: 14; 43: 14; 48: 17 etc; Ezekiel 37).

An extremely rich source of material for our theme is provided by the Psalms, which repeatedly express a powerful sense of the saving nature of the deity. In the words of Psalm 68:

Blessed be the Lord,
  who daily bears us up;
God is our salvation.
Our God is a God of salvation;
  And to GOD, the Lord, belongs
  escape from death (verses 19–20).

As any concordance of the Jewish and Christian Bible will show, there are many other Psalms which sound exactly the same note.

After the prophetic age the concept of salvation is Israel's religion underwent a few technical developments but never lost its basic implication of a divinely-given benefit. One such development was the idea that salvation was to be found by keeping the divine law as revealed in the books of Moses, an idea strongly linked with rabbinic Judaism. Another was the expectation of a coming national deliverance through the awaited messiah or king, possibly reflecting the frustrations felt by the Jewish people after their independence had been lost and their country fell under Seleucid and Roman government. There was also a tendency by some to think that salvation would not take place in the present world order but in a transcendental future, an idea that was current and influential when Christianity began (Bruce 1963: 51ff and Westermann 1972: 9–19). Finally, mediaeval and modern Jewish writers are reported as having continued to treat the concept as centrally important (*Encyclopaedia Judaica* vol. 14: 7–8).

Taken together these items from the leading figures and events in ancient Israel reveal a historical process of transformation from obscurity and slavery to nationhood and covenant and the promise of a more righteous and secure future. It is with good reason, then, that biblical theologians have spoken of this process as involving a salvation history (Westermann 1979: 15ff). In reviewing its high points we are not, of course, dealing with fresh information but rather focussing attention on a much neglected facet of well-known facts, namely the prominence of amelioration and benefit in the religion of the ancient Israelites. Taking a broad survey of the Hebrew scriptures, the investigator finds there a wealth of themes: covenant, law, prophecy, the revelation of Yahweh's nature and will, righteousness and the divine control of individual and national affairs. What pervades and unites them is the further theme of deliverance and blessing, of being saved from peril and preserved from something better, homelessness being transformed into a settled existence, slavery into freedom, exile into return, wickedness into repentence and uprightness of life, defeat into victory, apostacy into loyalty to one's god, and despair into hope. Hardship and sorrow were thus frequently experienced, but the crowning impression of the evidence is not one of suffering, evil and pessimism but, under Yahweh, of blessing and well-being. The blessings varied in kind and are certainly not to be regarded as purely spiritual, for prominent among them was deliverance from the physical bondage of slavery; but whatever the peril or problem from which Israel experienced rescue, in every case there was benefit, and no matter who the instrument was through whom the benefit came – whether Moses, Joshua, David, the prophets or the expected messiah – ultimately the source of Israel's salvation was believed to be Yahweh her god (but see Barr, 1973: 39–52).

Salvation in the New Testament

The themes of blessing and salvation are at least as prominent in the New Testament as in Judaism, though with greater emphasis on deliverance from sin and its consequences and on spiritual benefits and relatively less on this-worldly matters, though these are certainly present. The Greek verb *sozein*, meaning to save, additionally signifies to heal and to make whole, so covering also the physical dimension of the blessings which Christians claim to have found in their faith (*Interpreter's Dictionary of the Bible* 1962: vol. 4: 178). Not surprisingly, in view of this connotation, it was used by those who translated the Hebrew scriptures into Greek to render a range of words meaning to deliver, to rescue, to escape, to survive, to help and to keep alive, as well as simply to save (Friedrich 1971 vol. VII: 965–1024; Oxtoby 1973: 20).

Whatever Jesus of Nazareth thought and said of himself, his followers since the earliest days have regarded him not only as their own saviour but as the saviour of the world. In the words of the first epistle of John, 'the Father sent the Son to be the saviour of the world...' (4: 14). Jesus is only twice recorded as having used the noun salvation but he often used the verb to save, linking it with his own work (Hastings 1902: vol. IV: 362). According to Luke's Gospel, where the theme of salvation is especially prominent, Jesus clearly spoke of his mission in terms of liberation. In the Nazareth synagogue early in his ministry he read the following words from Isaiah 61:

> The spirit of the Lord is upon me because
>   he has anointed me;
> He has sent me to announce good news
>   to the poor,
> To proclaim release for prisoners and
>   recovery of sight for the blind;
> To let the broken victims go free,
> To proclaim the year of the Lord's favour.

Having read these words he told the congregation that this text had come true in their very hearing that selfsame day (Luke 4: 18–21). Furthermore, Matthew's gospel explains that the name Jesus means saviour and was given because he would save his people from their sins (ch. 1: 21). But the use of salvational terminology, striking though it is, constitutes only part of the evidence of the gospels and must be related to the accounts given of Jesus' deeds and their effects on the people who encountered him. As the enquirer examines the records of his healing, feeding, morally guiding and socially emancipating actions, his doctrines of a divine fatherliness pre-eminently loving and an impending divine intervention in history to establish the kingdom of God, and his injunction to the disciples to love one another, an impression forms of a figure of quite remarkable effectiveness in relieving the bodily, moral, social and spiritual distress of those who came to him for help. It has been calculated that as much as one fifth of all the gospel material consists of healing narratives, while another extremely prominent facet of Jesus' ministry was the forgiveness of sins. Whether through instruction, healing or forgiveness, those concerned can reasonably be thought to have experienced a profoundly beneficial transformation in their lives.

Thus we find in St Paul a dramatic personal change from being a fanatical persecutor of the early Christians into a dedicated servant of the gospel who thereby became one of the most influential figures in western history. Not surprisingly, his writings are much preoccupied with the theology of salvation, mostly in the legally-orientated idiom so natural to and typical of him, concerning the justification of the faithful before God through Christ. Significantly, he introduced his most famous epistle with the words, 'I am not ashamed of the gospel. It is the saving power of God for everyone who has faith – the Jew first, but the Greek also – because here is revealed God's way of righting wrong...' (Romans 1: 16). It is no surprise, then, that elsewhere in the New Testament there is a wealth of terminology for various aspects and implications of the saving work of Christ, such as redemption, ransom, reconciliation, atonement, sacrifice, the new creation, regeneration and others as well. In the words of W. Adams Brown, 'The salvation brought by Jesus is the theme of the entire apostolic age. Wherever we turn in the New Testament, whether it be Acts, Hebrews, St Paul or St John, we are conscious of a note of confidence and triumph, as of men possessing a supreme good, in which they not only themselves rojoice, but which they are anxious to share with others' (Adams Brown 1902: 365; cf Aulén 1976: 141ff; Bornkamm 1960: 64ff; Perrin 1967: 54ff; Vermes 1973: 225).

Although our main concern for the moment is to review the world's great scriptures, it is instructive to glance briefly also at the history of Christian thought down the centuries, for there too the investigator finds the theme of salvation in great prominence. Athanasius, arguably the thinker who most influenced the shaping of Christian orthodoxy in the great fourth century struggle to define the doctrine of the person of Christ, based his conception of Jesus as truly divine on the key notion that only a divine Christ could really save. And the Nicene Creed which emerged from the long debates and conflicts of that century to win acceptance to this day as a formal statement of Christian belief declares that Jesus came down from heaven and was made man 'for us men and for our salvation'. It is not too much to say that these words touch the heart of the Christian faith because they identify the purpose believers see in Christ's work, which is none other than salvation. This was also the theme of one of the most important books to be written during the mediaeval flowering of theology, Anselm's *Cur Deus Homo?* (Why did God become Man?), issued in 1098. As for the protestant reformation in the sixteenth century, the doctrine of salvation was one of its most important issues, if not the most important of them all. Martin Luther's actions and ideas are unintelligible except when seen in relation to his wrestlings with the question of salvation, personally as well as doctrinally. Nor can the missionary expansion of Christianity be separated from this concern, whatever other motives, more worldly in kind, may also have been present. These are merely a handful of the many pieces of evidence in the New Testament and in subsequent Christian writings testifying to the immense importance of salvation, understood as deliverance from sin and its damning consequences and as Christ's gift of reconciliation with God in this life and in the eternal life to come. In fact so rich is the evidence that it is a major puzzle why our inherited theories of religion, so often the products of Christian thinkers, have failed to give due prominence to these great themes of blessing and salvation. Whatever the cause of this faulty theological map-making, the Christian province of terra religiosa no less than its Jewish borderlands abounds with indications of profound spiritual, moral, social and material benefits, of men and women beyond number who report having found healing, hope and wholeness through faith in Christ, their saviour (Franks 1962).

The evidence of the Qur'ān

Although the themes of blessing, well-being, deliverance and salvation are not as frequently mentioned in the Qur'ān as the great Islamic doctrines of God and faith, they are implicitly as important there as they are overtly prominent in the Jewish and Christian scriptures. But whereas those two traditions were shaped by a combination of outstanding figures and decisive events from the exodus to the resurrection, in Islam it is the concept of divine revelation coming to a final climax in the Holy Qur'ān that dominates, and not the faithful prophet Muhammed or the dramatic developments associated with him, chiefly the *hijrah* or journey from Mecca to Medina in 622 CE, from which the Muslim era is dated. In other words, scriptural evidence is even more weighty in Islam than in Israelite religion or in Christianity except perhaps for some Christian fundamentalists because of the absolute authority of the Qur'ān in the lives of Muslims. And on its own terms it carries a message of salvation, as sura 40: 44 surely makes clear: 'O my people, how is it with me, that I call you to salvation and you call me to the Fire?' (Arberry, 1980). More explicit as to the predicaments from which God will save the upright is sura 39: 63:

> God shall deliver those that
>   were godfearing
> in their security; evil shall not visit
>   them,
> neither shall they sorrow (Yusuf Ali 1938).

Sura 76: 11 repeats this theme of salvation from evil but also specifies the benefits awaiting the righteous:

> But God will deliver
> Them from the evil
> Of that Day, and will
> Shed over them a Light
> Of Beauty and
> A blissful Joy (Yusuf Ali 1938).

That the blessings God gives apply to the present life as well as to life after death is stated early in the Qur'ān:

Now some men
there are who say, 'Our Lord, give to us
in this world'; such men shall have no part
    in the world to come.
And others there are who say, 'Our Lord,
Give to us in this world good, and good
in the world to come, and guard us against the
    chastisement of the Fire';
those — they shall have a portion from
what they have earned; and God is swift
    at the reckoning (Arberry 1980: sura 2: 197).

According to the Qur'ān, righteousness will be followed
ultimately by happiness:

As to the Righteous
They will be in Gardens,
And in Happiness, –

Enjoying the (Bliss) which
Their Lord hath bestowed
On them, and their Lord
Shall deliver them from
The penalty of the Fire (Yusuf Ali 1938: sura 52: 17–18).

The metaphor of the garden in this extract is explained by
Abdullah Yusuf Ali as signifying 'all the Bliss we can imagine
through our senses' (1938: vol. II, 1463). So we have here a
remarkably explicit conjunction of righteousness and happiness,
a most valuable and significant piece of evidence for the theory of
religion expounded in this book. The same metaphor and several
others appear in an extremely graphic passage about the goal of
the religious life in sura 54, verses 54 to 55:

As to the Righteous
They will be in the midst
of Gardens and Rivers,

In an Assembly of Truth,
In the Presence of
A Sovereign Omnipotent (Yusuf Ali 1938).

Commenting on this passage, Yusuf Ali writes that it comprises four metaphors of ascending sublimity. Firstly it speaks of gardens and rivers, signifying the sum of imaginable sensory bliss. Next there is reference to an assembly of truth, meaning 'intellectual and social satisfaction'. Then there follows the term Presence, a reference to maximum spiritual intensity, culminating in the fourth metaphor where omnipotent sovereignty stands for the inmost realization of God's complete mastery. Thus completeness of faith is conjoined with transcendence and the utmost well-being, a very revealing view of religion and a cornerstone of the theory contained in this book (Yusuf Ali 1938: vol. II, 1463).

Summarising these ideas, Yusuf Ali writes as follows: 'This is our idea of Salvation: the negative avoidance of all the consequences of evil, and the positive attainment of all – and more than all – that our hearts could possibly desire...' (1938: vol. II, 1353). In another place he is even more explicit, describing salvation as 'the achievement of a perfected Personality, a Bliss that grows up within us, and does not depend on external circumstances...it is the Supreme Achievement, the attainment of all desires, the Felicity *in excelsis*.' (Yusuf Ali 1938; vol. II, 1469).

Another way of showing the connection the Qur'ān upholds between faith and blessing is to consider what it says about human nature, as Kenneth Cragg has done in an essay called 'The Trouble of Man' (Cragg 1973: 93ff). The Qur'ān paints 'a stern and sombre picture,' he writes, quoting sura 90 verse 4: 'We have surely created man in trouble.' But this is only part of the picture. Much emphasis is also placed on the need to seek forgiveness from God and above all on his willingness to forgive. So the Qur'ānic view of humanity links with its doctrine of God's mercy, a doctrine recalled in the invocation that precedes all but one of the suras: 'In the name of God, the merciful, the compassionate.' So the Qur'ān teaches that God alone gives meaning and hope to human existence, through acceptance of his divine sovereignty, goodness and mercy. This, surely, is to assert that beyond the troubles of humanity there is an absolute ground of hope and amelioration.

Thus it transpires that although salvational language is less frequently used in the Qur'ān than some other kinds, yet logically its central message is indeed one of divine favour and blessing, a climactic revelation of the absolute sovereignty of God without an acceptance of which nobody can enter the peace and joy of heaven.

Zoroastrianism

The religious tradition launched by the ancient Iranian prophet Zoroaster in the sixth century BCE now survives as only a small community of Parsees in and around Bombay, but it possesses a collection of sacred writings called the Avesta and has been historically very influential, so we must refer to it in this discussion of religion and benefit. Here too we find the themes of deliverance, salvation, triumph over evil and blessing that mark the other near-eastern traditions. In the words of Yasna 30, a prominent text in the Zoroastrian scripture,

> If you, O man, understand the
> commandments which the Wise One
> has given,
> Well-being and suffering — long torment
> for the wicked and salvation for the
> righteous –
> All shall hereafter be for the best (Eliade 1977: 71).

Despite alleging that this religion does not have a doctrine of salvation 'in the proper sense of the term' (which is not specified), Geo Widengren none the less writes that it certainly does teach about 'liberation from the evil powers met with in man's existence as well as in the universe' and that people themselves must fight against evil. This falls within the coverage of the present discussion of religion and benefit (Widengren 1973: 315ff). Moreover, Willard Oxtoby writes in the same volume that the idea of salvation as the future reward of the righteous was present in ancient Iranian religion, and in any case there is in that tradition the doctrine of a saviour named Sōsyant, meaning 'he who brings benefits' (Oxtoby 1973: 23).

The Hindu religious tradition

A pre-occupation with enlightenment, the release of the soul from the cycle of rebirth, the elimination of suffering and other beneficial goals is arguably the main connecting thread in the

Indian tapestry of faiths. Hindu thought recognises several paths
to salvation, like the ways of transcendental insight and of action.
Perhaps the most widely followed is the way of devotion to a deity.
For worshippers of Lord Krishna, who is believed to incarnate the
divine preserver, Vishnu, the message of the Bhagavadgita is
especially cherished and must rank as one of the world's most
influential scriptures. Its salvational teachings and promises of
supreme bliss are unmistakable. Thus we find the following words
of Krishna in Book XII, verses 6—7:

> But those who, all actions
>   Casting on Me, intent on Me
> With utterly unswerving discipline
>   Meditating on Me, revere Me,
> For them I the Savior
>   From the sea of the rounds of death
> Become right soon, son of Prthā,
>   When they have made their thoughts
>   enter into Me. (Edgerton 1952).

In Book XVIII, called 'Discipline of Renunciation unto
Salvation', there is explicit reference to deliverance from evil. The
devotee is instructed thus:

> Abandoning all (other) duties,
>   Go to Me as thy sole refuge;
> From all evils I thee
>   Shall rescue: be not grieved! (Edgerton 1952: verse 66).

The promise of supreme bliss is given in Books V and VI. It is said
of the religious person:

> With self unattached to outside contacts,
>   When he finds happiness in the self,
> He, his self disciplined in Brahman-discipline,
> Attains imperishable bliss (Edgerton 1952: V: 21).

> Thus ever disciplining himself,
>   The disciplined man, free from stain,
> Easily to contact with Brahman,
>   To endless bliss, attains. (Edgerton 1952: VI: 28).

A different but equally liberating path is taken by those who obtain knowledge of the ultimate truths, perceiving, according to the Upanishadic writings, that our seemingly separate selfhoods are but an appearance, the deeper reality being our essential identity with Brahman, the supreme, transcendental reality. To know this is to break free of the cycle of births. The Maitri Upanishad asks:

> In this sort of cycle of existence (*samsara*) what is the good of enjoyment of desires, when after a man has fed on them there is seen repeatedly his return here to earth? Be pleased to deliver me. In this cycle of existence I am like a frog in a waterless well. Sir...you are our way of escape – yea, you are our way of escape! (Radhakrishnan and Moore 1967: 93f).

The central tenet in this philosophical form of religion is that *moksha*, liberation or release from the prison of rebirth, is possible through a conscious transcending of the illusions of phenomenal existence leading to awareness of the underlying unity of reality. Individual rebirth presupposes separate selfhoods; to overcome separateness is thus to overcome rebirth, and at base reality is not separateness but unity.

Popular Hinduism is replete with evidence of a rich seam of divine help and benefit. What is homage to Ganesh, the divine remover of obstacles symbolised by the elephant, if not a desire for help from on high in overcoming a seemingly intractable problem? So too with the worship of the mother goddess Mariamma, who is believed to be a protectress from disease. Villagers who live amidst the threat of measles and chicken pox participate in the annual temple ceremonies in honour of the goddess in the hope of receiving her help – what a researcher into this cult has called 'a functional response to a perceived threat' (Buijs, 1980: 7). Illness, especially among children and where medical resources are scarce, is one of the most menacing of all problems people face. The goddess is worshipped not, it seems, in a spirit of disinterested devotion but, quite naturally, with an eye to the acutely needed protection she is believed capable of giving, just as Krishna promises imperishable bliss to those who turn to him. In any event, the evidence we have reviewed is quite clear: salvation, blessing and related beneficial themes are just as prominent in the Hindu tradition as in the near-eastern ones (Zaehner 1962: ch. III and 1963: 218ff).

The evidence from Buddhism

The desire to overcome the evils that haunt human existence and to find supreme well-being is dramatically repeated in the teaching of the Buddha and in the two main forms of Buddhism. Nowhere else in the world's faiths is the concern for liberation from suffering as explicitly central as in the famous four noble truths which encapsulate the Tathagata's message. The first truth declares that life involves suffering. The second, that the cause of suffering is selfish desire or clinging. The third states that the way to overcome suffering is to remove its cause, selfish desire. And the fourth identifies the way to implement this quest for liberation as the eightfold path of right belief, aspiration, speech, conduct, livelihood, effort, mindfulness and meditation. Successfully implemented, it conveys the practitioner from the suffering round of rebirth to the boundless liberation of nirvana.

This programme of self-liberation, to which the gods and any other superhuman beings are declared irrelevant, is continued in the Theravada tradition of Buddhism in Sri Lanka and other regions and in Zen. The other great form of Buddhism, the Mahayana, is no less concerned with helping people. But now the individual can draw on the saving help of heavenly bodhisattvas or buddhas-to-be. Thus one Mahayana text expresses the bodhisattva ideal of saving humanity as follows: '. . . It is surely better that I alone should suffer than that all these beings should fall into misery. . . . I must give myself away as a substitute through which the whole universe is redeemed. . .' (Smart 1981: 142f). Another passage phrases this dedication to save humanity as follows:

> I take upon myself the burden of all suffering. . . . I have made the vow to save all beings. All beings I must set free. The whole world of living beings I must rescue, from the terrors of birth, of old age, of sickness, of death and rebirth, of all kinds of moral offence, of all states of woe. . . of the jungle of false views (Vajradhavada-Sutra in Eliade 1977: 48).

The Pure Land school is a particularly graphic expression of the Mahayana redemptive vision. It focusses on the saving grace of Amidha Buddha, through faith in whom devotees will gain entry to the Pure Land of the West. In the Twelve Adorations used in some forms of Pure Land worship, the following is said of Amidha Buddha:

> His Light, bright and clear as a cloudless sky, shines
> Serene and without peer through every darkness.
> His power to save men is unbounded and free.
> Thus I place my faith in Amidha Buddha (*Buddhist services and gathas for children*).

When we reviewed Christianity we noted that the Nicene Creed pivots on the belief that the Son of God became man in order to bring salvation. So too Pure Land Buddhists have a creed which sounds the same saving note:

> We rely upon Tathagata Amitabha with our whole heart for the Enlightenment in the life to come, abstaining from all sundry practices and teachings, and giving up the trust in our powerless self.

> We believe that the assurance of our Rebirth through his Salvation comes at the very moment we put our Faith in Him; and we call the name, Namu-Amida-Butsu, in happiness and thanksgiving for His mercy...' (*Buddhist service book* 1967: 43).

So John A. Hutchison writes that Mahayana Buddhism multiplied and transformed Buddha figures into 'sacrificial saviors holding out helping hands, dispensing grace, to the whole suffering creation; and vowing not to enter nirvana until the whole universe is saved' (Hutchison 1977: 173; Conze 1963: 67ff).

Not surprisingly, in view of the strong concern with well-being in the parts of Buddhism we have been surveying, the themes of blessing, benefit and the overcoming of evil also appear in Zen Buddhist literature. The famous 'Song of Meditation' by Hakuin (1685–1768), the father of modern Rinzai Zen, contains these words:

> As regards the Meditation practised in the Mahayana,
> We have no words to praise it fully:
> The Virtues of perfection such as charity, morality, etc.,

And the invocation of the Buddha's name, confession,
   and ascetic discipline,
And many other good deeds of merit, –
All these issue from the practice of Meditation;
Even those who have practised it just for one sitting
Will see all their evil karma wiped clean;
Nowhere will they find the evil paths,
But the Pure Land will be near at hand.
With a reverential heart, let them to this Truth
Listen even for once,
And let them praise it, and gladly embrace it,
And they will surely be blessed most infinitely (Suzuki 1970:
151f).

As the scriptural evidence shows, Buddhism's various strands give
prominence to the offer of a way to triumph over the ignorance,
illusion, rebirth and suffering of everyday existence, whether
through self-effort leading to nirvana or through the saving grace
of a heavenly being helping the faithful to reach the Pure Land.
Certainly the paths of liberation lead to a transcendental reality,
but it is not thought of as a god. This is of the utmost importance
for any who wish to understand the planetary meaning of
religion.

Religion and well-being in China

One of the regions in which Mahayana Buddhism took root and
flourished was China. This means that its vivid and comforting
message of salvation through the compassionate agency of
heavenly bodhisattvas won acceptance among the Chinese
people, so it would be very strange if the native traditions of that
country, Taoism, Confucianism and folk religion, were without
comparable elements of hope and benefit. In Taoist teaching as
enshrined in the *Tao Te Ching* ('The Way and its Power'), this is
easily found, for it is taught that the path to peace is through
unassertiveness and harmony with the flow of the cosmos. This is
certainly to offer people a means of overcoming or at least
minimising the wretchedness of ordinary living, and that is
obviously a benefit. Here are some relevant extracts from the *Tao
Te Ching* (Lin Yutang 1949):

He who knows the Eternal Law is tolerant;
Being tolerant, he is impartial;
Being impartial, he is kingly;
Being kingly, he is in accord with Nature;
Being in accord with nature, he is in accord with Tao;
Being in accord with Tao, he is eternal,
And his whole life is preserved from harm (ch. XVI).

The Sage does not accumulate (for himself)
He lives for other people
And grows richer himself;
He gives to other people,
And has greater abundance.
The Tao of Heaven
Blesses, but does not harm.
The Way of the Sage
Accomplishes, but does not contend (ch. LXXXI).

The message of these words is plainly more than just the existence of a way of harmony and non-assertiveness, of creative quietude, as the doctrine of *wu wei* is often translated; it is something explicitly more: such a way exists and is the way to minimise hardship and promote well-being.

Turning next to Confucianism, the investigator faces an initial difficulty as to whether to include it in a study of religion. Often it is regarded as a religious movement, but it does not focus attention on a transcendental realm. Everything depends, of course, on how one chooses to define religion. In the present book the aim is to arrive at an understanding of it after examining the movements we ordinarily associate with the word, and for this purpose the sensible policy is to cast the net widely and include phenomena whose status is a matter of debate as well as the accepted, typical candidates. Confucianism therefore qualifies for inclusion. In any case, its long history in China means that like Islam, Hinduism or Christianity it won and held the allegience of millions of people over many centuries, so that our exploration of the human qualities involved in religious existence will profit from drawing Confucianism into the discussion by revealing the nature of its appeal to people (Yang 1967:26). At least there is an interesting family resemblance with the other movements that have been examined, because Confucianism also provides ways of promoting human welfare. Master Kung is often seen as a social educator rather than a religious metaphysician or interpreter of the gods; his priority, to judge by the *Analects*, being to inculcate principles that would promote *jen*, goodness in the individual and in the community (Waley 1938: 28). Since this is obviously intended to minimise personal and communal hardship, it is clearly a way to promote benefit. The intention may have been social salvation rather than transcendental salvation, but is salvation none the less, and therein lies the family resemblance with movements like Buddhism and Christianity. In the words of the *Analects*: 'The Master said, he that is really Good can never be unhappy. He that is really wise can never be perplexed. He that is really brave is never afraid' (Waley 1938: IX: 28). Another passage reads similarly:

> The Master said, Without Goodness a man
> Cannot for long endure adversity
> Cannot for long enjoy prosperity.
> The Good Man rests content with Goodness;
> he that is merely wise pursues
> Goodness in the belief that it pays
> to do so (Waley 1938: IV: 2).

That goodness none the less involves benefit is asserted in the following passage:

> Jan Jung asked about Goodness. The Master said, Behave when away from home as though you were in the presence of an important guest. Deal with common people as though you were officiating at an important sacrifice. Do not do to others what you would not like yourself. Then there will be no feelings of opposition to you, whether it is the affairs of a State that you are handling or the affairs of a family (Waley 1938: XII: 2).

In other words, good behaviour results in favourable feelings towards the person who so acts, which is clearly a desirable consequence.

In his study of religion in Chinese society C. K. Yang presents a wealth of evidence that testifies to the benefits sought by the ordinary people in connection with popular or folk religious beliefs and practices, with their temples, priests and local deities (Yang 1967: 28ff). His data on the purpose of the temples and of prayer slips used by supplicants discloses a comprehensive search for individual, communal, farming, national and cosmic benefits. Concerning family life, for example, Yang writes:

> The Chinese people have always felt that, even with the utmost exertion, human abilities and efforts alone were not sufficient to guarantee physical well being, economic success, or family harmony. There was always the profound feeling that success or failure in these respects was not entirely within human control, but needed the blessing of spiritual forces (Yang 1967: 28).

There could hardly be a more explicit statement of the central part the desire for well-being plays in connection with religion than this. The same is true of the economic sphere:

> On behalf of the peasant, the emperor, provincial governors, and county magistrates throughout the country plowed ceremonial fields and offered sacrifices to the agricultural deities at (the) altars in the spring and sometimes also in the fall, praying for assistance from the supernatural forces to bring 'harmonious winds and timely rain' for the year (Yang 1967: 65).

Thus the religious experience of people living in China repeats the pattern of benefit and protection against adversity that we have found so abundantly in other societies. The sources of succour are differently conceived from people to people but all of them turn in their faiths to whatever they believe will help them to cope with the things that menace their existence (Thompson 1979). Details of doctrine, ritual, imagery and behaviour vary strikingly among the religions, as do the specific conceptions of how to find well-being. What is constant is the desire for that well-being. So the scriptural evidence confirms the personal reports of religious experience with which this discussion of evidence began, showing us that whatever else it may be, faith is certainly a call for help and a conviction of its availability amidst the multitude of destructive forces encountered in life.

Scholars' conclusions about non-scriptural religions

Two of the four categories of evidence about religion and well-being have now been examined, namely personal testimonies and scriptural material. Now it is time to look, albeit briefly, at the third category, the verdict of a selection of observers and other researchers who have investigated religions that do not have their own written forms of expression, from the many hundreds of which information is available.

Writing about American Indian religions, Ruth M. Underhill reports that the ceremonies which were so prominent in them were not intended for worship, but are better regarded 'as the renewing of a partnership between man and the supernaturals, to the benefit of both' (Underhill 1965: 4). Also in connection with the American Indian people, Mircea Eliade records a very revealing belief held by the Delaware Indians concerning the Creator's dwelling:

> When we reach that place, we shall not have to do anything or worry about anything, only live a happy life. We know there are many of our fathers who have left this earth and are now in this happy place in the Land of the Spirits. . . .
> Everything looks more beautiful there than here, everything looks new, and the waters and fruits of everything are lovely (Eliade 1977: 160).

This belief splendidly exemplifies the religious promise of something greatly, even infinitely superior to our present existence, a place or condition of happiness and beauty in contrast to the difficulties, sorrows and ugliness that physical existence involves. The desire for help in coping with such problems is a very natural one and is well illustrated in the following Delaware prayer: 'We come here to pray Him to have mercy on us for the year to come and to give us everything to make us happy; may we have good crops, and no dangerous storms, floods or earthquakes' (Eliade 1977: 159). Something similar has been reported of the Australian Aborigines. Referring to the performance of their secret ceremonies, an investigator writes that the participants return from these events refreshed mentally and spiritually, with 'an assurance that having performed the rites well and truly, all will be well with themselves and with that part of nature with which their lives are so intimately linked' (A. P. Elkin, in Eliade 1977: 164). And the Dayak people of Borneo are reported as believing that the area they inhabit, being 'supported and enclosed by the godhead,' is such that they can live there 'in divine peace and well-being' (Eliade 1977: 155).

The African traditional religions are a rich mosaic of faiths and in them the same phenomenon – the prominence of benefit and assistance in dealing with crippling problems – is present. Thus E. G. Parrinder discusses a West African form in his essay called 'An African Saviour God' (1963: 117ff); it is recorded as being part of the beliefs held on the eastern side of the continent (Werblowsky and Bleeker 1970: 181ff) and is certainly present in southern Africa. A splendid example is the rain-making cult of Zimbabwe's Matopos Hills situated in the south-western part of the country, which is notably drier than the rest. The link here between religion, rain and benefit is too obvious to require elaboration.

The purpose of citing these examples is to show that observers into widely separated forms of non-scriptural religion in Africa, America, Australia and Borneo have detected exactly the same concern as we saw in personal reports and the scriptures of the faiths of literate societies in the west, the near east, Indian, China and Japan: the desire to safeguard cherished values, to find assistance in withstanding the many threats posed to life and happiness, to achieve and retain a sense of peace and the assurance that there is something to hope for and hold to if not in this life then certainly in another. Jointly the three categories of evidence are sufficiently fundamental, sufficiently in touch with terra religiosa itself, and sufficiently representative to justify the conclusion that apart from anything else it may be, the religious life all over the world and in all the periods of which there is reliable information is most emphatically a pervasive concern for well-being, for deliverance from all kinds of danger and harm including physical danger, for liberation from whatever is found to confine and imprison, for salvation from suffering, sorrow, anxiety, mortality and evil, and for increase and abundance of the things that make for health, prosperity, wholeness and peace, in this life and beyond the grave. In all its provinces terra religiosa is pervaded by this comprehensive concern with well-being, and if

we would map it faithfully we must map this ubiquitous characteristic. Yet that is exactly what our received and widely held
theories about religion so often fail to do.

Scholarly confirmation

The concern to find help in coping with life's many adversities
and to generate benefit is recognised, in varying formulations, by
several experts who have worked in close, empirical contact with
religion, unlike those whose approach is heavily theoretical. Their
views provide valuable corroboration for the conclusion reached
above. In this connection William James is especially instructive
because of his influential and pioneering work in the analysis of
religious consciousness. In *The Varieties of Religious Experience*
he wrote, 'Happiness! happiness! religion is only one of the ways in
which men gain that gift. Easily, permanently and successfully, it
often transforms the most intolerable misery into the profoundest
and enduring happiness' (James 1902: 175). And near the end of
his book he set forth the following conclusion about spiritual
experience itself: 'The only thing that it unequivocally testifies to
is that we can experience union with *something* larger than
ourselves and in that union find our greatest peace' (James 1902:
525). There is no conceptual difficulty in grouping together the
key words in these two passages – profoundest joy, enduring
happiness and greatest peace — under the terms benefit and well-
being, because each of them stands for a quality of existence or
being in which all is well. On this score it is interesting that
Ninian Smart, whose work covers a far wider range of religions
than that of William James, should reach essentially the same
conclusion. He writes that 'religion itself functions as a slant on
welfare, a way of seeing the nature of true satisfaction' (Smart
1981: 282). In theistic terms Wilfred Cantwell Smith has written
that 'God saves us in any way He can, I suppose; but thus far,
primarily through our religious systems' (1981: 170). The eminent
Dutch phenomenologist of religion, Gerardus Van der Leeuw,
declared that salvation is the goal of all the faiths, defining it as
'the enhancing of life, improvement, beautifying, widening,
deepening' but also as a 'completely new life, a devaluation of all
that has preceded. . .' and finally asserting that 'all religion, with
no exception, is the religion of deliverance' (Van der Leeuw 1938:

681f). Very similar is the judgement of John R. Hinnells:

> Salvation is the essence of religion. Belief in God or gods is not a central part of a number of traditions, but salvation is the mainspring of much if not all religious experience (if by that term we mean release from the bonds which the believer is convinced ultimately oppress him, be those bonds the disintegration of tribal society, loneliness, suffering or death)' (Hinnells 1973: 125).

As defined by these writers, salvation is just as readily to be understood in terms of well-being as the words William James used. What they have in mind is a quality of existence in which all is well. Very similar is the eloquent verdict of the distinguished Indian philosopher and religious thinker, Sarvepalli Radhakrishnan. He wrote that the aim of religion is 'to lift us from our momentary meaningless provincialism to the status and significance of the eternal, to transform the chaos and confusion of life to that pure and immortal essence which is its ideal possibility' (Radhakrishnan and Moore 1967: 635). Meanwhile the American process theologian Henry Nelson Wieman wrote that the 'religious problem . . . can be stated thus: What can transform man in such a way as to save him from the depths of evil and bring him to the greatest good which human life can ever attain?' (Wieman 1958: 10). To be lifted from an unworthy and pointless existence, to escape chaos and confusion or the depths of evil, are variations on the themes of benefit and well-being and thus point in exactly the same direction as the views of William James, Ninian Smart, Wilfred Cantwell Smith, Gerardus Van der Leeuw and John Hinnells.

Lest this collection of expert judgement seem unwisely dominated by verdicts from people whose work is in theological and religious studies, let us include others from the social sciences. Peter Berger has written that in order to withstand the ubiquitous threat of chaos, the religious person infuses reality with his own meanings. 'Religion implies that human order is projected into the totality of being . . . religion is the audacious attempt to conceive of the entire universe as being humanly significant' (Berger 1973: 37). The reference to withstanding the forces of chaos is quite consistent with the benefit-giving quality we have seen in preceding pages. Anthropologist Melford E. Spiro sees religion as 'the belief in superhuman beings and in their power to assist or to harm man...' (Spiro 1966: 94). His definition places greater importance on the idea of spiritual beings than is consistent with the teachings of several of the movements we have considered, and the reference to harm touches a separate facet of religion, but by explicitly including the element of assistance Spiro supports the conclusions reached by the others. Perhaps the most forthright confirmation of all comes from social scientist C. K. Yang when he writes of religion as

> the system of beliefs, ritualistic practices, and organizational relationships designed to deal with ultimate matters of human life such as the tragedy of death, unjustifiable sufferings, unaccountable frustrations, uncontrollable hostilities that threaten to shatter human social ties, and the vindication of dogmas against contradictory evidences from realistic experience. Such matters transcend the conditional, finite world of empirical rational knowledge, and to cope with them as an inherent part of life man is impelled to seek strength from faith in such nonempirical realms as spiritual power inspired by man's conceptions of the supernatural' (Yang 1967: 1).

In view of this powerful body of evidence about religion as a way of seeking and finding significant well-being, Mother Julian of Norwich, the noted English mystic, can be seen to have spoken from the heartland of terra religiosa when she said, 'But all shall be well, all shall be well, all manner of thing shall be well' (in Neil 1975: 74). Undoubtedly, then, religion is in significant measure a concern for benefit in its many physical, moral and spiritual forms (Brandon 1962; Parker 1935; Shaw 1930).

The question of terminology

The preceding examination of personal testimonies, scripture, research findings and scholarly judgements has revealed the unmistakable prominence in the various religions of a large family of broadly synonymous words which jointly signify benefit. Starting with the material quoted from William James' work, we encountered a long series of such expressions: happiness, being saved from suicide, strength, vitality, support, the good of all, peace, security, freedom, increased energy and courage, deliverance, safety, health, hope, guidance, healing, prosperity, bliss, rescue, life after death, release from the cycle of rebirths, freedom from fear, infinite blessedness, timely rains, supreme enlightenment and many others. They form an impressive index of the qualities involved in the world's faiths, the more so because their prevalence in all areas indicates something deeper and more widespread than the localised variables of particular cultures. In these expressions we hear the heart beat of faith, we touch the virgin soil of terra religiosa.

But religious studies does not yet have a suitable covering term for this luminous spectrum. Salvation is favoured by some authorities but it has the severe drawback of doctrinal associations with Christianity, which unfits it for global use except possibly when heavily qualified. That carries the high price of laborious expression. The term used in this book is well-being. As an established phrase it is free of the problems of artificiality and strangeness that so often go hand in hand with coining new words; it has a desirable breadth of meaning without being uselessly vague; signifying 'a condition characterized by happiness, health or prosperity' (Webster), it covers exactly the kind of item that the devout themselves mention. Here and there believers themselves use it in connection with their faith, but nobody could say that well-being belongs to the special vocabulary of any of the world's religions, and it has the philosophical advantage of combining in a single phrase the twin concerns with existence and value so typical of much religious thinking. Of course there are also disadvantages; notably a certain lightness is some of the the associations of the word, unfortunate in regard to faith, for which people will on occasion die (and indeed kill). But any term will have blemishes; what counts is whether they are bearable. Weighed against the advantages the difficulties of the present proposal seem manageable.

With this terminological consideration out of the way we can now conclude the first and longest part of the global characterisation of religion to which this chapter is devoted. When explored on a planetary basis and with regular recourse to evidence coming directly from the various faiths themselves, the religious life turns out to involve a pronounced concern for and a finding, however incompletely, of significant forms of well-being in any of the great number known to human experience, from cures to asthma and the expectation of immortality to transcendental insight and the hope of surpassing finite existence itself. Such sweeping benefits as these remind us of the breath-taking promises made in some of the world's faiths, like eternal life, perfect and unending bliss or the peace that passes all understanding. They tell of an unsurpassable good to which religious faith is the key. Conversely, this striking and fertile theme of blessing has its counterpart in the grim realities of evil so much emphasised as well by sages, saints, martyrs and seers, and also by the ordinary citizens of terra religiosa. With this deeply significant point about religion and benefit established we can now move on to discuss the remaining global characteristics of religion. The discussions of them will be much shorter than with religious well-being because on the whole they are better established in our spiritual cartography.

POWERS THAT AFFECT HUMAN EXISTENCE AND ITS VALUES

Closely related to the beneficial transformations so typical of the spiritual life is the experience of powers that affect human existence. For example, one of William James' informants who was quoted above spoke of 'the Holy Trinity' and a related sense of immense happiness. Another told of a 'fundamental cosmical It' which gave endless vitality. Sir Alister Hardy's data included reports of a warm and beautiful Presence followed by a sense of peace, and of the wonderful feeling of freedom and flow of love that resulted from dedication to Jesus Christ. The Hebrew scriptures tell of the god Yahweh who caused a strong east wind to part the waters of the Red Sea and allow the Israelites to escape from the pharaoh's pursuing armies. According to the New Testament, Jesus of Nazareth was raised from death by God (Acts 2: 24), while for Muslims the infinite blessings made known by the revelation of the Qur'ān come from Allah himself. Zoroastrian teaching speaks of Sosyant, a superhuman figure who will bring benefit, and in the Bhagavadgita Lord Krishna promises to save those who focus their thoughts on him from the sea of the rounds of death. The Upanishads declare that transcendental knowledge has the power to liberate people from the prison of perpetual rebirth and ignorance and reveal our essential unity with Brahman. In Theravada Buddhism knowledge of the four noble truths likewise has liberating power, while in the Mahayana the heavenly boddhisattva bestows his saving grace on those who place their trust in him. According to the great Rinzai Zen master Hakuin, even those who practice meditation for only one sitting will have their evil karma wiped away, which surely implies a greatly beneficial power issuing from that practice. The *Tao Te Ching* speaks of the way of heaven which blesses, Confucius of principles that promote goodness, and sociologist C. K. Yang reports the common people's conviction in China that they need the help of spiritual forces for success in life. Ruth Underhill wrote of the supernaturals believed in by America's Indian peoples. Africans discern tiers of spirits and a high god, while in Melanesia anything extraordinary was attributed to mana, a diffused potency everywhere potentially operative.

As these expressions show, the world's religious vocabularies contain a large number of terms referring to the entities and activities that are believed to cause or be effectively associated with the blessings so persistently sought by believers. Very often but not always these terms denote invisible superhuman beings ranging in importance from local and ancestral spirits through the intermediate tier of gods and goddesses with limited spheres of operation, like Poseidon, the ancient Greek god of the sea, to the omnipotent supreme beings of the monotheistic faiths. We can also see this in the vast register of personal names invoked by devotees in many parts of the world as they pray or worship: Yahweh, Allah, Shiva, Zeus, Indra, Baal, Ra, Thor and Enlil, to name a handful of well-known ones. Judging by religious art, these divine beings are mostly conceived on the model of humans and described by words like king, judge, or warrior. There are, for example, ancient Canaanite depictions of Baal, lord of the rains, in the regalia of a king. But theriomorphism – concepts of divine beings based partly or wholly on the forms of animals – is also present, as with the elephant-headed symbolisation of Ganesh in Hinduism. An extremely widespread tendency in the religious life is therefore to think that human well-being depends ultimately on the power of personal spiritual beings with minds and wills of their own.

But our examples also show that the sources of well-being are not always thought of like this. The Buddha set forth a way of liberation that does not depend on spirits or a god but on the effectiveness of supreme insight into the nature of reality and a

related programme of emancipatory action, crowned by meditation. Something analogous is to be found in philosophical
Hinduism, in the teachings of the *Tao Te Ching* and evidently
also in that extremely widespread notion of many non-scriptural
religions, namely that there is around us a diffused potency
capable of causing remarkable effects, known as mana in parts of
the Pacific and by various other names elsewhere (Underhill 1965:
20). Shivesh Chandra Thakur is thus correct in saying that 'it is
entirely possible to have religion without God' (1981: 19). The
human mind has not been uniform in its understanding of the
sources of the well-being it so highly values.

What has not varied, however, is the conviction that human
existence and happiness are decisively affected by the operations
of these spirits, deities, diffused potencies and liberating truths,
which the devout invoke in their prayers, honour with their
sacrifices and accolades or base their lives on. It is not difficult to
find illustrations of this belief in virtually any society. The
material presented in the section of this chapter devoted to the
theme of religion and well-being contains many. What is
extremely tricky is to find a way of grouping the variously
conceived agents and sources of well-being under a single,
suitable category. The one chosen in the present book is power,
although the word force will also be used for stylistic variation. To
speak of powers or forces for what believers themselves call their
ancestral spirits, the risen and ascended Christ, Lord Krishna,
the Tao or the Dharma is to do four things: reflect the common,
logical meaning of those terms; avoid terminology strongly
associated with any of the spiritual traditions; avoid tacitly
endorsing or denying the believers' claim that such spirits, deities
or supernatural realities really exist; and reflect the fact that in
the religious life important effects are indeed experienced. Of this
there can be no legitimate doubt. People really do report peace of
mind or an inflow of strength or hope and other benefits from
their prayers, worship and meditation, and there is no reason to
suppose that they are being dishonest when they do so. They are,
after all, in the best position to report on what they experience.
Real effects, moreover, presuppose real causes, so it is in fact
uncontroversial to speak of these causes as forces or powers, for
whatever produces a change or an effect is, by definition, a force
or power. There is thus no question-begging or sacrificing of
scholarly impartiality involved in speaking of the believer's

claimed relationship with a god, for example, as contact with a power, so long as effects are indeed produced in that person. Whether or not that power is correctly regarded as a spiritual being or as a projection from the subconscious mind of the believer is of course an entirely separate question and not one we are called upon to debate in a phenomenological chapter like this.

There are further grounds for this choice of word. The theistic religions explicitly relate the concept of God to the exercise of power. In the words of the Qur'ān: 'God is powerful over everything' (Sura 24: 44). Hinduism's RigVeda X: 129 speaks of the primordial unity in terms of the concept of -*svadha*, meaning 'energy, intrinsic power which makes self-generation possible' (Eliade 1977: 111, Hutchison 1977: 38). William James summarised the spiritual life as the 'sense of a Presence of a higher and friendly Power' (James 1902: 274), while Sir Alister Hardy's research hinged on an appeal to people for reports of experiences involving 'some Power, whether they call it God or not, which may either appear to be beyond their individual selves or partly, or even entirely, within their being...' (Hardy 1979: 20). There is also some linguistic evidence that the Semitic word for deity, '*ēl*, actually meant 'be strong' and 'power' (Pope 1955: 16ff), while a similar meaning appears to be associated with the root of *kyrios*, the Greek word for Lord. Then there is the instructive example set by Van der Leeuw when he selected the term power to stand collectively for what he called the object of the religious consciousness (Van der Leeuw 1938: 23ff). On logical, methodological, factual and linguistic grounds the terms power and force are thus suitable for use as a descriptive generalisation about whatever religious people believe affects or is the cause of the well-being they desire so strongly.

Our mapping of the spiritual landscape can thus be taken a stage further by means of this second, equally ubiquitous characteristic. Among believers, in terra religiosa, so to speak, there is not only a yearning for and taste of significant well-being, but concomitantly a focus on the powers that appear to yield and, for that matter, frustrate it, whether conceived as spirits, gods, heavenly potencies or transcendental insight into the ultimate nature of reality itself. Thus Ninian Smart has written that the 'power of God is ultimate security', (1981: 204) just as the ancient Egyptian devotees of Aten, the deity symbolised by the solar disc, could say, memorably, 'Thy rays suckle every field' (Eliade 1977: 30). The connection between these forces and human well-being cannot be sufficiently emphasised because it is everywhere present in the religious life itself. That is why our inherited idea that religion is all about a spiritual realm is so misleadingly inadequate; it fails to make explicit this ubiquitous belief in an *ameliorating* potency of some kind or other. The connection between these higher powers and well-being is true even in the seemingly contrary view sometimes expounded by devout people, namely that God is worshipped for his own sake and not out of any desire for reward or any fear of punishment. Yet such people none the less hope to experience the everlasting peace and beauty of God. What is access to the everlasting peace and beauty of God if not supremely beneficial? The evidence itself therefore justifies H. N. Wieman's blunt comment: 'The word "God" is irrelevant to the religious problem *unless* the word is used to refer to *whatever in truth* operates to save men from evil and to the greater good...(Wieman 1958: 12). In any case, the point is surely established that the religious life everywhere involves experience of certain highly significant forces which believers regard as directly responsible for the benefits they so assiduously seek.

TRANSCENDENCE

In the eyes of believers the powers encountered or released during religious activities are of a very special kind, not on a par with the forces of nature or those at human command but higher than these, manifesting or giving access to a superior but imperceptible order of reality. To a westerner the words that probably capture this belief best are spirit, the supernatural, the sacred and the transcendent, each deriving from Latin and thus historically associated with western religious thought. To use them in the present project with its avowed intention of avoiding conceptual provincialism might therefore seem self-defeating, but since the same differentiation between physical or mundane existence and a superior, invisible order of existence with which we can have contact by special means but which is inaccessible to our senses is present in all the traditions explored in this book, it is not methodologically improper to use them, especially as there are no accepted alternatives. Of the four the word transcendence appears to be the most suitable for the present project because it is the least beset by disputed philosophical associations. The concepts of spirit and the supernatural are often used by those holding a strictly dualistic view of reality, sharply contrasting physical existence accessible to the senses with a postulated superior non-physical realm, that of spiritual or supernatural reality. Using these terms might thus seem to imply acceptance of dualism, and since this doctrine is disputed even inside religious circles (for example by advaitic Hindus and process metaphysicians), any apparent endorsement of it would conflict with the phenomenological method, in which such issues are bracketed. Transcendence, which means going beyond or surpassing, is semantically free of this difficulty and better suited for the purposes of descriptive generalisation. It stands for all those religious notions which assert that the powers affecting human well-being belong or lead to a reality which is more durable, reliable, beneficial, valuable, powerful or important than the supposedly lesser reality of everyday experience, with its impermanence, tragedy, pain and failure. On the other hand, the term transcendence does not exclude the possibility of a dualistic world-view being correct; such an exclusion would also be contrary to the phenomenological approach. As for terms like the sacred and the holy, these have acquired such strong conceptual links with disputed theories or views of religion, notably those of Rudolf Otto and Mircea Eliade, that their use here would be unwise. What they stand for in spiritual experience is of course immensely important and will be dealt with elsewhere in this book, for example in chapter five.

Another advantage in speaking of transcendence is that it can cover both the superhuman beings who figure so largely in many faiths and also those which do not have that concept but focus instead on a transcendental condition regarded as finally and ultimately real. It is simply more accurate to speak of religion as teaching that there is a transcendental order of reality than to speak of it as belief in spiritual beings, because only the former covers all the faiths - those that are directed towards conditions like nirvana or sunyata as well as towards spiritual beings like God.

So, to round off this third part of our picture of religion, terra religiosa is that form of human existence in which the quest for well-being through the forces that govern it, while often involving mundane benefits such as bodily health, none the less has primary reference to the concept of an unseen, transcendental reality as far exceeding our finite, mortal condition in power, durability and value as the heavens, in the prophet's mind, were higher than the earth. Thus Ninian Smart has fittingly written that 'what the great religions claim, against radically secular ideologies, is that there is a Beyond or an Unborn; and this is somehow accessible to the religious experience of the human race, and is not just a philosophical speculation or a theory about the world.' (Smart 1981: 178)

RELIGIOUS FAITH AS THE INVOLVEMENT OF THE WHOLE PERSON

It is sometimes supposed that religion, being orientated towards a transcendental dimension of reality, has little relevance to the material side of our existence, and that faith has its basis merely in one part of our make-up, namely our capacity to believe, interpreted as the acceptance of a set of ideas about spiritual entities for which there is little or no empirical evidence or rational foundation. Seen in this way, religious people are passive beings, heavily dependent on an external source of truth and direction and apt to neglect the physical side of life in favour of the spiritual, at least if they are really devout. This view is at odds with the evidence, which shows that faith is often anything but one-sidedly other-worldly. Instead it involves the whole personality of the believer in a comprehensive, creative effort to experience the blessings of a transcendental orientation in this life as well as in any other. No less an authority on faith than Jesus of Nazareth said as much when he taught his disciples to pray that the Father's kingdom should come on earth as it is in heaven, and to ask for daily bread as well as glorifying God.

Just how comprehensively people enter into their religious commitments can easily be seen in the material that was presented above in order to document the desire for well-being. There were references to our mental life, to the ability to experience the presence of beneficial powers, to have a sense of peace, to feel happy

or hopeful, to form concepts and to seek truth; there were references also to actions of all kinds, to making things, to leading and
being led, to listening and to speaking. The pains of the body and
the problems of daily living were cited along with moral issues,
profound philosophical wrestlings and the most rarified ascents of
the questing spirit. The only safe verdict to reach is that the entire
range of human resources comes into operation in the religious
life, as befits so paramount a concern as our greatest well-being.
This is also evident in the kinds of spiritual activity that are
especially prominent. Meditation, prayer, worship, processions,
chanting and other practices occur in many traditions and have
some right to be thought of as typically religious; each of them
involves the whole person, thoughts, words, bodily movements
and feelings (Hick, 1974).

It is also contrary to the evidence to view believers as necessarily
passive or as helplessly dependent on the powers that govern their
well-being. While it cannot be denied that such people consider
that their existence is crucially affected by those forces and
on occasion describe themselves self-deprecatingly as utterly
dependent on them, this must not be confused with passiveness.
Religion involves effort, however light that effort may seem to the
glad-hearted believer: effort of mind to understand saving truths,
to meditate, search the scriptures or formulate doctrines; effort of
will to discipline behaviour into salutary patterns; effort of body
to build cathedrals, and effort also to conduct services and use
words or deeds to the good of all. Often the effort is conspicuously
creative, as when a hymn in written, a melody composed, an
epistle penned to the Romans or a Zen koan devised in order to
promote transcendental insight. This holds for religions which
focus on the saving help of spiritual beings as well as for those
which call for self-help in the path to liberation, where human
action is obviously essential.

Just as the religious life involves the whole person, so too it is
something that requires seriousness of purpose. Faith certainly
generates happiness and joy but it does not go with levity. The
best illustration of this point is the extent to which the devout are
prepared to suffer for their faith. There are many martyrs in the
various traditions and although crucifixion, extreme self-denial
and death at the stake or in the arena are rare they have
happened and imply the utmost dedication. Much space has been
given in this chapter to documenting the pursuit and experience

of well-being in religion, and with good reason. But the full picture also includes an undeniable element of hardship, what Jesus of Nazareth spoke of as suffering for righteousness' sake, and which many believers know at first hand.

The best word for this comprehensive, ultimately enriching, transcendental orientation is faith, provided it is not confused with belief in the sense of accepting certain propositions on authority. This is a widely held but fallacious interpretation, as Wilfred Cantwell Smith has recently shown (1979: 170ff, Needham 1972). Belief in this sense is limited to concepts and propositions, and smacks of the tentative and the provisional. Yet in the religious life, in faith, people sense something profoundly real, transcending the capacity of words. Inestimably important to them, the telling of it is both imperative and yet at best a feeble echo of the reality itself. Wilfred Cantwell Smith has summarised it admirably as 'a capacity to live at a more than mundane level; to see, to feel, to act in terms of, a transcendent dimension.' Explicitly calling it a 'planetary human characteristic', he adds that faith 'involves man's capacity to perceive, to symbolize, and to live loyally and richly in terms of, a transcendent dimension to...life' (1979: 12, 140f). To be religious, then, to have faith, is to be wholly engaged, mentally, actively and spiritually, with the powers that generate well-being in this life and in relation to a surpassingly higher but unseen order of being. This is an advisedly broad definition of faith; anything narrower would fail to cover all the facts. But it is just as advisable to remember the specific modes of experience which it summarises. There is mystical experience – itself perhaps a complex phenomenon with inner varieties – rational reflection, a turning of the probing mind to the divine for explanations of the world's beginning or for answers to the mysteries around us, awe at those mysteries when they threaten to engulf us, life-changing revelatory visions, wonder, love sublime, the tenderest intimacy and even the anguish of the doubt-plagued or guilty soul. Caught up in a power which has overtones of transcendence, people have exhibited some striking variations of mind and feeling, and we would do well to keep at least the more prevalent ones in mind. Nor should we forget that so far as details are concerned, individuals appear to be unique in their personal faith, nuancing it to the needs, situations, opportunities, temperaments and choices which are different for every one of us. Faith reveals patterns but it does not seem to involve spiritual cloning.

THE PLURALITY OF RELIGIOUS TRADITIONS

To live religiously is not just to experience the beneficial transformations of an orientation towards the transcendent, it is also to
think, speak and act in a highly specific way in relation to that
experience, each individual appropriating and living in terms of a
common stock of ideas, expressions and behavioural patterns
from one (and nowadays more than one) of the world's spiritual
systems. In other words, the life of faith is also a matter of sharing
the resources of a specific tradition in whose shaping countless
people have played a part and which differs from other religious
traditions. Terra religiosa is watered by many streams, each with
its own characteristics; to be religious is thus to draw from a
native river shared by some but not by all one's fellow human
beings, most of whom live on the banks of other sustaining
streams.

Let us think of a religious tradition as an evolving complex of
shared ideas, words, action patterns, artifacts, institutions, roles
and associations which jointly facilitate, embody and express the
believers' experiences of benefit-giving powers which become
effective in an orientation towards the transcendent. People
participating in some or other tradition are of course what the
investigator first encounters when exploring the religious life:
devotees gathered at a temple or shrine to offer sacrifice to a
patron deity whom they think of as a protector from disease or
against famine and failure, pilgrims at Lourdes, the Ganges or
Mecca, and innumerable other examples. Philosophers and theologians deal in the abstract and talk generally about supernatural
powers, but the religious life itself is very specific. To be religious,
to seek and taste the benefits of a spiritual dimension, is to focus
one's life on specific supernatural beings or transcendental goals
with their own names and characteristics which differentiate
them from those of other traditions and also from a theorist's
abstract generalisations. To say, 'I take my refuge in the Buddha'
in company with other believers in a Pure Land temple is to take
part in something very particular and well defined. It is to accept
a system of ideas about the Buddha and about life at large which
may not be held even by other Buddhist groups; it is to be
involved in a ritual act of reaffirming membership of a particular
Buddhist sect, in a place and very probably in front of symbolic
objects whose design and shapes give spatial and visual expression

to that faith and distinguish it from other kinds; and it is to associate with others of the same persuasion. For the most part the life of faith anywhere in the world comprises some such complex of participations, some such system of myths, doctrines, rites, artifacts and associations, and on the whole a religious tradition lives in the involvement of persons in these things. The exceptions are very rare indeed, namely individuals who practice a solitary faith without altar or icon and beyond word or concept, to experience that pinnacle of pure and immediate insight which some hold to be the crown of religion. Even here, of course, the more usual style of the spiritual life is presupposed, for nobody reaches the summit of faith without first ascending the foothills, and to pass beyond icons or incense or companions is never the less to affirm for them a genuine although provisional reality. So it is fair to say that being religious includes participation in a specific tradition of ideas, actions, artifacts, roles, associations and institutions which express, facilitate and embody the believer's contact with or progress towards a superior order of reality, even if some adepts say that the sign of success is the ability to do without those things.

The earth contains many such participatory, evolving traditions, and the historians of religion of the past century or so have enabled us to recognise that they differ, often acutely, in point of detail. The world's spiritual systems are not, as some appear to hold, virtually the same except for minor differences. Certainly there are striking instances of close similarity and many important parallels. But there are also some very real divergences. The main ones are between people who understand the final and supreme reality as a personal god and ones who do not, a distinction often expressed as the difference between numinous and mystical types of religion, between those who believe in immortality for the individual with the retention of separate identities and others who see such identities as something to be transcended; and between belief in a divine creation of the physical universe and the doctrine of an eternal cosmos. There are other disagreements over specific doctrines like the finality of the Qur'ān or the Bible as God's supreme revelation, or the indispensability of faith in Christ for eternal life, but it is not necessary to be exhaustive about them. The point is simply that there are some very substantial disagreements among the world's believers, not just from tradition to tradition but also within individual religions. No two believers, to vary Heraclitus' famous saying, can ever draw from their native stream in quite the same way. An acceptable explanatory theory of religion must reflect these variations and say why human beings with their common, planetary quest for well-being and their common vision of a transcendental dimension none the less embody that quest and vision in such different systems or doctrine, ritual and institution.

There is much evidence supporting the statement that religions evolve, at least as far as cultures with written records are concerned. The faith of the ancient Hebrew prophets in the eighth century BCE is not identical to that of a contemporary orthodox rabbi; St Paul would doubtless have needed a good deal of briefing to make sense of a Lambeth Conference or a Vatican Council, or even of Luther's protests against Rome; and it is by no means clear that Muslims before and after the Islamic revolution are unchanged people. Often a religion will teach that there is an unchanging ultimate reality or that its own beliefs are immutable, but it is quite another matter to suppose that such religions themselves, moulded and carried as they are by changeable human beings, are immune to development and modification in the course of time. And of course even in a relatively stable spiritual tradition no individual is ever static. For this reason the use of the phrase 'the cumulative tradition' is particularly apt because it brings out the living, evolving character of our systems of religious belief and practice (Wilfred Cantwell Smith 1978: 154f). Christianity is an excellent example. A contemporary Anglican eucharist will often be conducted according to an order to service modernised in the last decade or two, with some of its prayers influenced by Thomas Cranmer in the sixteenth century, based on a liturgical tradition which reached the English through Rome from the early church. The creed will date from the year 381, the sermon be based on a gospel passage written in about 70 CE recording the words of Jesus spoken a generation earlier and applied, let us say, to the problem of racism in the modern world. The Gothic cathedral where it all happens may have been built in the middle ages, with music composed at the beginning of the twentieth century. And it could take place on a date which commemorates a saint who died in the fourth century. Of all this only the words of institution spoken by Jesus of Nazareth and the sacramental act of sharing the broken bread and the wine are known to go back to the original event in the Jerusalem upper room, barely hours before the arrest of Jesus. The rest has accumulated over the centuries, like the annual rings of a living tree.

To summarise these contentions let us visualise the earth's religions as many groups of people, each group possessing a distinctive stock of concepts, words, ways of viewing reality, patterns of personal and social behaviour, buildings, music, styles of dress and institutions; with each person daily using a unique selection from that distinctive, shared stock of resources to express a common sense of well-being and transcendence, occasionally also adding something lasting for others to use, like Cranmer and his eloquent prayers or the unknown architects who gave us the minaret and the pointed arch. All over the earth a multitude of such spiritual groupings has emerged, mostly in considerable isolation, often with quite striking differences of belief, ritual and organisation, while yet exhibiting a common concern with transcendence, blessing and the forces that yield it. To these regional variations must be added, or course, the conceptual bifurcation of the world's religions into the two great categories of faith, one focussing devotion and service upon personal, spiritual beings, the other proclaiming the experience of a non-personal spiritual paramountcy as the ultimate reality. In ages past virtually all people appear to have belonged to some such group, often as a matter of course and involving no element of personal choice at all. In our own time the groups are in ever greater mutual contact, with some of their boundaries – never absolute – becoming increasingly easy to cross. New, plural spiritual citizenships are evident. And at the same time the number of people renouncing any such citizenship steadily mounts.

RELIGION AND CONTEXT

As we have just seen, the spiritual life of the individual is expressed in an evolving tradition comprising myths, doctrines, rites, codes of behaviour, institutions, social roles and artifacts. This brings the mapping of religion in the present chapter to something that is conspicuously absent in most of our old theories: contextual influences on the shaping of a religious tradition. We can define these as the effect exerted on a tradition by formative factors like geography, culture, history, political pressures and any other phenomenon to which those who help produce, modify and transmit it are exposed. Traditions live in and through the people who participate in them, and people think, act and speak occasionally out of pure creativity but mostly under the influence of whatever external realities impinge on their consciousness. Among these external realities is the context or environment in which people live. To be human is therefore to be more or less affected by a particular set of conditions and to reflect its influence in what one thinks, does and says. Put the other way around, contextual conditioning means that a system of religious ideas and practices cannot be detached from its environment as though it were unrelated to the surroundings in which it formed. Judaism could not be what it is without Zion or Egypt, nor Christianity without Rome or the Emperor Constantine. Would we ever have spoken of Buddhism's larger and lesser rafts – the Mahayana and Hinayana traditions – without India's great and once unbridged rivers? The twenty-third psalm could not have been written in a society without shepherds, and who can doubt that traces of Arabia in the seventh century are visible in the imagery of the Qur'ān? Religions, in short, are covered by the finger prints of those who pass them on. This is not, of course, the same as saying that religion is entirely the product of the conditions in which it is found. It is merely an acknowledgement of the local colour that is visible in all faiths.

Since the world comprises a great many localities and has seen many historical, political, economic and cultural changes, and since people often differ greatly from one another in temperament, interests and abilities, their ideas and beliefs, as expressed in any of the natural languages, exist in a host of different, local forms and systems. They are like the plant kingdom, which comprises not one but many different species adapted to the weather and soils of a given locality in a world of varied terrain and climate. Or, to vary the analogy, they are like currency systems, each operating in a specific area and not directly equivalent or even similarly structured to the others. Outside that area of circulation a set of religious ideas and associated activities may, like sterling or the maluti, have a limited acceptability, or even none at all. Theology, or buddhology for that matter, is not globally, let alone universally, negotiable. It is not a kind of spiritual algebra, intelligible and meaningful anywhere on earth, independently of the circumstances in which it is formulated, as the examples given above make all too clear.

It requires a broad perspective, a measure of detachment and a good deal of comparative analysis of belief systems in relation to their contexts to bring all this to light. But if one knows only one's native Islam or Christianity things will seem very different. Prevailing ideas will seem to be unrestrictedly valid and their connection with local, conditioning factors will not be noticed. Our inherited views of religion have their origins in precisely such circumstances, and their formulators can hardly be faulted for not emphasising or even noticing a contextual influence that must have been virtually impossible to detect at that time. The fault is to persist with them now that the fuller, transformed picture is available. It is not an exaggeration to say that recognising at least some degree of contextual conditioning could necessitate a revolution in our view of religion, a paradigm shift to a radically new perspective, because the new view calls in question the possibility of perfectly expressing timeless, absolute truths, such as some religions say they possess, in any available language, influenced as it will be by passing, contextual factors and local concerns. For this reason alone much of our traditional spiritual cartography is obsolete, of no more use in mapping the paths to heaven than Ptolemy's cosmology could guide Mariner to Mars. A good deal more will be said on this issue in chapters four and five when we discuss the formation of cultures and doctrinal systems.

LEADERS, EVENTS AND SACRED WRITINGS

No picture of the world's religions could be complete without including the small group of great leaders from Moses to Muhammed, sacred writings like the Bible or the Vedas, and pivotal events such as the exodus, the crucifixion and the hijrah which have so profoundly affected some but not all of the faiths, notably those that have come to be called, unsatisfactorily, the world religions – Judaism, Christianity, Islam, Hinduism and Buddhism. Together these are the spiritual traditions of by far the most believers, often spreading well beyond the societies in which they began. Obviously, then, the figures, scriptures and events which played a fundamental, formative part in launching or steering these massively influential movements must be among the most important characteristics of terra religiosa. In connection with the people who so crucially shaped these so-called world religions, there is also the often-cited and intriguing fact that many of them lived within a century of the year 500 BCE, making that period an astonishingly fertile one for religion. Since the term 'the axial period' is often mentioned in religious studies for this development, it is convenient to speak of the traditions that were involved, directly or indirectly, as the axial religions and the others as non-axial, thereby avoiding the undesirable, judgemental connotations of a term like the great religions or the inaccuracy of 'world faiths' for what are in fact only the most populous provinces on the spiritual landscape (Jaspers 1957: 14ff; Geering 1980: 32f). In any event, the fact is that a small number of spiritual leaders, documents and critical events play an enormously important part in shaping the world's most widely followed faiths but are absent in others. A worthwhile map of terra religiosa must chart this fact and a worthwhile explanatory theory shed light on why it is so.

THE SECULAR CHALLENGE TO RELIGION

There are indications that for most of history religious faith of some kind was a universal feature of human existence, something that people acquired automatically as a natural, unquestioned part of their heritage. At all events the dissenters were exceedingly rare if they existed at all. But over the past few centuries a new situation has been developing, especially in Europe and America, namely the rise of non-religious ways of understanding reality and living, in which any kind of spiritual orientation is seen as mistaken and delusory. The new phenomenon goes under several names, like materialism, positivism and secularism. One of its signs is the idea that religion is an entirely private or personal matter. But the heart of the phenomenon is the repudiation of any talk about an ultimate spiritual reality independent of and superior to mundane existence. So far as we can tell from available statistics, most people now living continue to profess some form of religious affiliation or conviction, so that the number of wholly secular people would be relatively small. This is not, however, the point. What matters is not the statistical question but the fact that religion in the forms it has hitherto manifested and perhaps in any form is now increasingly bypassed in favour of a this-worldly life-style, while even believers must nowadays make a conscious choice about their faith. (Berger 1980) That a once-universal form of human existence is being challenged in this way by secularism is also something that must be entered on the contemporary map of religion.

*   *   *

With these remarks our planetary representation of the most important, recurring characteristics of religion is complete. The resultant map shows us a world-wide, age-old phenomenon of people reporting experiences of deeply significant well-being in connection with belief in a transcendental order of reality and the operations of a range of powers conceived often as personal, spiritual beings capable of aiding humanity and sometimes as beneficial truths and techniques which individuals must realise and apply on their own; involving the whole personality and taken with great seriousness of purpose, these experiences are embodied in a set of traditions all over the earth which contain striking mutual resemblances as well as powerful disagreements, each one forming at least in part under the conditioning influence of a range of local factors such as history, geography and culture, and, in the most numerically powerful faiths, under the impact of a handful of decisive leaders, events and inspiring scriptures. Well-being, transcendence, powers, faith, immortality, mythico-ritual traditions the world over, contextual conditioning, the great luminaries, the enduring scriptures and the secular alternative – these are the key words in a general description of religion which aspires to global validity in our time. And underlying these constituent themes there is, let us recall, the teeming spiritual landscape itself, comprising a myriad specific and personal details of religion on earth. For just as this fair planet of ours has brought forth her soft green carpet of plant life, plentiful and varied and marvellously fitted to the prospects for life in moist conditions or dry, temperateness and the tropics, hillside and valley, and just as she has mothered the family of human cultures from tent-dwelling Bedouin parents to their computer-minded son, so too is the earth the place of a richly-speciated faith. Some there are who look to ancestral spirits for guidance and correction, some to the gods and goddesses of sky, earth, rain and sea. Some, most numerous now, have found their soul's wings through the summons of that unifying vision which discerns a single god ruling providently over all lesser things. Elsewhere, others there are who tell of a formless spiritual finality, the all to which all else tends when elsehood fades. Thus a shared human sense of an unseen transcendent is refracted into the various, crisper, spiritual images of particular believers. Expressing and enhancing them is the prodigious growth of ritual, custom, myth, costume, life-style and world-view, never **exactly replicated anywhere yet exhibiting an unmistakable** family resemblance – regional variations on a global human melody heard and loved by an inner ear from Stonehenge to Silicon Valley. And with one voice this planetary, spiritual chorus declares that the only true and lasting satisfaction, the ultimate power and the ultimate blessing, lies in that unseen, transcendent order. Such is the real marvel and fascination of terra religiosa: that amidst the unmet pressures and the unfinished pleasures of the visible world, with which even now we have not nearly made our peace, there should be this massive, ancient and deeply rooted sense of another, better world, immediately to hand yet also mysteriously remote, suffusing, enthusing and surpassing the things of sight and sense. With all this in mind we can turn next to explanation, asking why this immense phenomenon has come to be part of human existence, why people down the ages have been convinced that their welfare and indeed their very lives depend in the last resort on an order of reality transcending perception, why some of them think of that reality as the realm of spiritual beings from the lowliest to the most high, while others see it as non-personal, why religious traditions and individual believers differ, and why sceptics repudiate all suggestion of such an order of existence. To answer these questions it is, however, first necessary to deal with a logically prior issue: what does the act of explaining involve?

3   The Art of Explaining

Attempts at explaining religion have seldom paid any attention to the crucial problem of working out an adequate and defensible explanatory method. Instead they plunge ahead and take this extremely important and difficult question for granted, as though it were perfectly obvious what was involved. The result, as we saw in chapter one, is a predictable impoverishment of the theories in question. This is as much true of believers as of sceptics, and it applies to the authors of all our best known accounts of religion: Feuerbach, Marx, Durkheim, Otto, Freud, Barth and others. In consequence valuable insights and proposals are undermined or even vitiated altogether. Explanatory theories of religion are thus badly in need of methodological rigour and refinement, and the best way to achieve these improvements is to build on and adapt the work done by thinkers who have explored the philosophy of explanation most thoroughly. It is they, chiefly in the physical and social sciences, who have made the greatest progress towards pin-pointing the steps that should be taken in order to explain a phenomenon satisfactorily. That is the purpose of the present chapter. After a review of the procedures recommended by these philosophers there is a systematic discussion of central issues in their work, followed in the last section by an adaptation of their methods for the special purpose of explaining why people think and behave religiously and why others choose a secular way of life. It turns out that the most promising approach is to construct a coherent explanatory theory of religion out of causal factors within our experience, broadly considered, some of them akin in scope and function to the laws of nature invoked in scientific explanations of physical phenomena. This would mean showing that religion in any form is the logical consequence of certain fundamental, far-reaching factors affecting our existence in general, our separate cultures and our personal situations, while also accounting for those who reject a spiritual approach to life

68

altogether. The most influential view of rigorous explanation at present is precisely this, namely to propose a testable theory such that all the phenomena under investigation will be logically derivable from it, as well as satisfying the usual, formal requirements to which all theories are subject, such as clarity, economy of terms and logical consistency.

CENTRAL ISSUES IN THE PHILOSOPHY OF EXPLANATION

When we use the word 'explain' we mostly have in mind one of four meanings: giving reasons for something we have done; clarifying an unclear statement, a process that has been analysed by linguistic philosophers; helping a learner to grasp something, which is an educational skill; and finding out why a phenomenon exists or works in a particular way. This fourth meaning relates to the discovery of new knowledge, and it is the one with which the present chapter deals. Each of the four has its own distinctive methods, and much confusion arises from failing to distinguish them. The question that first confronts us is how explanations of this fourth kind should be done. Let us review the available procedures.

The covering law model

As could be expected in view of their success, the physical sciences have been the basis for much of the work done in recent decades on the philosophy of explanation. From that work comes the covering law or nomological approach, its technical name from the Greek word *nomos*, a law, an approach which some influential thinkers regard as the ideal type and thus as a model for people working in other disciplines to follow if they also wish to achieve rigorous standards (Nagel 1961; Hempel 1970: 331ff). A characteristic of this procedure is that explanations in the strict sense are answers to why-questions and not merely to what-questions; they are called for whenever we pose problems like 'why do objects fall when there is nothing to support them?' and are provided whenever we introduce our replies with the word 'because', followed by a law of nature which embraces the problem and a description of the conditions in which it happens (Popper 1972: 193). By contrast, what-questions are logically less demanding. When we ask what happens if an object like the weather vane on a cathedral tower loses its support, the answer can be found by watching derelict spires in stormy weather, seeing what takes place and then stating it in an exact description, such as 'they fall to the ground'. This requires patient observation and care in the choice of words, but these are physical and technical difficulties, not logical or conceptual ones of the kind involved in trying to answer why-questions. The latter presuppose that a phenomenon has already been extensively observed and described, with the way now open to asking why it happens. Explanation therefore depends logically on description and is thus a more complex procedure. And it is made even more complex if the only really adequate way of carrying it out is to identify one or more covering laws, because finding them requires a vast, tested knowledge of nature, enormously surpassing the observation of specific phenomena.

Within the category of covering law explanations there are two kinds: a more ambitious kind involving deduction and a less ambitious one involving induction. The former is known technically as deductive-nomological explanation, and the details are as follows (Hempel 1970: 335ff). The problem to be solved is called the explicandum (or explanandum) while the solution is known as the explicans or explanans, and it must comprise two components: firstly one or more laws of nature, and secondly, a set of statements specifying the initial conditions of the problem – in other words, descriptions of the circumstances and conditions present when it happened. The really important requirement, however, is that the statement of the problem must be logically deducible from those two component parts of the explicans. It must follow necessarily from them. An illustration involving the law of gravity will be helpful at this point. Suppose we have observed a weather vane crashing to the ground from a church tower and we ask why it fell. The explanation is that the bolts which secured it to a steel bar rusted away so badly that in the next strong wind they sheared completely, and, with no support, the weather vane fell, because all objects fall to the ground unless prevented. Each of the requirements mentioned above is present here. The problem or explicandum is why the weather vane fell.

The covering law is the law of gravity, formulated as the general principle that all unsupported objects fall. The initial conditions are the severely rusted bolts and the strong gust of wind. And the deductive logical relationship between the explicans and the explicandum is honoured, because it follows of necessity that if all unsupported objects fall then this particular weather vane must fall too. Bearing in mind that the Greek word for law is *nomos*, we can now see why the procedure is known technically as deductive-nomological explanation: it involves deduction from a covering law. An important advantage of this procedure is precisely the ability to make deductions because these can be be formulated as predictions and tested in practice, an essential step in science. So the quest for explanations is greatly aided by a method with built-in testability such as the covering law approach. As C. G. Hempel has said, a 'proposed explanation is scientifically acceptable only if its explanans is capable of empirical test...(in Brodbeck 1968: 185).

Clearly, the concept of a law of nature is central to this method. It can be defined as a single statement of a genuine invariant or regularity in nature, (for instance, all unsupported objects fall), capable of being stated in hypothetical (if-then) form, discovered on the basis of empirical investigation and able to yield testable predictions. It is also said that a law should use only terms referring to observable phenomena (for example, 'unsupported objects' and 'fall') or at least only ones that can be related to observations, and that it should be capable of systematic linkage with other laws, so forming part of a coherent account of the world (Hesse 1967: 404ff; Hospers 1967: 229ff). Whether a law of nature can ever be known to state a genuine invariant or regularity of nature is a matter of dispute, because we can never observe all the possible instances of a proposed law. Therefore natural laws are often regarded, less ambitiously, as generalisations with a very high degree of probability rather than as absolute universal principles. This weakens the inferences we can make from them thus giving us the second of the two types of law-invoking explanation, namely the inductive-nomological type. Since it too appeals to a law of nature to account for problems, the term covering law is still logically applicable.

In summary, then, advocates of this model assert that 'the occurrence of an event is explained when it is subsumed under or covered by a law of nature...' (Kim 1967: 159). Similarly, Rudolf

Weingartner has said, 'To explain why an event occurred is to deduce the statement expressing what has occurred from initial condition statements and general laws.' (Weingartner, in Brodbeck 1968: 351)

As can be seen from the existence of two forms of the covering law model, this is not a clear-cut explanatory procedure. It is not surprising, then, to find that even in regard to the physical sciences there are thinkers who seriously question at least the strong or deductive form of the model, also raising other problems like the concept of a natural law (Toulmin 1964, Harré 1970, Feyerabend 1978, Hesse 1980). None the less it continues to have many defenders, and it is easy to see why. In theory the strong or deductive form of this kind of explanation could provide the most thorough treatment of a problem by relating it to a universal, unvarying pattern of nature. The very universality involved is the attraction of the model, because it means that the relevant pattern admits of no exceptions whatever. Therefore it would logically provide a complete explanation. The weak form of the model naturally falls somewhat short of such comprehensiveness. It may be closer to actual scientific practice but its explanatory power amounts to an extremely high probability rather than to a logical certainty.

Underlying the appeal to laws of nature in order to account for phenomena is, of course, a view of the universe as an orderly aggregate functioning according to regular, uniform processes which can be discovered through observation and formulated very accurately as testable laws of nature. This implication is present irrespective of whether adherents of law-invoking explanations recognise it or not. Two questions arise in this connection. Firstly, how reliable is the idea of an orderly universe, in view of the fact that it is itself derived from a limited (though numerically immense) number of observations, while none the less purporting to state the basic character of a limitless cosmos? And secondly, even if we grant that it is a reliable concept, why is there such a universal orderliness in the first place? This is, of course, to take the search from explanation to an ultimate point and it raises the problem of whether science can ever complete the search. We shall return to this problem later in the chapter. The purpose of raising it now is to draw attention to the influence our basic world-views can have on what we judge to be the correct or best method of explaining phenomena. It has been said that '. . . conflicts of method are much more than differences of opinion about the technique of human enquiry. They are immense struggles between competing empires of the mind' (Woods 1958: 13; cf von Wright 1971: 2ff).

Explanation in the humanities and the social sciences

The key question that arises at this point is whether the covering law model of explanation is appropriate in disciplines dealing with human behaviour. Some prominent theorists think that it is. Thus Hempel has written that 'all adequate scientific explanations and their everyday counterparts claim or presuppose at least implicitly the deductive or inductive subsumability of whatever is to be explained under general laws or theoretical principles (Hempel, in Brodbeck 1968: 411; Gardiner 1965). But there are also thinkers who deny this, holding that human behaviour is not such as to be explicable, or at least wholly explicable, in terms of covering laws (Dray 1957, 1964; Gallie 1964; Popper 1961; Winch 1958; Cobb 1981). Their standpoint calls to mind the celebrated view of Wilhelm Dilthey, the nineteenth-century German philosopher of history, who held that there are separate methods for the natural and human sciences. Logically, the heart of the issue so far as history is concerned is said to be its distinctive subject matter. Individual actions and events are the raw materials of history and being unique they cannot, in principle, be referred to laws, since these apply to classes of events, not to unique particulars. Classes presuppose similarity whereas every historical event is different. Therefore it would be wrong to demand covering law explanations in such a subject. Instead the historian refers to illuminating concepts, prior events and the reasons or motives governing individual actions. Others remain unconvinced by this point. Thus Gardiner has written as follows:

> The engineer is concerned with building particular bridges. The architect is concerned with designing particular houses. Like the engineer and the architect, the historian is concerned with reconstructing particular situations in the past. But, just as neither the architect nor the engineer is free to ignore the laws of mechanics in his work, so, I shall argue, the historian, for all his attention to the individual and the unique, is not free

to disregard general laws in his work of reconstruction
(Gardiner 1965: 45).

Arguing against the extension of the covering law model to
history, William Dray contended that historians have explanatory
methods of their own. One of them, for example, involves showing what an event is, which he called 'explanation by means of a
general concept' (Dray, in Brodbeck 1968: 344). The investigator
proceeds, in effect, by classifying the problem. This need not
involve a general law or yield predictions, though it may. He concluded that 'it would thus still be a mistake to regard the covering
law theory as setting forth a genuinely necessary condition of explanation' (Dray, in Brodbeck 1968: 345). According to this view,
a reference to the industrial revolution as, for instance, a triumph
of ingenuity over conscience, could count as a valid historical
explanation. This is similar to an earlier proposal (Walsh 1942)
suggesting the term colligation for the act of bringing a phenomenon under a subsuming or covering principle or concept, from
the verb colligate, meaning 'to bind, unite, or group together
often according to a subsuming principle', and 'to organize under
one conception' (Webster). Other explanatory methods open to
the student of human activity are to identify the origins of the
problem under investigation, sometimes called genetic explanation, and to refer to the intentions that accompany or give rise to
the things people do, for which the technical term is teleological
explanation.

An important issue in the literature about methods of explaining in the life sciences is precisely this reference to intentions and
to purposive or goal-directed behaviour. Unlike weather vanes
and other inanimate objects, living organisms adapt their
behaviour into patterns designed to realise goals, consciously and
unconsciously. Any satisfactory explanation would have to take
this factor into account. Let us look briefly at the example of a
man who spends many hours in the evenings and over week-ends
doing over-time work to finance a holiday abroad for the family.
Clearly his goal or purpose leads to those over-time activities, so
that some theorists regard the goal as explaining his behaviour,
because what he then does will realise it. A conscious intention is
present and effective. Goal-orientated behaviour need not,
however, be conscious. Depth psychology has brought to light the
fact that human actions are sometimes governed by factors like

repressed fears or hostilities of which the agent can be quite unaware. The resultant actions need be no less goal-directed for that reason, as in the case of a person whose unrecognised fear of failure leads to an aversion towards anything that involves an uncertain outcome. Both varieties are spoken of technically as teleological behaviour.

The point to consider now is whether the covering law approach is applicable to this kind of behaviour. Here too opinions differ. According to some it can be. Referring to this view Charles Taylor has written that 'the laws by which we explain the behaviour of (living organisms) are teleological in form' (Taylor 1964: 17). Similarly Wright has written that 'the very identification of teleological behaviour is at bottom a matter of determining the underlying, causal regularities and boundary conditions which conspire to produce it...the explanation in each case is of the standard covering-law/causal-deterministic kind' (Wright 1976: 29). The reference here to determinism is important, and one we shall return to later. For the moment the point to emphasise is that purposeful behaviour is not regarded by Taylor and Wright as incompatible with law-invoking methods of explanation.

A contrary view is, however, expressed by Georg von Wright in his book *Explanation and Understanding* (1971). He denies that all real explanation is of the covering law type, holding that cybernetics, for instance, involves a different kind and that the covering law approach does not account for action (von Wright 1971: 15ff). Logically, the issue depends on whether goal-directed behaviour necessarily excludes the possibility of its being an instance of a law. It would be if such behaviour were randomly irregular or idiosyncratic, because that would in principle rule out the very notion of a law, because a law of nature is precisely a testable statement of a regular or uniform phenomenon. Conversely, if regular patterns of goal-directed behaviour were to be observed, law-invoking methods of explanation would in principle be valid. After all, hibernating animals all maximise their chances of surviving the winter shortage of food by hibernating, so there are examples of goal-directed uniformities of behaviour. In principle, therefore, goal-referring and law-invoking explanations could be compatible, so that the logical possibility exists of purposeful activity among humans or in any other life-form being accounted for in terms of the covering law model of explanation.

Whether all human behaviour can be so handled is, of course, another question altogether.

Functional analysis has also been proposed as a valid explanatory device, especially in the biological and social sciences (Hempel, in Brodbeck 1968: 179ff). This means finding out what a component does in a working system of which it is part, for example the beating of the heart in the body of an animal or the regulation of interest rates in a modern economy. We say these organs and measures exist in order to oxygenate the body or, by influencing the money supply, promote or restrict investment, and so forth. This is a revealing way of putting things, the phrase 'in order to' being a sign that functional analysis belongs to teleological methods of explaining. There is no doubt that it is illuminating to know the function of a given item, but whether this amounts to rigorous explanation will depend on one's view of the latter. Thinkers like Hempel consider functional analysis to fall short of having a genuinely explanatory value, the reason being the absence of a relevant law capable of being tested empirically. So Hempel concludes that a 'class of phenomena has been scientifically understood to the extent that they can be fitted into a testable, and adequately confirmed, theory or a system of laws; and the merits of functional analysis will eventually have to be judged by its ability to lead to this kind of understanding' (Hempel, in Brodbeck 1968: 209). As with goal-directed behaviour in living organisms, the analysis of functions may or may not be part of a law-invoking method of explanation; it all depends on whether those functions instantiate a general or regular pattern of phenomena. Failure to do so would not deprive the analysis of value, but it would be explanatory in a less ambitious sense than in cases where an appropriate law or set of laws can be invoked. In any case, it is noteworthy that functional analysis can certainly be a way of answering a why-question, as may be seen in the following questions: 'Why do motor car engines have carburettors?' or 'why do banks raise and lower interest rates?' The answers tell us about the part played by carburettors in petrol engines and by interest rates in attracting investors and making a profit, so taking the form of functional analyses.

The viewpoints so far considered have contained no logical grounds for concluding that the covering law type of explanation is out of place in the human sciences, except in relation to unique, particular phenomena. Dray's covering concept in history, the idea of colligation proposed by Walsh, teleological methods and functional analysis each provide illuminating techniques without necessarily invoking laws, but none constitutes grounds for ruling laws out as being unsuitable in principle, except for unique particulars. The human sciences are not, of course, confined to these. There is, however, a viewpoint from which the covering law model can be resisted as logically mistaken. It is based on the claim that human behaviour involves free will. This entails the possibility, not to say certainty, of unpredictable variations in the choices people make, which would be logically incompatible with an appeal to covering laws for the simple reason that where there is randomness and unpredictability there cannot be regularity, and without regularity we have no basis for speaking of laws in the first place. Another way to put the issue is to say that making deductions from covering laws to account for everything implies a determinist view of reality, with all events being predictable, at least in principle. But a genuinely free choice cannot be predicted, so if people do in fact make such choices, their actions cannot be completely explained by the deductive-nomological method. The point is valid, and if human behaviour does contain such a random element, it will to that extent not be exhaustively explicable by means of nomological techniques. Everything depends on the evidence. If people's actions reveal uniformities that could be stated as testable generalisations, like 'All criminals come from deprived backgrounds', then there is justification for seeking explanatory methods that make use of covering laws. But if their actions reveal idiosyncracies unique to each individual, then covering laws would be out of the question.

Explanation and religion

Turning next to explanation theory in relation to religion, the enquirer finds some valuable suggestions by social scientists but no comprehensive treatment, and, apart from a few recent exceptions, very little by philosophers of religion. One such exception is Donald A. Crosby's book *Interpretive Theories of Religion* (1981). Crosby helpfully distinguishes theory from definition, which deals with the meaning of words and has to be succinct; from descriptions, which present particular details; from descriptive generalisations, where patterns and similarities in such particulars are identified and classes of phenomena described, and from normative theories, which say what a religion ought to be. Theories, he asserts, are constructed, posited or invented, unlike descriptions of data; and their purpose is either to interpret or explain. They interpret by telling us what it means to be religious. On the other hand, explanatory theories, which he says depend logically on interpretive theories, are mainly intended to identify the causes of religion (Crosby 1981: 4-17). Most of these are relevant observations, suggesting an inter-related investigative complex that begins with the description of religious phenomena, moves next to descriptive generalisation involving the identification of patterns and resemblances in the data as a whole; then turns to the construction of interpretive theories designed to say what religion means, and culminates in the devising of explanatory theories where the objective is to reveal what causes religion. In due course it will be necessary to amend somewhat this view of explanation in the light of Popper's work, but that does not detract from the usefulness of Crosby's set of distinctions.

Another useful contribution from Crosby is his list of criteria for theory-building. Although the items in it are intended for interpretive theories, most of them are equally applicable to explanatory work. The relevant criteria, somewhat paraphrased in a few cases, are as follows. There should be no judgemental or normative element in a theory, which is of course also what the phenomenological approach stipulates. It should provide a structure of categories capable of illuminating the religious life; and where possible, make use of previous theories. Next, a theory ought to help the enquirer understand single religious systems and should also clarify why the various faiths both resemble and differ from one another. Then there must be due attention to both the personal side of the religious life and to the objects on which believers focus their faith. Furthermore, theories should be 'adequately general, not provincial, in scope', and they should 'enable us to distinguish religious interests from other basic types of human interest and yet do justice to the interdependence of religious and other interests'. Finally, a theory should help the investigator classify difficult examples of the phenomenon it purports to cover (Crosby 1981: 298). There is clearly much in Crosby's work that is extremely useful and readers are invited to apply his criteria to the theory set forth in this book. The limitation, so far as the present project is concerned, lies in the restriction of his subject matter to interpretive as distinct from explanatory activity. This is perfectly legitimate but it does leave undeveloped the question of how to explain faith, and Crosby's own definition of an explanatory theory as the identification of causes is, as we shall see, unsatisfactory.

Also of interest is Shivesh Chandra Thakur's treatment of the question 'Does Religion Explain?' in a book with the title *Religion and Rational Choice* (1981: 47ff). He argues – correctly, in view of the massive amount of aetiological or cause-orientated mythology in religions the world over – that spiritual beliefs do indeed often have an explanatory function, parallel to but not the same as that of science, and he offers an extremely instructive account of the way religious explanations arise and take shape, seeing them 'as appearing in extraordinary experiences by unique individuals, peculiar when first experienced but from then on capable of serving as moulds of perception for others' (1981: 49). These are instructive ideas but Thakur's project differs significantly from the one dealt with in this book. He sees religions as explaining the world; here it is the religions that must be explained, not the world. When he does discuss methods of scientific explanation his lucid account deals mainly with the covering law model.

The reference just made to religious explanations of the world is a convenient point at which to mention the work of two philosophical theologians who have given extensive treatments to this very question (Woods 1958; Swinburne 1979). Both writers expound a view of theistic religion as providing a complete or ultimate account of things, or as being superior to rival accounts. G. F. Woods, the earlier of the two, sets out 'to show that theology is the consummation of our best methods of explaining the world' (Woods: 39). He makes much of the idea that we explain as persons but gives no great attention to the methods of explanation discussed in the philosophy of science or the humanities. Swinburne, on the other hand, pays careful attention to them, though his main aim is to contend that personal explanation involving purposes and intentions is quite distinct from scientific explanation (Swinburne 1979: 36ff). All this is done in the context of a highly technical inductive argument for the existence of God, making ingenious use of probability theory. Both writers thus work in the area covered by Thakur's book, namely religious explanations of the world, except that their proposals are confined to theism. As such they appeal to religion to function as the explicans or explanatory factor for the problem of why there is a world, which is precisely the opposite procedure to the one called for in this book, where spiritual phenomena are the explicandum or problem that requires a solution. Put differently, Woods and Swinburne operate theologically rather than scientifically or as investigators looking for an explanation for theology and all other manifestations of religion. This naturally limits the relevance of their work for the present project. What remains relevant is their notion of personal or agent explanation as a distinctive type not to be assimilated to covering law methods, which places them in the same position as thinkers like Dray who also resist the notion that the only adequate explanations are ones which involve laws. We shall return in the next section to this issue. Meanwhile there is another point arising from the theories of Woods and Swinburne which requires discussion, namely the attempt to provide ultimate or complete explanations for things, whether by appealing to the concept of God or to any other factor.

This prompts the question of the cognitive status of such ultimate facors. Are they self-explanatory or not, and if not, what could conceivably explain them, since they are supposed to be the key to everything else? It seems that the search for a complete explanation must either involve unexplained categories, in which case it falls short of being wholly explanatory, or those categories must be clarified in terms of other items in the theory, which is plainly circular. Either way the attempt seems logically incapable of yielding a complete explanation of reality as a whole. It is perhaps in this light that Popper's objection to the idea should be understood, though his own reason is formulated as the impossibility of 'a self-explanatory description of an essence (Popper 1972: 195). In any case his familiar statement that scientific discovery involves 'the explanation of the known by the unknown' appears to imply that at least in empirical investigations there cannot be ultimate or final explanations (Popper 1972: 191). Excluded from empirical research by the most influential contemporary philosopher of science and logically incapable of being either wholly explanatory or wholly comprehensive in either theology or metaphysics, the project of finding an ultimate account of all reality appears as problematical as it is attractive to those who are not satisfied with an incomplete picture of things.

The most helpful contribution from a social scientist to the question of how religion is to be explained is Melford Spiro's essay on 'Religion: Problems of Definition and Explanation' (Spiro, in Banton 1966: 85ff; cf Hammond-Tooke 1982). He asserts that a full account of religion must be both causal and functional, defining these two methods as seeking 'some antecedent condition' and 'some consequent condition', respectively. He writes that the 'causes of religious behaviour are to be found in the desires by which it is motivated, and its functions consist in the satisfaction of those desires. . .'. In a slightly varied formulation of the same idea he proposes that 'an explanation for the practice of religion must be sought in the set of needs whose expected satisfaction motivates religious belief and the performance of religious ritual' (Spiro, in Banton 1966: 100, 117, 107). In other words, the spiritual life is brought about or caused by certain needs, and consists in the measures that are thought to satisfy them. What those needs are is a separate question and one which those who construct theories of religion must establish; Spiro's aim in the essay under discussion is not to deal with that, but to specify the basic requirements for a satisfactory explanation of religion.

There is a two-fold justification for his suggested method and an important limitation. The two justifications are firstly the enormous emphasis believers themselves place on finding true well-being, which is easily construable in terms of needs and their satisfaction; and secondly, the fertility of the method in the actual construction of an explanatory theory of religion, though this must await a later chapter for demonstration. The drawback about Spiro's causal-functional model is its apparent limitation to the believers who experience those needs and whose faith satisfies them. There is more to religion, however, than just the believer; an external component comprising the powers that affect well-being is also involved. This is what Donald Crosby calls the cosmic side of religion, as distinct from the personal side (Crosby 1981: 298; cf Smart 1973: 74ff). To affirm these powers is simply to respect the empirical evidence of the effects faith has on the devout. As was explained in chapter two, wherever there are effects there must be powers or forces in operation. While Spiro himself makes no such claim, on its own a needs-satisfaction method of explanation might seem to imply that there is nothing more to religion than the people who feel those needs and take steps to satisfy them, and this would certainly be to ignore relevant evidence. So Spiro's explanatory model is valuable as a tool for establishing why faith exists and persists, but will have to be supplemented by other methods with respect to the forces that generate religious satisfaction, especially when objective phenomena like the fall of Jerusalem or the monsoon rains are associated with that satisfaction. And for this Spiro has himself given a neatly worded directive: an explanation of religion, he writes, should comprise 'the specification of those conditions without which it could not exist' (Spiro: 118). As the wording implies, those conditions might be external as well as internal to the believer.

ESSENTIALS OF EXPLANATION

The preceding discussion shows that the philosophy of explanation consists of a number of prominent, debated themes mostly relating to the nature and scope of the covering law model. A great deal of valuable progress has been made: necessary distinctions have been drawn, guidelines proposed and positions defined. All this is immensely helpful, but it has not been coordinated into a systematic discussion of the subject. What we need now is precisely such a treatment of the main items that have emerged so far.

What-questions and why-questions

In every day speech the word explain is used in connection with what-questions as well as why-questions, and indeed also with ones beginning with the word how. So, for example, we might ask a suspect in a police investigation to explain what happened on the fateful night, or how he managed to own a luxury car without being employed, or why he was living under an assumed name. This ambiguity makes it essential to say exactly which of these logically distinct meanings we intend and then use the chosen one consistently. In this book explanation means answering why-questions and in a few specified cases, how-questions, unless the other meaning is specifically indicated. Mostly, however, issues like 'what does faith involve?' will be regarded as requests for descriptions of observable phenomena or for interpretations. It will become clear in chapter five that constructing an explanatory theory of religion involves a good deal of interpretive activity in addition to the descriptive generalisations given in chapter two. These are thus important topics and must now be dealt with in greater detail than previously.

Descriptions, interpretations and models

The policy adopted in this project means that the task of saying what religion is belongs to the preparation for rather than to the actual construction of an explanatory theory. Here it is helpful to recall the various facets involved in that preparation and add one that has not previously been mentioned. The first facet is recording information about religion on the basis of observation. Ideally this should be done with as much empirical terminology as possible, but in practice no observer can completely separate descriptions from interpretations caused by his or her existing notions. In the well-known phrase, our descriptions are apt to be more or less theory-laden, because even the act of observing is affected by the ideas already present in the observer's mind (Hanson 1969: 61ff). None the less, a skilled investigator who is aware of this problem can produce reports that are much less affected by observer-bias than others less practised in their craft, so it remains useful to speak of the first stage in preparing for explanatory activity as the description of individual phenomena. So far as religious studies are concerned, this refers to the long and exacting labours of historians of religion and anthropologists mainly over the past century.

A second, partly preparatory, step is to transform the mass of descriptive material into a representative model of the phenomenon. This is a term that has not previously been discussed but what it stands for has certainly figured prominently. A model can usefully be defined as a systematically developed and comprehensive representation of a complex phenomenon designed to identify and co-ordinate its elements (cf Barbour 1974: 6ff). The operative words here are representation, elements and co-ordination, so that the crux of modelling religion is to identify its typical, constituent parts and then relate them to one another in a way that will set forth accurately the processes and connections present in the spiritual life itself. The idea is to enhance understanding by means of representative simplification in which richness of detail is sacrificed in order to give prominence to important structural and functional properties. So far as this book is concerned, the modelling stage corresponds partly to chapter two where the dominant characteristics of religion were identified. Co-ordinating them is, however, best left to chapter five because it depends on certain explanatory considerations relating to the desire for well-being, which will only be presented in chapter four. To revert to an earlier set of distinctions, devising a descriptive model is a way of saying what religion is, so it forms part of the preparation for explanation. Co-ordinating the elements of the model is a way of saying how they interrelate, and is thus best located separately. In any event, constructing a model of religion is partly a matter of descriptive generalisation of the kind that was done in a previous chapter, and partly an explanatory procedure that will be tackled in later chapters.

As for interpretation, this too can be regarded as preparatory to the finding of an explanation, but here the essential operation is to provide an imaginative, revealing way of crystallising or epitomising the information. An example will be helpful. Suppose someone declares that the earth is best thought of not as an organism but as a single, living cell (Thomas 1975). To do this with any degree of acceptability requires firstly that the originator of the idea has mastered the available information about the earth and next that a concept or phrase is found which covers and highlights all that information. The success of the exercise depends on the closeness of the fit between that covering concept (to use Dray's expression) and the data, and on how striking the concept is. More is thus required than just the data, and the extra requirement is an imaginative, creative act of matching a metaphor to the material in hand. This justifies the distinction between describing and interpreting a phenomenon. To say that the earth is twenty-five thousand miles in circumference at the equator, with three quarters of its surface covered by salt water is to describe it; to say that it is a living cell is to interpret it. Both are ways of saying what it is; neither tells us why it exists or why the oceans are so extensive; but they certainly prepare us for those explanation-seeking questions. With these clarifications in mind we can now return to the topic of explanation itself.

The various kinds of explanatory method

As we have seen, explanation is itself a complex of methods, a cluster of questions beginning with 'why'. It is important to bear in mind the main ones. One type amounts to a search for causes, technically known as aetiology. 'Cause' is a much debated concept, (Mackie 1974) but usually it is taken to mean that which produces something. This calls to mind John Stuart Mill's definition of a cause as 'a uniform antecedent of a phenomenon' but the insistence on the cause preceding its effect would be disputed by some thinkers today (Taylor 1967: 56ff). Among philosophers of science there is widespread agreement, however, that the identification of causes cannot be separated from our theories about nature. As N. R. Hanson has said, 'when we use the word "cause" we bring a causal law and its associated theory to bear on a particular matter of fact so as to explain the latter by the former' (Hanson 1969: 308). Our earlier example of the falling weather vane is a case in point; to say what caused it to fall we invoked the law of gravity and thereby also the Newtonian theory of mechanics. So the search for causes is bound up with the logically more complex process of creating explanatory theories involving laws of nature. This fact is directly relevant to the method used in the present book.

Another way of explaining is to find out which goals, ends, purposes or intentions an agent or organism pursues. From aetiology we thus proceed to the various kinds of teleology. Here too the procedure can at least in some cases be developed into a law-invoking explanation, as we saw earlier. Then there is functional analysis, which is also to be classified as answering a why-question, even if there are doubts about whether it can or should be developed into a covering law approach. Genetic explanations uncover the events out of which a phenomenon arises and are common in history and biography. But except for unique, particular events, the most rigorous way of showing why a phenomenon exists, happens or has certain properties would be to subsume it deductively or inductively under a covering law or generalisation, or several of them, plus initial conditions, and, in the interests of coherence and comprehensiveness, to create an explanatory theory in which those factors are systematically related to one another. With these two related measures the explanatory process reaches its climax. The only logical exceptions to it would be unique or random phenomena, for reasons that have already been mentioned. More will be said in a moment about theories, but first there is the question of whether law-invoking or nomological explanation is universally applicable.

The scope of covering law explanations

The rule governing the scope of nomological explanations is that they are logically appropriate whenever the problem being investigated contains regularities such as can be expressed in testable, general or universal statements like 'all unsupported objects fall.' We must examine the relevant phenomenon and see whether there is uniformity and pattern or whether there is random variation. This last is extremely important, because mere variation does not count logically against law-invoking procedures. The variation must be random and disorderly, evincing no pattern at all to be logically incompatible with the concept of a covering law. Genuinely random human actions would be a case in point, explicable perhaps in terms of individual choices or ad hoc manipulation by alien minds. So, as long as the debate about freedom and determinism continues, nomological procedures cannot justifiably be seen as unrestrictedly applicable. Likewise unique particulars cannot in principle be explained in terms of laws. But despite this limitation law-invoking methods are still the most rigorous and comprehensive ones available, especially in view of the fact that the other ways of saying why something happens or exists can often be transformed into this more rigorous technique. Generally speaking, then, explanation is a process of specifying the necessitating or at least predisposing factors and conditions that give rise to the problem in question, where possible by recourse to covering laws. The rule of thumb to follow is that the method used must match the material that needs explaining.

It is worth commenting at this stage on just how different the modern conception of explanation, based on the procedures so

fruitfully developed in the sciences, is from the classical doctrine
formulated by Aristotle. He distinguished four types of explanation, namely the identification of the material cause of a
phenomenon, that is, what it is made of; the formal cause, or
what it is made into; the efficient cause, which states who or what
made it, and the final cause, which specifies what it is made for.
None of these is directly equivalent to anything in the modern
doctrine, though final causation is clearly akin to the concept of
purposive explanation (Hanson 1969: 279f). In view of the differences only confusion can arise from failing to keep the two doctrines separate.

Requirements for rigorous explanation

Karl Popper has greatly refined our awareness of the formal
criteria for adequate explanation (Popper 1972: 193ff). He
specifies four main norms, beginning with the stipulation that
'the most satisfactory explanation will be the one that is most
severely testable and most severely tested...' (p. 203). Secondly,
the explanation must (of course) be true or at least not known to
be false and it must, thirdly, be independently testable. This is to
ensure that the explicans is not just another way of stating the
problem, which would amount merely to circularity and not to
explanation. To avoid this danger the proposed solution must, as
it were, cover more than the phenomenon that needs explaining,
and this would be ensured if it could be tested by other consequences than the problem in question. As Popper himself
wrote: 'satisfactory theories must, as a matter of principle,
transcend the empirical instances which gave rise to them; otherwise they would...merely lead to explanations which are
circular' (Popper 1972: 355). Fourthly, the proposed explicans
should use laws of nature. These criteria of testability, truth, non-
circularity and universality have been borne in mind in the
construction of the present theory of religion, as well as the ones
listed by Crosby in connection with theories of religion.

Explanation by means of theories

The process of showing why a phenomenon exists does not end

with an identification of relevant covering laws, initial conditions and other explanatory procedures like functional analysis. There is, as was noted a while ago, another vital step involving the need to co-ordinate these items into a coherent account or theory. The main property of a theory is that it is constructed, whether to provide a new understanding of a problem or to systematise existing explanatory ingredients. This means that alongside the ability to account for as large a range of relevant facts as possible, an essential requirement of a good theory is logical coherence. The underlying assumption governing this requirement is the orderliness and coherence of reality as a whole, but since science and most if not all religions share this assumption, though for very different reasons, it is unlikely to be widely resisted. Another canon of theory-building that is generally accepted is the so-called principle of parsimony, according to which the best theory is the simplest one that will fit the facts.

Because theories are constructed by finite investigators, they can in principle always be superseded. Thus May Brodbeck has defined a theory as 'a deductively connected set of empirical generalizations. These generalizations... are always subject to possible refutation by future experience and are, therefore, hypothetical. A theory, accordingly, is often referred to as a hypothetico-deductive system...' (Brodbeck 1968: 457). This of course implies that there is a touch of paradox about theoretical explanation. To explain a problem we invoke covering laws and specify initial conditions. To systematise these we construct theories. But as constructs those theories are inherently corrigible. So the very process of enhancing our knowledge and solving our problems also involves something inescapably provisional. As Hanson has succinctly commented, hypotheses are 'theory-laden conjectures' (Hanson 1969: 227). The implications of this comment for religious belief-systems are, incidentally, of the very greatest importance, as we shall see in the next two chapters. They undermine the idea that such belief-systems are immune to correction.

The words just quoted might seem to imply that the terms 'theory' and 'hypothesis' are used interchangeably. This is not so. The prevailing convention is to speak of hypotheses as particular statements, often in what is known as 'if-then' form and usually in connection with a law or theory. Theories, as we have seen, consist of systems of statements correlating the elements of an explanation, and are thus more complicated than hypotheses. They overlap, of course, in the sense that hypotheses form part of a theory and both are provisional devices formulated in order to help us explain things.

Once again it is Popper who has especially enriched our understanding of the nature and function of theories in the search for knowledge (Popper 1965, 1968, 1972). His suggestions apply mainly to the discovery of new knowledge and should be assessed in that context rather than in relation to situations governed by established or accepted proposals. The main point to grasp is that in the quest for fresh insight theories play a crucial, fundamental part, strongly affecting the direction the explanatory process takes and the kinds of observations that are made in order to test it. There is a widely held belief that theories are the result of observations, arising inductively from them. Popper has persuasively challenged this conception. He argues that the quest for new knowledge begins with some or other problem, often caused by anomalies resulting from existing theories (cf. Kuhn 1970). A solution is then proposed in the form of a new theory or potential explanation of the problem. It is pointed out that this can happen in all sorts of ways, from sudden intuitions or flashes of insight to deliberate inductive generalisations, but the way the new theory emerges does not in the least affect its potential value. What counts is that it should give rise to tests that could refute or falsify the proposal. When these come to hand theorists should not try to save their proposals by qualifying them and reducing their **coverage but should look for a theory which will keep the strengths but overcome the faults of the earlier one.** The cycle of investigation then begins again with knowledge growing through the key processes of conjecture and refutation (Popper 1968: 32ff; Magee 1973: 56).

Several points in this account of theorising call for further comment. Firstly, there is something inescapably creative about theory-building, calling for imaginativeness and innovation, often involving the use of metaphors, a point that has been valuably made by Mary Hesse (Hesse 1980: 111ff). As a result the exercise is clearly tentative and provisional, even when there has been enough successful testing for a given theory to be widely accepted, because the possibility always exists that a new discovery or insight would falsify it. Next, there is no such thing as a pure observation, entirely free from the influence of existing theories or beliefs. None the less, our ability to observe critically is not imprisoned by the beliefs we already hold, for if it were we would never question those beliefs on empirical grounds, as we undoubtedly to (of Hesse 1980: 63ff). Observations are theory-laden but not necessarily theory-bound, and there is the world of difference between naive and critical handling of evidence. This brings us to consider situations where a decision has to be made between rival theories. Popper's advice is to understand the situation as a choice between more and less satisfactory candidates, not between a true theory and a false one, (O'Hear 1980: 47ff) which oversimplifies the complex, subtle character of theories, comprising as they do much more than collections of facts (Magee 1973: 27f). Clearly, no theory could never enlarge our knowledge unless it also contained something new like a fresh concept or a revolutionary way of relating the relevant facts. And just as Popper has proposed guidelines for deductive-nomological explanations, so also he has indicated the criteria for assessing theories (Magee 1973: 40). They are that the proposed theory must provide a solution to the problem which gives rise to it; there must be compatibility with all known observational evidence; the theory must embrace earlier ones but overcome and account for their shortcomings; and the more thoroughly a theory be testable the better it will be. Summarising these contentions in a striking passage based in an aphorism by Novalis, Popper once wrote that theories 'are nets cast to catch what we call 'the world': to rationalize, to explain, and to master it. We endeavour to make the mesh ever finer and finer' (Popper 1968: 59). All this amounts to a much richer and more fundamental method of explaining than the logically simpler procedures of invoking covering laws, looking for intentions and functions and identifying causes. In fact Popper's work enable us to recognise explanatory theories as a highly creative way of bringing these other methods together in an illuminating network of of ideas, involving what Mary Hesse has suggestively called the 'metaphoric redescription of the domain of the explanandum' (Hesse 1980: 120).

Theory-building is thus an essential part of the explanatory process, called for by the need to solve problems and find new knowledge as well as by the pressure to systematise the items contained in a given explanans into a coherent, testable statement of the factors and conditions without which the phenomenon in question could not exist or function. This being so we can hardly expect to account for religion with anything less than a fully elaborated explanatory theory.

A STRATEGY FOR EXPLAINING RELIGION

It is time to apply the guidelines contained in the preceding pages to the subject matter of religion, starting with a crystallisation of those guidelines. The fundamental one is the logical principle implicit in the debate about the scope of explanations that make use of laws of nature, namely that explanatory methods must match the material being treated. Where there is order, pattern or regularity in the data a search for covering generalisations, perhaps even laws, is valid, but where there is none, other methods more specific in kind are needed. For the same reason it is impossible at present to invoke well-established laws in all the sectors of human enquiry because not all of them have identified any, and perhaps never will. The humanities are the obvious example. Even here, however, a search for possible laws that might be involved in human behaviour would be valid if existing research could point to patterns and regularities in the things people do. A second lesson for us is that to explain rigorously by any method is to say fully why a given problem or phenomenon exists or functions as it does, and this means identifying all the factors, whether laws, specific causes, initial conditions, intentions, needs and personal choices, without which the phenomenon in question could not exist. In the third place, the identification of these factors may call for creativity, for imaginative and perhaps even bold new ways of seeing the problem, because previous research may not have brought all the necessary considerations to light. It might also be necessary to rethink and restate earlier ideas or rearrange factors that have long been known but have not so far been satisfactorily related to one another. In this sense the exercise involves a mental venture into the unknown, rather like Popper's idea of proceeding by means of testable conjectures. A fourth lesson is that the only adequate way of attempting a comprehensive new explanation of something is to devise a theory that will coherently embrace all the particular factors involved, meet the usual formal standards of clarity, conciseness and logical consistency, and enable all the data to be covered by logical derivations in a manner not done by earlier or rival views, which is another way of saying that it must be amenable to extensive testing by the available evidence. Of vital importance, too, is the requirement that the proposed explanans be wider in scope than the problem being treated, otherwise the account given will merely be circular. The best way to ensure this is to adopt an explanans from which other consequences follow than just the phenomenon to be explicated. Naturally the items in the explanation must be true or at least not known to be false, because facts cannot be accounted for by means of fictions. Additionally, the new theory should strive for logical simplicity by using the fewest possible explanatory factors, and it must be an improvement over its rivals and predecessors especially so far as factual coverage is concerned.

Bearing these guidelines in mind we can now take up the question of how to explain religion. The problem before us could helpfully be stated in a series of five questions:

1   Why do people in all known societies seek benefit and especially perfect or everlasting well-being with all their personal resources and those of their traditions through relevant powers from or in a transcendent, unseen world?

2   Why do believers fall into two main categories, one kind thinking of that transcendental world and its power as a plurality of personal, spiritual beings and acting accordingly, while the other kind sees it as an undifferentiated, ultimate spiritual reality in which all distinctions fall away?

3   Why are there different religious traditions, some believers thinking of the spiritual beings as divine kings, others as divine warriors, judges or fatherly creators; with some of them looking to Jesus of Nazareth, some to the Torah, others to the Qur'ān, the Gita or the Dharma as their guide to supreme blessing?

4   Why are individuals unique in their personal ways of being religious?

5   Why have many people, especially over the past few centuries, moved away from religion altogether?

We saw right at the start of this book that established views of religion provide inadequate explanations for the phenomena referred to in these questions. Naturalistic theories fail to cover enough data and make the error of subjective reductionism, as if religion were solely a matter of the people who practice it. On the other hand religious theories hardly do any better. As classically formulated, none of the world's faiths even mentions all the others that were in existence at that time, let alone accounts for them. To mention only one indication of this difficulty, the great founding figures of religious history are much more imposing, even compelling, than the interpretations implied by the doctrines of the other religions would imply. The situation in regard to our understanding of religion and, for that matter, human existence in general is thus extremely unsatisfactory. We have here a phenomenon of colossal power in the lives of billions, faith in the realm of spirit evoking from them as from innumerable forebears in all lands a staggeringly enormous dedication of time, energy, talent and loyalty. But we do not yet know why this should be so, nor why the music of faith, so captivating to some, should be inaudible or meaningless to others. Ordinary curiosity, not to mention faith itself, can scarcely resist the force of the challenge contained in this situation. We are, then, at a frontier of knowledge. Religion is too massive and magnetic to ignore but at the same time it simply will not do to explain it either as illusion born of fear, ignorance, oppression or whatever, or as justified fidelity to the evocations of an objectively real, transcendent world of the spirit, accurately perceived by the eye of faith.

In this situation the way ahead is to look for fresh solutions despite the riskiness inherent in such ventures. We need an explanatory experiment to illuminate the phenomena of religious faith and, by further implication, the greater phenomenon of existence itself. The present theory is a contribution to that quest for an enlarged understanding of things, evoked by the magnitude and urgency of the problem as well as by the timeliness of the moment. Now that historians of religion and anthropologists have documented the world-wide family of faiths in minute detail, and philosophers strengthened our grasp of the explanatory arts, there is every justification for those of us who think that religious studies should now add to its splendid achievements in telling us what faith is, a comparable investment of effort into finding out why it exists and works as it does.

We have seen that the way to construct the necessary experiment depends on the nature of the material to be explained. In chapter two we found that the spiritual life involves a number of regular, recurrent characteristics. These we might call its global or constant properties, or its deep structure. In all ages and societies known to us the desire for significant well-being has been felt; believers invariably look to a transcendent realm as profoundly relevant to that well-being, and always there are powers in operation affecting it. There is, recurringly, a deep need, and, no less recurringly, an equally deep conviction that satisfaction is available, if not in this life then certainly in another. For every believer there is also an enveloping tradition, a sort of mythico-ritual matrix in which faith is conceived, carried, delivered and nursed. Faith is for all who have it an absorption of body, mind and all else in this quest for supreme blessing.

Regularities like these, which correspond to the first question in the list above, require from the would-be explainer the identification of one or more general causal factors applying to all people; fundamental truths of our condition that are wider in scope than the religious data lest circularity bedevil the exercise, and capable of identifying and accounting for the needs and satisfactions implied by the religious quest for and taste of supreme well-being, but without lapsing into the notorious pitfall of subjective reductionism. Religious studies and the human sciences in general are not, as yet anyway, nomological disciplines with accepted causal laws of human or spiritual nature to appeal to, so the general factors needed for the explanation of the data can scarcely be laws, at least for the time being. But the regularities in the data give every justification for proposing something analogous, namely that affecting all people there are pervasive, global factors with explanatory potential to which we can appeal as covering existential generalisations. The initial conditions in which these general causal factors are activated into producing the global characteristics of religious existence would of course also have to be specified, as well as those that issue in secular life-styles. This will be done in the final chapter. Thus question 5 in our list is also covered.

From the global properties of religion we turn next to what could be called its regional characteristics as referred to in questions 2 and 3 in our list. Terra religiosa also exhibits patterned, provincial pecularities. Some believers focus their faith on ancestral spirits, others on pantheons, yet others on solitary divine lords both unitarian and trinitarian. These are obviously variations but since each speaks of a type of transcendental, personal spirit, there is also present an embracing pattern. Then there are those whose faith has no need for such personal spirits at all and who yet report the foretaste of an equally superlative spiritual peace. Concerning the different religious traditions there is also patterned variation. All over the earth we find shrines and temples but the designs differ. The faithful everywhere have myths whose contents are never identical, so that the Valkyries, Baal and Indra and doubtless others besides jostle for lordship of the clouds. And in all the faiths there is devotion patterned by the power of different words, whether of holy people or holy books. Some acknowledge the Torah, some the traditions of the ancients, others Lord Krishna, others the Galilean. But all are shaped by them, like iron filings around some magnet of the soul. One way or another all these things present us with patterned variations whereby the global properties of faith are differentiated into all the varieties of the earth's religious traditions. In response to them the would-be explainer must additionally identify differentiating factors which would factually and logically account for this regional speciation of the spiritual life.

To these we must add the numberless personal expressions of the devout, evidently unique for every participating individual, like the teenager who once told the author that the church was a cageful of begging monkeys or the nameless ancient Zimbabwean who first spoke of Mwari, the divine being, as a great, great pool of water. We touch here the problem listed in question 4 above, and to explain it we shall need a set of agent-specific factors, for example personal intentions, whims, temperament, talent, the idiosyncrasies of place, time and circumstance and the exercise of individual choice. And in all three classes of data, global, regional and personal, scope may also have to be given to functional analysis as a handy way of illuminating the part played in religion by things like ritual, creed or hierarchy.

It is clear, then, that the subject matter of religion requires a battery of methods tailored to its complexities, and that to systematise them a comprehensive theory will be essential, from which factually accurate descriptions of religious phenomena will be logically derivable. The theory will of course also have to meet the other standards that were discussed earlier in the chapter. It is helpful to gather them together at this point into a consolidated list.

1   The formal criteria of clarity, non-circularity, economy of explanatory factors, and logical consistency.
2   The general material criteria of proposing explanatory factors for which there is empirical or other public justification, yielding a theory which most closely fits all the relevant data, squares with other sectors of knowledge, is extensively and rigorously testable, and offers advantages over other theories in its proposed solution of the problems of religion as set forth in our list of five questions.
3   Special criteria applying to religion, adapted from Crosby's list, namely the provision of a set of concepts capable of explaining the global, regional and personal characteristics of religion; the use of valid parts of earlier theories; an adequate account of the objective factors involved in the religious life which believers regard as spiritual realities; provision of the means of differentiate religious from non-religious interests; and finally the furnishing of criteria for deciding whether to classify border-line phenomena as religious or not.

This brings us to a sensitive but unavoidable consideration. What kind of explanatory factor must be invoked? To propose spiritual causes raises the presently insuperable problem of establishing which ones to invoke, because the believers of the world are disunited as to exactly what they are, and it evidently also involves circularity because it is precisely the belief in a realm of spirit that we need to explain. In this context it would tell us nothing to say that people believe in that realm because spirit is real; such an assertion in no way clarifies or explains that concept. In any case, to adopt this option would be to take sides in the debate between believer and sceptic instead of accounting for that debate, thereby shirking one of the main functions that ought to be fulfilled by a book like this. But if a supernaturalist view of the causes of religion presents fatal methodological problems, so too does its materialist rival. It would of course be just as tactically mistaken to side with the materialists in the explanation of religion as with believers. After all, the rejection of spiritual notions is as much to be accounted for in this book as belief in them. Nor do the available explanations of faith from writers in the materialist camp inspire much confidence in the merits of their method, as we saw right at the beginning of this book. Both they and their believing opponents have merits and,

The Art of Explaining 97

more important, both have severe explanatory shortcomings. Neither believer not sceptic is the thoroughly deluded person that each would have the other be, nor is each party nearly as justified as it appears to its own members. The position is altogether more subtle and complex than a simplistic, true-versus-false contest between supernaturalists and materialists. Let the contending parties come up with better theories of religion if they can; in the meantime the issue is much too important to wait, and the only option left is an explanatory strategy which proceeds along another path altogether.

The one followed in this book is experiential: the factors invoked as causing people to live religiously will be ones which any person, believer or sceptic, can experience. What could be fairer than a policy open to all parties to follow? So the theory worked out in the next two chapters could be called an experiment in open-ended empiricism, as distinct from a doctrinaire or reductionist empiricism. The latter asserts that there is no spiritual reality, and it is no more part of the present book to endorse this assertion than to side with its rival. By contrast, open-ended empiricism is simply an investigative strategy. Investigations must begin somewhere, and this one begins with the things that are available to the personal experience of any one, a starting point which does not compromise the aims of the book and avoids the circularity and question-begging of the alternatives. Where the investigation will lead depends entirely on how much such an approach can explain, and for that reason it is open-ended and experimental. In short, it is an attempt to find out to what extent certain commonly experienceable factors can account for belief in a spiritual realm. In any event, what we have here is an open-endedly empirical attempt to establish the factors and conditions which necessitate the existence of religion in all its various forms, including of course the massively powerful but disputed conviction that there indeed is a spiritual realm. Naturally, the project has all the risks of any experiment, but it fits the pattern described by Karl Popper when he wrote that 'the fundamental procedure of the growth of knowledge remains that of conjecture and refutation, of the elimination of unfit explanations...' (Popper 1972: 264).

To conclude: is there a set of general, regional and personal factors affecting human existence and accessible to the experience of any of us which would suffice to account for religion, secularity and all the variations in the forms of the spiritual life? I

believe that there is. In the next chapter those factors will be
identified and in the one after that they will be synthesised into an
explanatory theory of religion, in the course of which the initial
conditions which are associated with the rise and diversification of
religion into its many historical forms will also be identified.

4 Human Existence and Its Setting

Whatever else it may be for a pilgrim in Mecca, a Buddhist medi-
tator in California, an English country parson or a Zulu diviner in
Africa, religion everywhere involves a hunger for blessing from or
in an invisible, transcendental world of the spirit, a sensing of the
powers that give and withold that favour, a sharing of traditional
modes of thought, speech, ritual and lifestyle, a faith-filled quest
involving the whole personality. To understand why people have
come to live like this in such huge numbers for so long we must
grasp two basic points. Firstly, human existence is part and parcel
of and must come to terms with an environing, pulsating, partly
unseen external reality, alive and mobile with power. To live is
thus to interact with a larger, enveloping, conditioning totality,
like a plant rooted in and fed by the soil, with leaves spread to
draw on the sun and the surrounding air. Secondly, human existence is marvellously though fallibly equipped to navigate the
cosmic ocean with its fair winds and foul: vulnerable and limited,
to be sure, but also creative and resourceful, powered by an
immense need for satisfaction and steered across those unknown
seas by the ability to tell with some skill the difference between
success and failure. To cope with the force-filled cosmos people
must use all their resourcefulness to think, feel, communicate and
be endlessly inventive, and among the most remarkable pieces of
equipment they have ever made to help them find a safe anchor-
age is religion. Such is the main thesis of this chapter and the
next. Faith in its global form is the inevitable product of our
human struggle to cope with and find well-being in a vast, surrounding world which far surpasses us in power and duration,
which ceaselessly affects us and which even now we do not fully
understand and cannot control. Consequently, to explain the
global qualities of religion we must focus attention on those two

general, causal factors, anthropological and cosmological, as I shall call them. Afterwards the differentiating factors which result in regional and individual variations of religious existence will also be identified. The purpose of this chapter is therefore to propose, substantiate and formulate these explanatory items in such a way that accurate descriptions of religious phenomena will be logically derivable from them. A discussion of the concept of culture will be given at the end to round off the chapter in a suitable way.

A formal statement of the two main factors will be helpful at this point. The cosmological cause of religion is the incompletely understood and fractionally controlled field of largely unseen, interacting forces within which human life germinates and grows and by which it is conditioned, some of those forces favourable, others harmful. The anthropological cause can be expressed as a basic drive in people, vulnerable but creative as they are, to maximise well-being by all available mans, guided by their affective sense (as I shall call the ability to feel and reason about the difference between benefit and hardship) amidst and in response to the environing forces, and coming to different expressions depending on physical, cultural, historical, social and personal factors that will be discussed later in the chapter.

THE COSMOLOGICAL FACTOR: REALITY AT LARGE

What does it mean to say that one of the two globally-effective sources from which religion results is an encompassing field of interacting, conditioning, largely unseen forces, some helping and others injuring human existence? The operative word here is forces and it means, as was explained in chapter two, anything that produces an effect. So we may speak of whatever makes it rain, produces a bad harvest, disturbs a human conscience, triggers community action, opens the eyes of a Buddha to the sufferings of life or converts someone to Christ as a force or power, because all of these have experienceable effects of one kind or another. By the same token each one is associated with change from whatever was happening beforehand. To say that these forces are largely unseen is likewise to echo our common experience that very often the things that affect us are beyond sight and hearing, like bacteria, gravity, the good or ill will of others, the powers known to believers as spirits or the causes of tragedy and death. The metaphor 'field' has been used as a way of drawing attention to the apparent unity and coherence of the various forces to which we respond and contribute. Things seem to fit together into an orderly, living whole and another way of expressing this is to speak of a field of interacting forces (Harré and Madden 1975: 161ff). As for the terms cosmos and world, these are to be taken in the broadest sense, standing for reality at large whatever it may be, and not just for the planet earth or the physically measurable universe. The words 'whatever it may be' in the previous sentence are vitally important here in avoiding tacitly taking sides with either materialism or belief in a spiritual realm. Thus to say that people are involved in a changing world of incompletely understood, largely uncontrolled and often unseen powers is only a way of making explicit our common experience of a larger reality than just ourselves, of alterations around and in us, of perplexity at the precise nature, grounds and direction of those alterations when obvious explanations are not to hand, and limited ability to shape them to our will. Since the process of change affects us all for both good and ill, it is clearly a matter of universal human experience to include in the formulation of the cosmological factor the assertion that the field of interacting forces in which we participate sometimes promotes and sometimes diminishes our well-being.

So the first of the two general causes of religion turns out to be a common-place of human experience and its most elementary implications. To invoke it to explain the life of faith is not to usher a new actor on to the stage but to find that a familiar veteran was a mainstay of the company all along. As Wittgenstein once said, 'God grant the philosopher insight into what lies in front of everyone's eyes' (Wittgenstein 1980: 63e). Ordinary sensory experience and the inferences to which it naturally gives rise reveal that we are members of a wider, enveloping totality comprising all the myriad events and objects of everyday encounter, visible and invisible: family, society, nation, habitat, planetary system, galaxy, spatio-temporal universe and onward to the inclusive totality of all that is. A. E. Housman once wrote about a dead friend as wearing the turning globe like an overcoat forever. The truth about life in general is that all of us must wear the world or perish. This justifies the statement that human existence is conditioned by the enveloping cosmos. Being prior to our advent on the earth, nurturing, chastening and sometimes destroying us as they do, the forces that constitute our world inevitably affect what we can make of our lives. Here is the basis for both the age-old religious sense of the earth as a mother-goddess and the philosopher's perception of determinism. Each is aware of the external world as a conditioning matrix.

When we experience change in ourselves and in the wider world around us we are alerted to the dynamic character of things, for where there is change there must be powers at work, either as separate forces or as operations of a single, unifying potency. And when those changes affect us directly without our bidding, perhaps coming against our most ardent efforts to resist, then we know at first hand that the forceful cosmos affects us whether we like it or not, that we are ever involved willy-nilly in and part of a wider reality. Thus the justification for proposing the cosmological factor is firstly our own experience and its most elementary, natural implications, phrased as neutrally as possible to avoid begging questions and giving a circular theory of religion; and secondly its ability to function as a necessitating condition for the genesis of faith in the lives of people at any time and place. Precisely how it performs this function will be shown in the next chapter. For the moment the important step is to point out that only a general factor is logically capable of explaining human spirituality at any time or place; and the cosmological principle just presented is precisely that. It reminds us that we live in a larger, partly unseen and obscure totality of things which sustains but also menaces and destroys us, conditions our thoughts and actions, and constitutes the permanent setting for all that we imagine or contrive. Womb, playground, anvil and grave, it is the enduring envelope of our existence. With this firmly in mind we can turn now to the second general factor and describe the humanness which gives rise to religion. This takes the form of a philosophical anthropology, as the basic categories in which our existence is conceived have been called (Charles Taylor 1964: 4).

THE ANTHROPOLOGICAL FACTOR

The second general factor underlying the global characteristics of religion relates to a deeply-seated feature of personal life which can be formulated as follows. Human existence involves a powerful, pervasive drive to maximise well-being by all available means in a dynamic, conditioning cosmos on the part of creatures who are vulnerable and finite but also resourceful, adaptable and constitutionally equipped to tell with some accuracy, though not infallibly, what will prosper that drive and what will frustrate it. Such is the anthropological factor needed for an explanation of the spiritual life. For it to be acceptable two requirements must be met. The drive to generate maximum well-being must be shown to be a pervasive human characteristic; and the relevant circumstances in which it gives rise to religious faith must be identified. The way to meet the first of these requirements is to unpack or systematically expound the proposed factor, while the second one will be handled in the next chapter. But first it is necessary to explain what this anthropological factor means and give the reasons for suggesting it.

Terminology

The key word in formulating the present view of human existence is well-being. It is used here in the ordinary sense meaning the state of being or doing well in life (OED), a condition characterised by happiness, health or prosperity (Webster). It stands for that cluster of conditions the experience of which we all desire to have, perpetuate, increase or regain as being inherently satisfying: bodily and emotional health, the love and esteem of family and friends, social harmony, a sustaining, pleasant, physical environment, peace, the meeting of bodily needs, freedom from unwanted constraint or interference, self-fulfilment, the happiness of those whom we love, grounds for optimism, values for which hardship becomes acceptable and relief from distress. This is not meant to be a complete catalogue but only a typical list of examples with which anyone would be familiar. The word well-being has been chosen to encapsulate them all and provide us with a conscise, accurate, key term. That it has been defined ostensively by referring to the experiences it involves should occasion no surprise because that is to be expected of the basic or primitive concept in a systematic, experiential theory. The point to grasp is that the present view of human life as a desire for well-being rests on the common experience of people everywhere. The terminology may be novel but what it refers to is known immediately to and wanted by us all as satisfying and enjoyable. This much we seem to share, but there is no consensus about the best way to achieve the desired conditions, a fact that is of great importance for the present theory. Everybody wants to be well and happy but we have been unable to agree on a formula for achieving those goals. A further point is that there is more to well-being than just personal experience, since the possibility of having it often depends on certain objective conditions being present, such as food and friends.

The next word to consider is maximise. This means to attain the greatest possible amount, intensity or quality of something. As for the idea that we have a drive to achieve the greatest well-being, what is intended is an impelling natural disposition to satisfy a need by means of goal-directed effort, often but not always consciously. When consciously pursued it can be spoken of as a desire. To say, next, that the drive is basic is to say that it underlies, causes or pervades other aspects of our make-up as human beings. Another expression that will be used in the rest of this book is the adjective 'euonic', which has been formed from the Greek words *eu* (= well) and *ōn* (= being), as a handy alternative to the English phrase well-being. The last word to explain is the phrase the affective sense, signifying our natural ability to experience well-being and its opposites of pain, discomfort and misery. An entire subsection below is devoted to elaborating the point so no more need be said for the moment except that the reason for adopting this verbal contrivance is convenience. It is easier to talk about an affective sense than to keep repeating the full phrase that we possess the means of making a sensory discrimination between agreeable and distressing states of awareness. Taken together these definitions mean that the drive to maximise well-being is an underlying, natural disposition impelling people to realise and experience to the greatest possible extent the conditions that they find either inherently or instrumentally satisfying, such as those listed a few paragraphs ago. But what are the grounds for characterising human existence in this way? They are of two kinds, experiential and theoretical.

Experiential justification

The best ways to justify the present proposal are to examine how people in fact behave and to reflect on one's own experience. When this is done there is little doubt that for much of the time anyway we do indeed organise our lives and cultures in ways that are intended to satisfy our desire for well-being. As biological organisms we are equipped for pain-avoidance and pleasure-seeking, and sometimes our very survival depends on that equipment, as with finding water, shelter, warmth and food. Whole empires of human effort have grown in order to provide those things, which we so revealingly call 'the basics'. As we reflect on this fact let us call to mind the grim, even agonising experiences which attend the failure to obtain them and conversely the relief that we feel when they are met. It is a pleasure many of us are lucky enough to take for granted most of the time, but let it once be seriously threatened and we know with a fierce knot of anxiety that a drive to ensure physical well-being is most certainly built into us. People have gone cannibal in the desperate pains of starvation, which surely means that the euonic drive is a dominant force in us at the physical level.

A similar though less acutely felt desire for satisfaction can be seen in our dealings with other people and in our ethical, political and religious actions. For good reason we speak about a social contract to refer to the patterns of communal life in which individual needs and obligations are meshed into a workable system of corporate existence, as agreeable to each as is possible in prevailing circumstances. After all, obeying the law has better prospects of personal comfort than breaking it, so long as policing is efficient and penalties a deterrent. We may find social institutions and rules of conduct irksome but we also find that not having them is even more unpleasant. Truth-telling and doing one's duty may be noble; they are also, on balance, socially beneficial.

But our actions are not confined to gratifying bodily needs and maintaining supportive social structures, essential though these are for the physical survival of individuals and their groups. Sometimes we act in ways that are painful to us, sacrificing comfort or even life itself. Does this not refute the assertion that human existence involves a powerful, pervasive drive to maximise well-being? It is a fact that people can accept pain and death, and do not invariably try to avoid them. How can this be squared with the undoubted power of our desire for life and personal happiness? The answer is firstly that a drive is not the same as an irresistable force which completely governs the things in its power. Our hunger for happiness and other benefits is powerful but not omnipotent. If it were we should always avoid painful experiences. Since we can and do choose to endure them in certain circumstances, our drive to maximise well-being clearly does not amount to an invariable, relentless pursuit of our own, exclusively personal interests. Those interests can be overridden and sometimes they are. The drive is strong enough to protect us from many destructive problems but not so strong as to leave us no freedom at all to act for the benefit of others even at our own expense. And since this quality has withstood the evolutionary process, clearly it is not without survival value even to the individual. All this is made possible by a disposition that is powerful without being dictatorial.

The second reason why voluntary acts involving physical suffering or death do not nullify the view that human behaviour is impelled by a desire for well-being is that the drive is not confined to the physical part of existence, any more than it is solely self-centred. The phrase 'well-being' is deliberately broad at this point, as it must be to fit the evidence. Had the assertion been that people's actions are invariably governed by an impulse to promote their own physical pleasure, then clearly it would clash with the facts of altruistic and moral behaviour. The present formulation is broad enough to cover both bodily satisfaction and bodily sacrifice in the interests of ethical, religious or other goals, or for the sake of other people.

Of great relevance here is our ability to experience different degrees of enjoyment or pain and assign different values to their causes, so far as these are known to us. Given this ability we can subordinate the less prized to the more prized, or find a degree of suffering acceptable if it promises to yield a sufficiently great benefit. A case in point is the well-known behavioural phenomenon of delayed gratification, in which present hardship is accepted in the interests of a later benefit greater than any immediately available kind. It has been defined as 'the willingness to defer immediate, less valued rewards for the sake of more valuable but temporally deferred outcomes' (Fairchild, in Strommen 1978: 158). People discover that honourable behaviour, loyalty to friends or to a cause, adherence to principle and devotion to a god also involve satisfaction of a kind which can be much richer and deeper than the physical pleasures of a narrowly self-serving life. They too are maximising well-being but at a different,

logically higher level. Evidently this means that our equipment
for experiencing satisfaction, whatever it is, can function at different levels and with sufficient complexity to enable us to endure
extreme suffering at what would for us be a lower level, in order
to promote something we find more important, and it enables us
to derive a sense of satisfaction from doing so. The sacrifices of
religious heroes appear to be in this category. Martyrs who die in
the flames or the arena rather than deny their faith are
awesomely courageous but can hardly be seen as totally selfless
because they expect thereby to be in the joyous presence of their
saviour for ever. Psychologist of religion Roy Fairchild puts the
point admirably, commenting that:

> In the mainstream of Christian tradition the teaching of self-
> denial has been persuasive. The faithful are to defer the
> expression of many desires, especially the "base" emotions of
> sexuality and aggression, to live in self-discipline, confident
> that the promises of God will be fulfilled in the future and will
> bring true human beatitude.... To the Christian theologian,
> delayed gratification, or even renunciation of gratification, is
> *not* an end in itself; it is always related to one's goals and moti-
> vation. While the *ability* to delay or renounce gratification is
> crucial to discipleship, the "willingness to sacrifice" per se
> cannot be exalted indiscriminately. To do so is to provide
> masochistic people grounds for believing they are the most
> faithful Christians; and it confuses deeply religious people who
> find themselves baulking at the so-called "demands" of the
> gospel.... In traditional Christianity the urging of self-denial
> has frequently been justified on the basis of future rewards. A
> *postponement* or delay of gratification was preached, not a
> renunciation of gratification or a substitution of gratification.
> Often the resultant self-denial was a desire for one's own
> advantage, and obedience was motivated by the perceived
> power of God to punish and reward. However, an even deeper
> strain in the prophetic tradition of Judais and Christianity has
> stressed the serving of God and his will because of God's own
> loving-kindness to men and because such service *is* the
> abundant life in the present...' (Fairchild, in Strommen
> 1978: 156, 165, 169f).

Secular people who die in the service of a political movement are in a different position because they have no expectation of post-mortem benefit. But there usually is a dedication to the view that the cause is more important than the self, so that it is better to die for it if need be than to fail the movement in order to preserve one's own life. That too is within the logic of the drive to maximise well-being; except that here a contribution to the welfare of others through the progress of the cause is found more satisfying than the alternative of giving priority to personal survival.

Emerging from these reflections is a picture of human existence in which the effort is repeatedly made to realise a variety of conditions which are found satisfying by those who experience them, and to avoid or minimise others associated with unacceptable forms of suffering or discomfort. Many of those conditions are concerned with physical needs but others involve ethical, aesthetic, political and religious interests, according to individual priorities. But whatever the goal, pursuing it means that it is judged more satisfying to experience than its alternatives by the person concerned. It is seen as bringing about an improved state of affairs, as enhancing the well-being of the relevant party or parties. The massive amount of mental and physical energy we give to obtaining a food supply, shelter and clothing, to forming and keeping social groups for the support and guidance of individuals, to health care, to entertainment, to security, to instructing the young to cope similarly, to career-satisfaction and the pursuit of happiness are ample justification for asserting that our behaviour manifests a pervasive drive to maximise well-being. That it is a basic part of our make-up means that many other facets of human existence depend on and issue from it; a contention that is demonstrated in the elaborations given later in this chapter. And in view of the persistence with which we seek to improve our condition and diminish the likelihood of suffering, it is hardly an exaggeration to speak of this drive as involving a desire to maximise the benefits we prize so greatly. In short, there is plenty of experiential justification for the anthropological factor being proposed in this chapter.

Theoretical support

From various disciplines much direct and indirect support for the present view is forthcoming. Ever since Aristotle's pioneering account of human behaviour in the *Nichomachean Ethics* there has been an influential philosophical case for the view that a yearning for happiness is the mainspring of our activity (Kenny 1973: 51ff). So the great Greek thinker wrote that happiness is 'something final and self-sufficient, and is the end of action...the best, noblest and most pleasant thing in the world' (McKeon 1947: 317, 321). As in the present theory, Aristotle distinguished between happiness and pleasure, regarding the latter as of a lower order, though extremely important in training the young and an influential factor in the behaviour of many people. He wrote that pleasure 'is thought to be most intimately connected with our human nature, which is the reason why in educating the young we steer them by the rudders of pleasure and pain...since men choose what is pleasant and avoid what is painful...' (McKeon 1947: 518). In modern times utilitarian forms of ethics holding that actions are good in proportion to the happiness they engender have continued to find support from philosophers, though critics have not been slow to draw attention to the problems of such theories, especially alleging that to give priority to happiness is to diminish or jeopardise liberty. So far as the present project is concerned the point is not so much where the balance of critical opinion lies as the fact that the issue is still a live one among moral philosophers. (Sen and Williams 1982) The main reason for preferring the word well-being to happiness in this book is that the latter has subjective connotations at odds with the evidence. People do not merely look for the experience of happiness, they also work for the conditions in which that experience is fostered. 'Well-being' comes somewhat closer to capturing this fact than any word referring only to a state of mind besides also summarising the many other desirable states to which we aspire, apart from happiness.

Existentialist thought is of interest at this point because thinkers like Kierkegaard, Heidegger, Jaspers, Marcel and Sartre have also suggested categories for understanding human existence. Of special importance is the attention they pay to the concepts of dread or anxiety and choice, which are very similar to the creative anxiety and vulnerability so central to the present philosophical anthropology (Kierkegaard 1980; Tillich 1951: 186ff; 1965: 41ff). But the evidence of human behaviour requires a broader theory than the ones given by the existentialists. Their categories do not always sufficiently reflect the indications of well-being in our experience, perhaps because they were less directly concerned than this author with descriptive generalisations about human life based on empirical evidence. Setting this limitation aside, we may none the less see valuable support in aspects of their work (Heidegger 1962; Macquarrie 1955; Sartre 1957; Jaspers 1970).

The same holds for the social sciences. Economist Gary S. Becker has made the interesting suggestion that a general theory of human behaviour can be developed by combining the concept of utility, well-known in economic theory, with the idea of maximisation to form the basic dictum that people try to obtain the greatest utility in whatever they do (Becker 1976). For example, 'a person decides to marry when the utility expected from marriage exceeds that expected from remaining single or from additional search for a more suitable mate' (Becker 1976: 10). According to Becker the proposal provides 'a valuable unified framework for understanding *all* human behaviour' (p. 14). Whether this judgement is one which others will share is less important than the fact that maximisation is recognised by Becker as a central concept for understanding what people do in general, and not just as consumers. It may be that utility will come to be accepted as a suitable expression for the things people value in areas of life other than economics, but it strikes the present writer as less suitable than well-being because we need a term that expresses the enjoyable sense of satisfaction gained from the objectives of human behaviour. Utility is rather too austere to do that.

The concept of maximisation also receives a great deal of attention in the new sociobiological perspective associated with writers like E. O. Wilson and David Barash, except that this time it is not utility but genetic fitness that human behaviour is said to maximise (Wilson 1975; Barash 1979; Trigg 1982). As Barash writes, 'A guiding principle of sociobiology is that individuals tend to behave in a manner that maximizes their fitness' (Barash 1979: 25). Critics of this standpoint have objected to the genetic determinism of the doctrine but do not appear at all disturbed by the notions that our actions are purposeful and designed to maximise something; instead the dispute is about what it is that we try to maximise whenever we act, a further indication of how useful the concept is proving.

Another new field supporting aspects of the anthropological

theory being proposed here is cybernetics, together with general systems theory. This has been defined as the science of effective organisation, though its originators, Norbert Wiener and Arturo Rosenbleuth, saw it as 'the science of control and communication in the animal and the machine' (Bullock and Stallybrass 1979: 151). Since a great many of the things people do, like managing businesses or households successfully, are examples of the effective organisation which is the focus of this discipline, cybernetics has an obvious general relevance to philosophical anthropology and particularly to the attempt to identify whatever governs human behaviour, by indicating that there are indeed such controls and by devising models of how they function and process information. Cybernetics also supports the view of human existence being proposed here by recognising the importance of goal-seeking in the things people do. As one commentator has said, 'cyberneticians feel that purposiveness, that is teleology, is at the heart of goal-seeking mechanisms' (Aleksander 1981: 9).

The longer-established human sciences also provide some important corroborations for the suggestion that many of our actions are guided by the desire to maximise well-being. The psychological theory of Abraham H. Maslow is a case in point, it being Maslow's view that satisfaction and fulfilment at all levels of our existence are the goals towards which we aspire (Maslow 1954, 1962: Goble 1970). Support also comes from the ideas of the American wholistic health movement which closely resemble the notion of comprehensive well-being for all. And sociologist Peter Berger has argued persuasively that stability and security, which we can surely regard as forms of well-being, are immensely important in the creation and maintenance of social structures and the world-views which rest in part upon them (Berger 1973).

These and other theories do not and cannot prove that the anthropology outlined in this chapter is correct. No appeal to the judgements of expert authorities can do that on its own. But taken in conjunction with the practical evidence discussed previously they establish the present hypothesis as one with very firm empirical groundings and no shortage of backing from relevant quarters of philosophy and the human sciences. At the very least the proposal deserves to be considered seriously as an accurate depiction of a fundamental, pervasive factor in human behaviour. The drive to maximise well-being is certainly real and potent in all of us, strong and regular enough to cover the greater

part of all that we do, think, contrive and say. Confronted by
forces which we experience as causing pain, anxiety and
suffering, we mobilise our resources to contain and where possible
diminish or eliminate them, while those that we find a source of
benefit and satisfaction we foster and conserve so far as we can;
and we shall continue to do this as long as harmful powers
confront us and we ourselves remain vulnerable to the pain and
anguish they bring.

With these remarks the discussion of the evidence supporting
the definition of personal life as manifesting a drive to maximise
well-being reaches an end, and it is time now to unpack systematically the contents of this anthropological factor. Doing so will
bring to light the ways we as living beings are equipped to pursue
beneficial courses of action, enabling us thereafter in chapter five
to see how and why we have evolved our spiritual systems.

ASPECTS OF THE ANTHROPOLOGICAL FACTOR

What are the constituent qualities of the drive for ever greater
welfare in a changing world of interacting and often unseen
forces which both help and harm us but which we do not fully
grasp and cannot greatly affect, a world, none the less, where so
far we have managed to survive and even prosper, however unevenly? The phrases that crystallise those qualities are ones like
resourceful finitude and creative, anxious vulnerability, but what
exactly do they mean? To bring them into sharper focus let us
analyse a familiar, simple example of one way we take steps to
ensure benefit, namely by arranging for life insurance. The main
problem here is death at an age that would deprive a family of its
breadwinner, adding financial hardship to emotional tragedy.
For breadwinner and dependents alike the possibility is grim to
contemplate. Life insurance is a popular way to solve or at least
ease the financial side of the difficulty and bring some peace of
mind to those involved. Here we have all the ingredients of the
drive to maximise well-being. First there is the worry felt by the
family together with their desire to overcome the problem and
ease the apprehension. Our label in this book for the ability to
experience these unsettling and unwanted states of awareness is
the affective sense. Secondly there is the knowledge of what would

solve or at least alleviate the problem. Next comes the action of arranging for the necessary insurance. The fourth aspect of the example is the ability to talk about the fears, need for help and knowledge of what can be done to assist matters. But despite the undoubted value off these remedial measures the solution still falls far short of total relief from anxiety. Death still waits for us; inflation can erode the value of the pay-out and future unemployment could wreck the whole exercise by ending the ability to pay premiums. So, fifthly, there are limits to what we can do to banish anxiety and hardship. The sixth aspect of the example could be called sociality, meaning the presence not just of individuals but of groups, this time the family and the way group involvement affects what is felt, said and done. Similar but broader is the seventh point to notice, namely the existence of a conditioning context in which the episode takes place, with its own physical, cultural, social and historical characteristics, all of which influence what happens in some way or another. Finally there are the uniquely personal characteristics of the people in question. Such are the contents of the euonic package, discernible in a great deal, maybe even in most of the things that we do. Readers are encouraged to analyse their own experiences similarly and see for themselves how naturally and revealingly they lend themselves to this approach. Meanwhile we can now go ahead to a discussion of each of these aspects, some in connection with our anthropological factor and others in connection with the regional and personal factors that are described near the end of this chapter.

The affective sense

This phrase stands, it will be recalled, for our ability to find certain situations satisfying while disliking others. It is our steering and navigating equipment for the voyage to greater well-being, and, to change the metaphor, it also triggers the energies needed to keep us moving. Having an affective sense is a convenient way of saying that we are able to experience well-being and suffering, prizing the one and recoiling from the other and organising our lives as far as possible to increase the one and diminish the other. It is even possible to change the metaphors yet again and think of the affective sense as a sort of mental radar receiving signals from sources of benefit in the form of satisfying sensations and ones from harmful quarters as feelings of pain or discomfort. In response to these we then monitor and if necessary alter course, which is why the affective sense was likened to a ship's steering equipment a few sentences ago. And if we reflect on our own mental experiences it will be clear that the ability to experience these sensations is an exceedingly important part of our make-up, a pervasive and powerful force behind much that we do. Exposed to a live electrical wire our reaction, involving what physiologists call a flexor reflex, is swift and vigorous (Young 1978: 100). Drawn by a noble, all-embracing ideal our reaction would be a growing, life-long dedication. The former resembles a spurting fountain, the latter an ocean current, but both in their own ways are powerful. The affective sense has the further function of sparking these reactions and countless others like them. It detects promising directions for us to take in life, sets us in motion towards them and monitors our progress. In view of these deeply important, literally life-saving functions, it is surely correct to regard our ability to have these experiences as a basic part of our human make-up, governing many other abilities and organs. To speak of it as the affective sense is simply to use a convenient label. What counts is the reality for which it stands.

Support is available from physiology and psychology for this account of our mental equipment (Milner 1971: 163ff; Sage 1977: 319ff). J. Z. Young wrote in his Gifford Lectures that 'We now know that satisfaction and happiness depend upon the proper functioning of certain reward centres in the brain' (Young 1978: 142). Later he continued this theme, writing that 'Our daily lives and perceptual activities continue satisfactorily because of the rewards that come from those pleasure systems. They are the guarantors for the continuation of life. They alone can provide the smooth and integrated working of the whole brain program that ensures a successful life. They are continually influencing our thoughts, words and actions, urging us, as it were, to do things that are satisfactory' (Young 1978: 232). While the technical details of these alleged reward mechanisms in the brain are not relevant to the discussion, it is important to note that the account of our mental equipment given in this chapter is closely similar to the one provided in physiological theory. Summarising the matter, Young wrote that some of the brain's central regions are pleasure centres, containing 'what we might call the reference systems that set the course of the whole living control system. Their operation largely determines the ends or aims of the animal or man.... Other types of program intervene, as it were, on top of these fundamental ones of pleasure and pain that are produced by the actions of the reticular and reward centres' (Young 1978: 114f). This is strongly reminiscent of the distinction made earlier in the chapter between lower-order and higher-order satisfactions. As Young goes on to say, 'all these reward centres, are also connected with the operations of the parts of the brain that are involved in the satisfactions we obtain from higher intellectual, social, moral, and even religious activities' (p. 139).

The psychologist from whom the most direct corroboration for the present account can be taken is Abraham Maslow, apart from Fairchild whose views were quoted previously in connection with delayed gratification. Maslow sees human needs in a hierarchy of urgency, physiological survival being the most pressing, followed by safety, a stable world, love and what he calls belongingness, esteem, and finally self-actualisation. He holds that the ability in adults to renounce or delay satisfying a lower need is causally related to the meeting of basic needs in early years, and suggests, interestingly for a theory of religion, that so-called 'peak experiences' which give people insight into their place in the universe seem to be crucial for this kind of sacrificial behaviour (Fairchild, in Strommen 1978: 180; cf Maslow 1976; Goble 1970: 50). The clear implication is that the affective sense is indeed not limited to the physical gratification of its owner. Satisfaction can be felt for other reasons than merely bodily pleasure and is even available at the expense of such pleasure, provided the person concerned has come to experience a stronger kind of well-being from those non-physical sources. It is this hierarchical structure of ascending levels of well-being that matters rather than Maslow's views about the exact nature of each one. In any event, the ability to experience satisfaction is possible at several levels, so that there is no need to think of moral or spiritual activity as necessarily divorced from feelings of gratification. Meditation is a good example of this versatility in the affective sense. As J. Z. Young reports, 'There is indeed evidence that when a person successfully undertakes a Zen Buddhist meditation (Zazen), by breathing exercises, his brain shows much alpha rhythm. During this time, while he is in the state of Satori or enlightenment, he will report various mostly pleasant sensations...' (Young 1978: 201).

It is time now to discuss other facets of the affective sense, most of them implied by the points that have already been made. Perhaps the main one is its contribution to the formation of values. The affective sense may in fact be our means of developing them. A value is something prized or deemed important as shown by efforts taken to secure it, and the link between having values and experiencing well-being is captured in the following definition: to find something valuable is 'to assert that it is such as to give satisfaction to people in general in the long run' (Quinton 1973: 366). Without the ability to have satisfaction we would scarcely be able to form values. According to the theory being developed here the greatest value open to us is supreme well-being, and existence as a whole can therefore be seen as a quest to realise value, made possible by the affective sense. An alternative way of making the same point is that our ability to discover and pursue goals depends directly on that sense. Another of its fruits, though additional factors are also involved, is critical discernment. Precisely because things affect us differently, some being more enjoyable or painful than others, we must be correspondingly equipped to discriminate and judge the things that influence us on a scale of importance in relation to our desire for benefit, apportioning effort accordingly. This obviously amounts to critical discernment. In fact such a critical faculty is absolutely vital. Imagine the results of failing to rank the things we encounter or could expect in life according to their euonic impact. To refuse to heed persistent warnings or follow the advice of component judges in connection, for instance, with child-care, is, as we all know, to risk failure and suffering. Just to have survived as a species is an indication that the necessary rankings have been made. If so, life itself is a successful experiment in the detection and realisation of dominant values. To be is to value competently. And in that case there would be no existential or even biological foundation for the so-called fact/value dichotomy in the sciences and philosophy. As Young has said, 'study of the brain and its programs shows that there is no possibility of making such sharp separation of capacities. The parts of the brain that operate when we experience pleasure or love, fear or anxiety are closely linked with all those parts that are used in more intellectual activities and vice versa' (Young 1978: 134; cf Hall 1976).

Another facet of the affective sense, immensely important in this book, is its persistence and scope. We do not find that after achieving a modicum of enjoyment or a brief respite from suffering we are content. Quite the contrary happens. Having secured for ourselves a degree of well-being we at once wish it to continue and if possible increase. It is simply not in our nature to be satisfied with anything less. And that is why it is necessary to speak about a drive to maximise well-being rather than just a drive for well-being. The word maximise captures the persistence and comprehensive scope of our desire for satisfaction. As evidence of this scope let us consider for a moment the experience of aesthetic enjoyment. One of the greatest attractions of the concept of a pervasive affective sense is precisely its ability to account for our love of beauty and show that prominent among the satisfactions open to us, whether as artists or observers, must be the relish of those harmonies and adventures of shape, colour, arrangement, movement and sound for which our word is beauty. The link between the relish of these things and other facets of the affective sense is too obvious to require explanation. And the opposite experience of revulsion at other things found ugly or hideous is just as much a function of that sense.

The discovery of knowledge as a means of benefit

Our mental equipment involves much more, of course, than just the affective sense. To dread vulnerability, to want security and to act beneficially people must be able to discover what threatens and favours them. This brings us to discuss a second aspect of the drive to maximise well-being, the discovery of new knowledge. What follows is an indication of essential points relating to this topic, all of them well-known and experienceable by anybody. Once more, then, the explanatory factors being invoked are perfectly normal and ordinary, as was undertaken in terms of the strategy worked out at the end of the previous chapter. And as we begin the discussion of our cognitive or learning processes let us recall the steps in the argument thus far. We live in an environing cosmos which profoundly affects us all the time but whose workings are far from obvious. The things that affect us involve an unseen element. Yet we have no choice about their impact on us and must do as best we can to maximise benefit in relation to them. To do this with any degree of success means that we must discover what can help and harm us, and adjust our lives accordingly. In other words, knowledge is essential if we are to have that success. How, then, do we acquire it? Let us look at the various steps that are involved, beginning with memory. A sentient being exposed to fire will recoil from it, but unless the experience is remembered the next fire would sound no alarm and the scars would worsen, though the worsening would mean nothing to the burnt person. The affective sense enables us to discover what is important to us, that is, whatever promotes or threatens our well-being. Memory then leads us to build on previous successes and avoid old mistakes in future. Far from being merely a dispassionate recorder of events like a barometer, the brain or mind seems to be equipped to promote well-being by alerting us to whatever menaces and favours us. The outer senses transmit, the affective sense evaluates and memory retains the impact of the environment upon us in one and the same learning experience. Facts, we quickly discover, are often charged with value and knowledge can be a decided benefit even when it is initially painful. None of this could happen without memory.

The next part of the learning process that concerns us is the forming of a causal awareness of the things around us and of our own actions. The warm autumn sun that ripens a fruit crop strikes us very satisfyingly, signifying nourishment and good health before the winter's cold. All this is clearly relevant to the sense of well-being. But that very sense is simultaneously an awareness of an outside world affecting us. So, at any rate, it seems to all but the most inveterate philosophical solipsists. For the rest of us these are signals of an external cosmos, charged with importance as well as being straightforwardly informative. And where there is an effect, there we may look for a cause. As J. Z. Young has yet again said, 'In order to learn the symbolic significance of signals that come in from the outside world an animal or man must be able to relate them to its own life and needs, by the subsequent satisfaction or pain that results when it acts in a certain way' (Young 1978: 88). The affective sense establishes facts as it registers values; it is the hallmark of successful selfhood and reminds us that we need to look beyond ourselves for our own good. When changes take place around us we register shifts in our awareness, some of them pleasant, others disturbing. Memory enables us to recognise conjunctions between these outer and inner events, seeing the one as the cause of the other. This may be a logically uncertain move, as Hume pointed out, but it is undoubtedly prominent in our thinking and learning processes, enabling us to suspect significant links between such things as smoking or radiation and cancer, fluoride deficiencies and dental decay. Often the linked events can be observed and felt, for example a sudden fall in temperature and a bout of sneezing. But how do we discover causes when none can be perceived, as with radiation and cancer? This is directly relevant to the emergence of many religious beliefs because these often speak of invisible causal entities like the spirits or gods. The process is complicated but the key to it is our ability to create theories. Before exploring it there is however something else to discuss first, also relevant to the explanation of religion. This is the phenomenon of perception, which we now know to be a theory-laden activity and not a series of passive sensory reactions preserved by the brain like a collection of mental photographs of the things we see (Hanson 1969: 61ff). Interpretation, memory and even language are involved in perception and affect what is registered. A mediaeval observer looking at the eastern horizon early in the morning sees the sun rising. A scientifically-aware modern counterpart with Copernicus' theory in mind rather than Ptolemy's sees the earth turning. So once again we find that the process of learning involves more than the observable facts.

If perceptions are theory-laden then the theories with which they are laden must already be present in the mind or brain when the perceptions take place. This raises an exceedingly important question: how do we acquire theories in the first place, since they are not themselves something we can observe? The question is similar to one that was posed in the previous paragraph, namely how we identify imperceptible causes. Whatever the answer, it is clear that theory-building is another important part of the learning process. It influences what we observe, synthesises observations into coherent attempts to explain them and affects the search for causes where none can be detected. We saw in chapter three that theories are created or constructed, not discovered, so that in principle it is always possible for them to be superseded. But how do we create them? To judge by the characteristics of some widely influential examples like evolution, punctuated equilibrium, continental drift and ancient India's idea of the dance of Shiva, theory-building typically involves a process of analogical guesswork in the service of the facts being explained. An example will enable this phrase to be unpacked and clarify the steps that are taken when we construct these remarkable devices for enlarging our knowledge. The example is from philology. To explain the striking resemblances in Sanskrit, Greek, Latin, Persian and the Germanic languages, a long-extinct proto-Indo-European language has been proposed and widely accepted as the common ancestor of this linguistic family. Groups from the ancestral community migrated to different regions where their descendents developed separately, so accounting for the differences between them, while the similarities are seen as family resemblances stemming from shared parentage. We have here all the main steps of theory-building. The problem concerns the remarkable similarities between otherwise different languages and is simply a matter of perception. It reminds the theory-builder of the way siblings or perhaps cousins often look alike because of inherited physical qualities. Here the analogical part of the process comes into effect as the theorist finds something comparable to the problem in his or her existing knowledge. This gives rise to the conjecture that linguistic resemblances derive from a common ancestor, just like family resemblances, which is why the process was said to require an element of analogical guess-work. So the theory is born of the union between analogy and surmise, the familiar being used to hazard an answer to the question posed by the unknown. And as so often happens, this particular conjecture takes an aspect of personal life and projects it into a non-personal phenomenon in the well-known process of anthropomorphism. The use of association or contrast with the familiar seems to be a crucial device in the learning process, not confined to theory-building, so we shall look more closely into it a little later (Burrell 1973; Palmer 1973; Nagel 1961: 107ff).

In applying a seemingly promising item from existing knowledge to the problem under investigation the theorist often makes an inductive inference. Once the facts have been examined a conclusion is formed which contains more than just those facts. In the philological example this extra ingredient is the proposal that behind today's Indo-European languages there is a common origin. Such a surmise fits the evidence very well but it is nowhere contained in that evidence. We apply it from another source, our repertoire of potential explanatory and interpretive analogies as stored in the memory and different for every person. Those with rich, diverse experiences will clearly have a more fertile stock of material for their theory-building than meagerly equipped minds. Conclusions reached inductively, then, involve a creative mental act. They are not imprinted on observable data like the marks on a coin. A slashed car tyre is not itself proof of malicious damage to property, however clearly it may seem to warrant such a verdict. To make it we invoke past experiences of vandals and the damage they do. Confronted with a gap in our knowledge we reach into the granaries of our mental past for the seeds with which to sow a fresh crop of knowledge. And as on the soil, so in the mind the harvest can fail.

This brings us to consider the main cognitive drawback of inductive reasoning, which is that it never yields a logically certain conclusion. The way induction and all other theory-forming processes like hunches or intuitions take place makes this quite clear. Faced with an uncertainty or gap in our knowledge we venture a surmise to solve it, using whatever will fit the evidence most closely. But at several points the process is fraught with insecurity. No theorist can ever have a complete knowledge of the evidence, so that it is always possible that fresh facts will come to light which contradict a given theory. Then there is the dependence of the whole process on the proposed explanatory device, which can only be as fertile and elaborate as its author's ingenuity and experience will allow. As for the testing of the idea, this cannot be more rigorous than prevailing critical standards, and these are themselves being continually sharpened. And finally there is the fallibility of all our efforts. Clearly, then, inductive conclusions and the theories they help form are always provisional. They are what the fallible do with the unknown by means of the provisional. So we find that our theories, for all their importance, are never as cognitively secure as observed and tested data. Yet without them the data may often be mute and unco-ordinated. This is one of the reasons why we create theories. Another reason is simply the nature of things. The cosmos is more than we can ever observe. What we do observe is only a fragment of the totality. So observation alone can never be cognitively enough and we need other learning methods to disclose to us something of that larger, hidden part. Theories help us do just that.

These explorations enable us to answer an earlier question, namely how we find causes when none is observable. We find them by means of this splendid if insecure device of analogical guess-work, subjected to every test we can apply because tests are the best way to compensate for the inherently provisional nature of the exercise and save us as much as possible from the delusions wrought by unfit theories. The critical ability mentioned earlier as a product of the discriminating capacity of our affective sense is thus an absolutely essential part of the process of discovering what kind of wider world we are part of, just as an attitude of acceptance is also sometimes needed, for example in the earliest stages of education or when a theory has survived enough rigorous testing to deserve widespread assent. Only so can it act as a sort of conceptual platform on which other cognitive activity can be based. People who spend all their time checking foundations never build anything on them. *In The Biology of God* Sir Alister Hardy showed just how vital the ability to accept information can be in the evolution and survival of human life (Hardy 1975: 65f). Without it children could not learn and unless they learn they cannot lead independent lives. Essential though this accepting attitude is in the transmission of knowledge, it must none the less take second place to criticism in the discovery of new knowledge where that ability is indispensable for success.

This is a convenient point to return to the device of using the familiar to deal with the unfamiliar. Nowadays the world is a well-known place. Virtually everything we encounter in daily life is already recognised by all except the very young. By the time we are adults there is little or nothing really strange to experience, except at the fringes of scientific research or at the experimental edges of life which affect very few of us. As a result we may find it hard to imagine what it was like when the world was less well-known, when elephants or kangaroos or Saturn's rings were seen for the first time. Yet the long search for knowledge of the cosmos has been precisely that: a passage into unknown territory. Hence the techniques for dealing with the strange and the obscure are immensely important in themselves, while in a theory of religion they take on added significance because the spiritual life is precisely a way of making contact with the mysterious and the unknown. Believers in God, for instance, invariably speak of the deity as ineffable or of the peace of God as something which passes all understanding. And Rudolf Otto's celebrated theory of religion early this century even generalised the category of the mysterious into the focus of all spiritual experience, referring to it with due grandeur as a dreadful but compelling mystery (Otto

1931). So it is extremely important to look more closely into the processes we are naturally equipped to use when confronted by the unknown and the mysterious.

To start with let us note that the affective sense is active in such situations. Face to face with an entirely strange object or phenomenon, most of us would be wary or apprehensive because experience has taught us that it can be harmful and possibly fatal to march briskly into the unknown. But we would also be curious. Judging by past performances that curiosity is exceedingly persistent, for we seldom mentally ignore new phenomena, even menacing ones, being ill at ease until we know what they are. We desire well-being and alien phenomena could jeopardise it. That possibility is disturbing enough to goad us into investigative action. What we know we can come to terms with, even if only as slaves. The unknown in our midst is thus a deeply disquieting reality and to get rid of the disquiet we need information. So the affective sense and the discovery of new knowledge work in tandem, and curiosity tempered with caution has immense survival value. Thus motivated the discoverer in us tries to fathom the unknown object, assimilating it by seeking resemblances and contrasts with things already known. 'It looks like an otter but it has a bill like a duck' says an imaginary explorer in Australia on first seeing a platypus. We saw above that this device of using the familiar to form a concept of the strange plays a part in theory-building. It also comes into operation when we encounter new phenomena, giving us a way of making that essential first step of forming an idea of the novel item. Afterwards other cognitive skills can be put to work, from magnifying glasses to radio telescopes and linear accelerators. But the first step is usually that of naming, typically through the modification of familiar ideas. It is a splendidly creative and richly metaphorical venture, giving us in recent times such gems of technical precision as the cosmic big-bang, black holes and those adorable celestial twins, the red giant and the white dwarf.

Another facet of the cognitive process that needs to be discussed is the creation of large-scale theories or megatheories intended to cover reality as a whole, known variously as world-views, cosmologies and paradigms of reality, perhaps associated with the activities of the right hemisphere of the brain (Parry 1976: 5ff). Mental activity of this kind is a striking feature of the search for knowledge all over the earth because in theory it is unnecessary.

People could simply have concluded that they did not know the whole story about the cosmos and left it at that. In fact, however, we tend to do the opposite, creating world-views to serve as co-ordinating frameworks with a place of sorts for everything known to us. So the folklore, mythology and belief-systems of cultures everywhere provide accounts of the origins of customs and clans, natural phenomena, the world and the gods themselves, all far surpassing the limits of established human knowledge. Ancient Hebrew mythology is probably the best known example with its comprehensive picture of all things being created by God and its accounts of the origins of evil through the primaeval sin of Adam and Eve, of language and labour pains and the tensions that often arise between those who raise crops and those who herd animals, personified in the figures of Cain and Abel. But comparable world-views have been found in other cultures as well all over the world. There are surely reasons for this phenomenon, and in due course some will be suggested. But first let us notice the charac-teristics of world-views in addition to their prevalence and the fact that, theoretically anyway, people need not have produced and retained them but could have chosen an attitude of agnostic-ism, a fairer reflection of their lack of knowledge about such large-scale issues.

World-views are invariably conditioned by the circumstances of their origin. They give a picture of the cosmos at large as seen from a particular cultural, geographical, historical and personal standpoint. Each of these varies in space and time. So, for example, the ancient Greeks produced a mental map of reality that differs from the one thought up by the San of southern Africa. The sages of classical Athens would have been exceeding-ly baffled to learn from the San that all things were made by Kaggen, the creator-spirit who sometimes takes the form of an eland bull and dearly loves that mighty species of antelope (Lewis-Williams 1981: 117ff). The idea has no relevance at all to the Mediterranean territories but is exquisitely contoured to the landscapes of southern Africa and particularly to the life-style of the San people. The cosmologies of localised cultures – and until recently all cultures were confined to specific localities – turn out, paradoxically, to be indicators of their creators' circumstances rather than reliable maps of the cosmos at large, a sort of mental brass-rubbing from a highly confined society. This is another manifestation of the ubiquitous influence of the known on the unknown, except that with world-views the known is minute and the unknown infinite. Lest this seem breathtakingly audacious, let us remember that it is also admirably intrepid. World-view construction is done in the same way as theory-building but on a much more ambitious scale. An apparently dominant feature of the known is generalised into the explanation of the whole of reality, which is conjectural reasoning in the grandest manner.

Important consequences follow from all this. World-views, with their inevitable local colour and their frequently analogical origins, are culturally relative products of finite human ingenuity in the search for insight into the nature of reality as a whole. This relativity can be illustrated from mathematics. There is in the universe a plurality of things and to express accurately the extent of the plurality we need a system of numbering. Most of us are familiar with three systems: roman, arabic and nowadays also the binary method. Let us think of them as analogous with different ways of conceiving of reality as a whole. The number-systems enable us to count and calculate, the world-views give us a basic map of reality with which to identify and co-ordinate our experiences. But the numbering systems are not identical. Arabic and binary numeration permit operations that are either very clumsy or even inconceivable in the roman system, such as working with place values, numbers less than one or programming computers, besides being able to do all that is possible in the old system much more efficiently. This does not mean that the roman system is false and the others true. It means that it is an awkward, restrictive and largely obsolete mental tool. Similarly, the mind has produced a series of world-views designed to give people an overall picture of things. But none of them is immune to replacement. Interestingly, the Jain religion of India has a doctrine of intellectual relativism that supports this contention. It is known as *syadyada*, meaning 'the way of perhaps'. According to philosopher of religion John A. Hutchison, this doctrine holds that the world is 'too complex for any single predicate or statement to grasp fully or adequately; hence, truth lies in holding to the relativity of all viewpoints and statements. All assertions may have some measure of truth, but none by itself is simply true or false' (Hutchison 1977: 164). Similarly William James wrote that 'the world can be handled according to many systems of ideas, and is so handled by different men, (James 1902: 122) while Albert Einstein is reported as having said that 'so far as our categories refer to reality, they are not certain; and so far as they are certain, they do not refer to reality' (Needham 1972: 223). Given the fallible process of creating world-views only the best will survive critical scrutiny and establish themselves in our thinking as reliable maps of reality. When they do this they become the foundation for other kinds of cognitive activity, and as with any foundation, they affect the kind of structure that can be built on them. To vary the metaphor, they provide unifying frameworks for more specific pieces of information but in return they affect them unmistakably, so that even our acts of perceiving are theory-laden rather than neutral retinal responses to visual prods from outside. It takes the utmost observational skill to disentangle what we see from what we have been taught, as Copernicus and Galileo found. And as soon as an old pattern of thought has been removed, like cobwebs from a window, another network of ideas promptly takes its place. What else should we expect of creatures who see so little of what there is, yet are involved in and buffetted by it all?

As could be expected, world-views once established are seldom recognised for what they are. Their human origins become invisible and unsuspected. Everyday experience appears to confirm them, as is natural for an accepted cosmology, since acceptance means that experience and conceptual system fit well together, with no discernible anomalies. The mark of a good marionetteer is to be unobstrusive, to control from behind and out of sight. By the same token an accepted, functioning world-view exercises immense covert power, becoming deeply embedded in our mental processes, giving rise to actions and social structures that further reinforce it, as the sociologists of knowledge have so splendidly shown, and thus tending to be extremely long-lasting (Berger 1973). But no amount of mental, behavioural and social power can alter the true origins of a cosmology or change its purely provisional character, and as knowledge grows and critical standards become more demanding the old fit between the frame and its contents will sooner or later come under increasing pressure till the mounting mass of ill-fitting items bursts its conceptual shell. The reliability of a world-view is directly related to the amount of proven knowledge used in its creation; the smaller the known, the larger will be the step needed to reach a general verdict about reality in toto, known and unknown; and the larger that step, the less secure the resultant cosmology. From this purely logical observation we can make an enormously important deduction: so long as knowledge increases, all world-views must sooner or later break when their ability to co-ordinate data falls short of the things that need co-ordinating. So although we might in theory have done without these large-scale mega-theories, once we adopt them we are in for periodic conceptual revolutions. The way our finite minds work and our setting in a wider, partially unknown world makes this completely inevitable. If intellectual history is likened to the course of a river, then every so often a placid stretch of water leads to rapids or waterfalls or the inflow of a major tributary with its tricky cross currents, before the next stretch of calmer water is reached. Until that happens the way ahead for the questing mind will be challenging, dangerous and uncomfortable, exciting for some though deeply upsetting for others, and the only placid waters will be the back waters. The mental history of the human race cannot be seen in evolutionary terms as a linear process of steady, continuous growth like a rising line on a graph. Instead it has developed through a series of major discontinuities, known nowadays as paradigm shifts or quantum jumps, in which an existing mega-theory is displaced by a radically different alternative which deals better with the facts in hand. The history of human consciousness turns out to be a case study in punctuated equilibrium. None of those punctuations would happen if we did not possess critical abilities by which to dethrone an unfit cosmology and the creativity to produce a superior successor. Both are facilitated by the affective sense. In chapter five, when we consider the genesis of religion, it will be necessary to return to the topic of world-views for an identification of the main ones in the history of religion. In the meantime the reasons for devising them need attention.

One has already been mentioned. Megatheories provide co-ordinating frame-works for specific items of knowledge. This is a cognitive function in the sense that it enables us to build up a coherent view of the cosmos and to fit our discoveries into a map of reality at large. There is evidence, incidentally, that the brain is programmed to create these general schemes, according to J. Z. Young, who reckons that 'this is one of its special talents.' (Young 1978: 40). He writes as follows:

A characteristic of our method of brain modelling is that we require what we call 'explanations' for all the occurrences around us. We expect them to fit into one coherent scheme. Yet all of us, however wise, reach, in the end, points where our knowledge and understanding fail and some form of hypothesis, or guess, or faith, or religion becomes the only possible way to provide the explanations. This is therefore the mode of brain activity that relates a man to ultimates that he cannot know about logically. Many people believe that they can do this by cultivating modes of mystical experience, which they enshrine in beliefs about some spirit or god. Others may find that a logical belief in the unity of nature is sufficiently satisfying. Neither of them can *prove* that they are right (Young 1978: 253f).

This judgement refers to cognitive reasons for producing large-scale, all-embracing theories. But there is also a euonic reason for producing them. The clue to it is precisely the all-embracing nature of a genuine megatheory, for example the belief that the entire universe is an orderly totality functioning in stable patterns that can be expressed as laws of nature, or that all things rest in the hands of a benevolent divine creator. Such notions mean that everything can in principle be explained. Reality may confront us with unsolved problems, gaps in our technical knowledge, but these are covered by the principles of cosmic orderliness or divine providence. The darkness is thus only relative, not absolute, and there are no real cognitive aliens in our midst. We abhor the possibility of truly unfathomable crevices in the cosmos because hurtful forces may lurk there. It soothes us to have assurance against this thought and world-views provide it by implying that there are no such crevices. What we know we can come to terms with, however unwelcome it may be at first, whereas what is forever dark will forever menace.

What shall we call the cognitively-significant activity of accepting, holding and building on cosmological ideas that transcend what can strictly speaking qualify as knowledge? The obvious candidate is belief. It is improper to say that we know there is a pervasive orderliness or divine providence embracing all things in the same sense as knowing that late frosts can damage deciduous fruit crops or that the earth is the third planet counting outwards from the sun. We can verify these two assertions empirically but not the former. So we need a different label for whatever it is that we accomplish when we entertain and accept as true a notion which goes beyond any possibility of conclusive verification, and believing seems altogether more appropriate than knowing. Its ordinary associations are quite compatible with this proposal, since they amount to the acceptance of an assertion which goes beyond available proof or demonstration. In philosophical circles it has become customary to distinguish between believing in somebody or something, and believing that such-and-such is the case. Assuming this to be a genuinely serviceable distinction, it is the second meaning that is intended here. The disadvantage of the word belief is its ambiguity. Rodney Needham has documented in considerable detail the varied uses of the word in modern philosophy, the range of meanings it carries in ordinary usage and their highly complicated linguistic origins. He comments that 'an increasingly extensive and complex conglomeration of meanings has come lengthily down to us; and after all the accretions and giddy twists of sense we now find ourselves, even within a specifically Christian context, with a notion of belief so dispersed, intricate, and ambiguous as to create yet more perplexity and uncertainty (Needham 1972: 50). Seen through the eyes of the lexical experts this is certainly true, but common parlance none the less doggedly regards acceptance as the central meaning of belief. This gives one justification for its retention in the present book. Another is the fact that our ordinary mental processes involve just such an accepting mechanism and cannot evidently function without it. J. Z. Young even regards this as a precondition of knowing and attributes it to 'the trusting capacity of the human brain...' (Young 1978: 251). Hence belief is not restricted to religion; it is generically human. But in view of the ambiguities so minutely identified by Needham, the only responsible way to use the word is by stipulating how it is used. To believe, then, is to accept as true a notion which transcends the available methods of empirical and rational proof. Thus there is a direct link between believing and producing world-views. The euonic perspective outlined here reveals why: having a world-view is not only cognitively essential; it is also deeply reassuring. Therefore people will hold to their world-views very firmly indeed as orientating items of the utmost importance to their well-being. And this fits perfectly the linguistic origins of the word believe. As shown by Needham and Wilfred Cantwell Smith, it originally signified to hold dear, a meaning still discernible in the related

German term *belieben*, to love (Needham 1972: 43; Smith 1979: 105ff). Given the direct connection we have seen between benefit and believing, it is scarcely surprising that the latter should derive from an expression which stood for holding something dear. What else would we do to that which benefits us?

From this account of the chief methods available to us for learning what the world at large is like we must now turn to a consideration of the main mental forms in which such knowledge is obtained and kept. The evidence suggests two kinds: pictorial and abstract, imagerial and conceptual, with the former being acquired before the latter (Hallpike 1979; Piaget 1954, 1978; Bronowski 1978). Let us deal first with the pictorial form of knowledge. Here the things we discover are registered as mental pictures or images. This takes place, obviously, in all cases of visual encounter but is not limited to them, another application being situations where we need to grasp something imperceptible. We saw above that existing knowledge provides the only naturally available resources for thinking about such things, and among our stocks of existing knowledge much will be in the form of mental images. This enables us to try picturing whatever we are attempting to understand on the analogy of some well-known mental image, and often those images will be personal. In fact the use of personal images in the discovery process seems to be logically inevitable. Analogical thinking like this always involves an epistemic given; X cannot be seen as Y if we do not already know Y. But the only given with which we commence our quest for knowledge is ourselves and other persons. So the human is an inevitable basic model for all that is other than we are, with anthropomorphism being a natural part of the learning process (Strawson 1959). In due course the grosser distortions inherent in the device come to be recognised and refined or dropped, but so far the device has yet to run out of value. Stellar red giants are proof of that. The great danger to avoid is literalising or reifying what is always a metaphor. Taken figuratively, imagerial forms of knowledge can be immensely vivid and valuable, but when literalism creeps in the results can be ridiculous. In any event, imagerial knowledge is not restricted to single bits and pieces of information and conjecture but can accumulate and grow into a comprehensive picture of reality as a whole, a world-view composed of mental images. The mythologies of old are of this kind, supposing as they do that the cosmos is the domain of invisible

gods and goddesses who are none the less visualised on the model
of human beings. Mythology is a tricky term, of course, with
popular associations of falseness that are deeply offensive to many
believers. But it is too useful a technical term to be dropped, so
long as a suitable definition is given and consistency followed in
using it. In this book mythology means all discourse about the
actions of gods or a god or any other kind of spiritual being which
affects events on earth. Myths are thus the linguistic expression of
belief in such visualisable divine entities, distinguished further
by the use of narrative and by evocative power rather than by
conceptual precision or logical analysis. This must not be seen as
automatically implying falseness. The truth or falseness of a myth
is an entirely separate question. People who believe in God may
baulk at this view, disliking the categorisation of their faith as
mythological or semi-mythological in form, but such an objection
is usually illogical. It is absurd for them to regard ancient Greek
or Indian religion as mythological but not that of the Jews,
Christians, or Arabs. All of them believe in spiritual beings and
tell stories of their deeds. Believing in one supreme god rather
than many is not enough difference to preclude both monotheism
and polytheism from being logically classified as mythological in
form.

Humanity has not, however, been limited to pictorial represen-
tations of reality but also uses those abstract, generalised rep-
resentations for which the usual names are metaphysics and
cosmology. Here the basic mental ingredient is the concept, in
the strict sense of a general notion abstracted from particular,
empirical instances. As such, concepts cannot by definition be
visualised, though visual experiences and memories seem to
underlie them. Given this difference between visualisable images
and abstract concepts, the distinction we have made between
world-view and cosmology or between mythology and metaphysics is valid, though perhaps not absolutely clear-cut. One
example is the difference between visualising the creator of the
cosmos along the lines of Blake's famous painting of the Ancient
of Days creating the universe or Michaelangelo's depiction of the
biblical story of creation, and on the other hand thinking in
abstract terms of a primary cause, which need not involve
visualisation at all. Within this second category of abstract,
conceptual representation there are of course different constituent kinds. One is the linguistic type just exemplified.

Another is mathematical. These kinds all lack the vividness and impact of visual images but are much more exact and versatile. We can conceive of a million-sided figure in geometry but we cannot visualise one. The learning process needs both forms but suffers when they are confused.

In concluding the discussion of how we discover and express knowledge it is important to emphasise several points that have emerged. Firstly, knowledge is an indispensable part of the drive to maximise well-being. We can no more find satisfaction without knowledge than a prospector can strike it rich without finding out where to dig. To say this is not, of course, to imply that people can never seek information in a spirit of disinterested enquiry. But it does imply that the search for health, happiness, peace or any other benefit necessarily involves a related search for knowledge. The second point to emphasise is that the cognitive processes and forms just discussed have a direct bearing on the explanation of religious beliefs in the next chapter. To explain these we must first know what our learning equipment is. Thirdly, it is essential to recognise that these processes take place *sub specie humanitatis*, in other words under the conditioning influence of our own learning mechanisms, especially our dependence on conjecture and analogy, as well as that of the contexts in which we live. It is natural for Laplanders to place the problem of better heating at the top of their agendas and refrigeration at the bottom. In the Sahara the exact opposite is natural. To survive we must come to terms with our immediate surroundings, therefore whatever dominates them will dominate and in the end shape our thoughts. We can minimise these conditioning factors by guarding against gross subjectivisms but they can never be entirely eliminated from the thoughts of finite minds. Local and personal colour is inescapable in what we conclude about reality at large. The important point is to recognise and compensate for it, and not mistake our human notions for a perfect, God's-eye view of things. We cannot overemphasise this present point. A world-view or cosmology based on experience only of Lapland or Egypt will in fact tell us more about snow or the Nile than about the cosmos, and to a greater or lesser extent any world-view is the victim of its creators' limitations. So while we understandably hold our accepted beliefs about reality at large dear, it would be harmful to the quest for maximum benefit to stake our lives on them. In other words, to

find greater well-being we must discover the nature and possibilities of the wider cosmos to which we belong, and to do that
an experimental approach is best because that is how finite minds
function most effectively in their search for knowledge.

Activity as a pursuit of benefit

In this sub-section the focus of attention is on human activity as a
means of finding benefit in life, on our multi-faceted, practical
resourcefulness in maximising well-being. Clearly we cannot
experience the satisfactions we desire merely by finding out what
would produce them, though discovery is often in itself an enjoyable activity. We must also act in order to bring about the situations that provide us with benefit, like hunting or foraging or
healing diseases. The brain or mind thus has the vital power of
directing and disposing us to act in ways that will promote
satisfaction. The affective sense can then be seen as providing the
motivation for a great deal of what we do. This enables the
present view of human existence to account for the concept of the
will so dominant in some religions and in voluntarist philosophies.
The will signifies powerful, directed effort, often with an
implication of free choice about the direction it takes. The
concept of a drive to maximise well-being provides a logical way
of dealing with this notion. The will can then be seen as our
ability to initiate and maintain a course of action in the face of
resistance, governed by a belief that by doing so benefit will be
enhanced. The belief may of course be mistaken with the chosen
course of action producing more harm than good, but powerful,
directed effort as such is not surprising in view of the strength of
our desire to experience well-being.

Not all behaviour is of course conscious or intentional. Modern
psychology has taught us that some of the things we do spring
from motives hidden to our own awareness in the depths of the
mind or brain. There may be repressed fears or passions, deeply
embedded notions dating from mental conditioning in early
childhood and perhaps also inborn dispositions of which we are
entirely unaware. Then there is Michael Polanyi's important
distinction between focal and subsidiary forms of awareness,
(Polanyi 1978: 55ff) or the one between instinctive and acquired
behaviours. These distinctions and the empirical evidence

supporting them mean that the day is forever gone when human actions could be seen as deliberate steps taken by rational agents always aware of what they were doing. We shall be on much safer ground if we set this idea firmly aside and accept that behaviour is a more complex phenomenon, not always consciously or intentionally done. At the very least some sort of dual model is needed according to which conscious acts are seen as only one part of our total performance. This much we must conclude from modern behavioural science. But the field is still marked by competing theories as to exactly how we should map the mind's hidden regions, so it would be unwise and unnecessary to adopt any of these disputed theories and distinctions into the present account. The important points are that not all our deeds are deliberate and that those which arise from unconscious or subconscious promptings do not contradict the present, euonic view of human existence. The very survival of such a mental characteristic depends on whether it contributes to satisfying and hence repeated activities, or at least not to harmful ones and thence to extinction. Either way the present thesis stands.

Attention therefore shifts to the rich and varied complex of activities where some degree of deliberation is present, whether in each individual performance or only in the originating of a habit, custom or convention, of which later enactments may be rather mechanical. According to the present theory of human existence, these are the deliberate, practical steps we take to foster well-being so far as our own limitations and prevailing circumstances allow. Before the ability to act deliberately or consciously was acquired, our forebears were already evolutionary successes. They managed to survive by repeatedly practising some behaviours and avoiding others. The repetition, on the present view, resulted from the satisfactions experienced, while the avoidances point to a remembered sense of discomfort. At some point, however, the ability to extend and ramify the web of activity through consciously selected and attempted policies arrived, and having survived, the new ability must also be a euonic advantage. Dangers are increased but benefits even more so, with an overall net gain in the harvest of satisfaction. So the bare phenomenon of consciously undertaken activity is itself an aid to increased welfare or lessened pain. We can see this borne out in the many specific activities that take place very day for all of us, and readers are encouraged to examine their own pattern of behaviour to test for themselves the fertility of the proposal. The list of actions done in a single day for a single person is long, but every example analysed in preparing this book yielded quite naturally and revealingly to analysis in terms of the euonic quest, from child-raising to suicide, altruism to gangsterism and numerous other instances.

Just as knowledge is influenced by the context in which it forms, so too human activity must be seen in relation to the conditions in which it takes place. The southern San people believed that Kaggen, the creator-spirit, dearly loved the eland, and their pattern of activity showed a parallel, practical focus on that animal, especially in hunting and in the marvellous rock-art that is the main surviving indicator of their existence. A major function of the euonic drive is precisely to find out what a given set of local conditions will allow to prosper, like corn in Kansas, and then concentrate effort on it. The evidence here is that people are very pragmatic, quickly abandoning policies that get them nowhere, as we say. This is an important clue to the explanation of religion, to be kept in mind when we come to ask why mediaeval Europeans built such economically doubtful edifices as Notre Dame and Salisbury cathedral, or why the Muslims created El Aksa or the Dome of the Rock. In any event, we must expect human activity, especially successful, enduring kinds of activity, to have a close link with the possibilities of the situation in which they take place.

In view of the importance of environmental constraints on the things people do it is necessary to consider briefly the question of freedom and determinism. The debate between those who say that we possess free will and those who say that our actions stem from determining factors like economic pressures or divine control is another perennial philosophical issue whose maze of argument and counter-argument we would do well to avoid. The reasons for including the topic in the present anthropology are the sheer importance of the issues involved, their direct relevance to the discussion and the fact that some unsystematised remarks on the subject have already been made in preceding pages. What light, then, does this theory of human existence cast on the debate? Two points arise. Firstly, the euonic model of life means that our behaviour is neither rigidly determined by external factors nor wholly the product of our choices. Instead it is strongly influenced by those outside factors but not so much that we became automata grinding away with complete predictability at whatever we do. The drive to maximise well-being is not, as was said earlier, a dictatorial force. Its strength makes particular policies extremely likely but not absolutely certain. That leaves scope for freely chosen modes of action, a state of affairs made even less predictable by the nature of our mental, behavioural and linguistic equipment, none of which obliges us to act in set ways. Words can be used to speak the truth and to lie, intentions can be helpful or harmful; the arm can assist as well as strike. Our ignorance also invites freely chosen courses of action because sometimes we do not know how beneficial or harmful an option will be. If we knew in advance what was best we would not need to deliberate about and then select a course of action. Another factor permitting such choices is the variety of enjoyable pursuits open to us. All sorts of things can be equally satisfying. If this were not so we should invariably opt for whatever rated most highly on the euonic scale, and there would be no real choice open to us. So a cluster of very real factors can be cited as creating a sort of behavioural free area in which individuals can do as they please. But it would run counter to the evidence to overstate the leeway. The wearisome uniformities of suburban house designs, breakfast menus and denim jeans, let alone the pressures of climate, restricted environmental resources and the sheer power of the hunger for well-being itself, prove that much is beyond our ability to change. There is nothing whatever we can do about the basic conditions of survival. These will always include food, shelter, water and the other basics, and we are so constituted as to find them enjoyable and to seek them again and again. We have no choice whatsoever about shivering when cold and wet or dying if the misery goes on for too long. But we can, and do, decline the whole package in the form of suicide. Even this, however, affirms the euonic quest. It is the euonic quest when living no longer offers any hope of satisfying the yearning to escape misery and find happiness. The present theory therefore supports what is technically known as compatibilism, which means holding that it is possible to view all actions as caused without thereby having to abandon the claim that people can act freely. Hard determinism and fatalism deny this and both are thus incompatible with the present theory.

Before finalising this discussion of activity we must notice how the euonic perspective explains the importance of hope in human experience and its link with action. Signifying desire accompanied by expectation of or belief in its fulfilment, hope is a well-known condition of healthy behaviour. To hope for something implies that we want it and have reason to think that it can be obtained. Those who believe are thus also able to hope provided their belief is in something desirable. This fits the present anthropology very neatly. And once felt, hope can give rise to actions which make its fulfilment more likely, whereas its absence can be crippling because activity will seem pointless.

A behavioural pattern thus emerges. Experience of the external world activates the euonic sense and enables us to link some phenomena with benefit and others with harm. Memory preserves the link and enables us to develop regularities of repetition and avoidance in what we do. This sets up hope in us, from which it is a short step to formulating rules to preserve the practical import of previous experiences, warnings about danger, admonitions and encouragements to the inexperienced, and instructions to transmit precious skills to our allies, partners and dependents. And thus we find the discussion of activity leading naturally to the next sub-section dealing with utterance.

Language

The nature and origins of language are another much-discussed and complex subject, and there is no need to cover that ground in this book (Chomsky 1966, 1968). By now the euonic model of human existence is sufficiently developed for it to be clear in advance that our linguistic competence can be as much a means of conducting the drive for well-being as anything else we can do. In fact it is an exceptionally potent euonic skill, as a stroll down Madison Avenue, literally and figuratively, will surely show, enormously enhancing the range, precision and depth of the satisfactions we can conceive, communicate or hear from others. Language is often defined in terms of intentional communication among individuals, itself a massive asset in the pursuit or conservation of benefit, but there is more involved than just inter-personal value. Language makes possible an exponential increase in the ability of some individuals at least to conceive of well-being, quite apart from whether or not they tell others about their thoughts. Without linguistic competence we would presumably be limited to visual and other sensory indications of the things we have found satisfying or painful, with little or no conceptual skills to augment them because abstract thought appears to be very much bound up with language. And our methods of communication would be appropriately brutish. The thesis, then, is that language is an integral part of the euonic package; it involves the act of verbally enhancing beneficial knowledge through vastly improved conceptualisation, making it readily available to others and greatly increasing the effectiveness and potential satisfaction of behavioural options.

This is does, of course, in an immense range of ways: straightforwardly informing, warning, beguiling, ordering, asking questions, praising, admonishing, belittling, hinting, prevaricating, insulting, agreeing, being blunt or even, oddly, being silent; and of course also by lying, deceiving and distorting. There can hardly be any doubt that the dissembler's craft would have persisted as it has unless it too, ironically, has verifiable benefits. Like the common cockroach, lies are an evolutionary success. But since it takes the truth to establish this, honesty appears to have the euonic edge. Likewise it is obvious that words wound, sometimes with horrifying savagery. The claim being made is that those who do the wounding often think it is necessary for the benefits they want or want to keep. The drive to maximise well-being does not allege that we are inveterate truth-tellers and angelic models of altruism. What it does is to explain human harm-doing, verbal or physical, as caused by the perpetrators' desire for satisfaction, coupled to the belief that well-being for themselves and their group sometimes depends on injury or death to those who threaten it or seem to do so. We have already seen that the affective sense experiences certain forces as pain, which are then remembered as threats. It is as much part of the drive to resist these as to cultivate the sources of enjoyment. In a cosmos some of whose forces hurt us, what else should we expect? Given the limits of our knowledge in comparison with the sharpness and power of our sensitivity to pain, and given also the gap between the appetite for and the ability to achieve satisfaction, deliberate harm-doing takes place. Sometimes people destroy in order to live. If that seems an unpalatable claim let us call to mind the last meal and how it reached the table. In short then, language does not cease to create scope for benefit by being capable of causing pain. The position is rather more subtle than a simplistic correlation of truth and altruism with well-being, though there are grounds for holding that ultimately falsehood and injury are less beneficial than their opposites. In any event, it looks very much as if in the meantime we shall have to make a deliberate choice about how to seek satisfaction. Linguistic, behavioural and mental capabilities are not going to make the choice for us by having some built-in incapacity for deception, harm-doing or malicious intent. This they clearly do not have.

What grounds are there for asserting that in the long run truth has a euonic edge over falsehood? The reasons are firstly, as mentioned already, that it takes truth to confirm the enjoyable or painful consequences of lies, so that dishonesty is the dependent, logically parasitical policy, always presupposing and requiring the more fundamental reality of honesty. Secondly, there is an inescapable euonic premium on the truth. We have seen that survival itself, let alone happiness, depends on the ability, on balance, to feel enjoyment from the things that foster life and pain from destructive agencies. What we relish we return to, and if we relish fires or freezing temperatures we should die happy but without delay. Similarly were we suddenly to hate food or water. Life itself depends on love of the things that sustain it. Since we have to find most of those things outside ourselves, the ability to identify them is clearly vital. But to identify is the same as establishing facts correctly, and because a fact is by definition true, life depends ultimately on truth just as much as it depends on euonic success. Facts are assets; and at the deepest level of existence, at bedrock, truth goes hand in hand with the greatest well-being. If we were automata or gods we would never deviate from this correlation. As automata we could not and as gods we would have no need to. But being somewhere in the middle we do find situations where our finite freedom makes falsehood attractive. Another way of putting the point is that the environment is harsh on those who misidentify its favourable and menacing ingredients. Coping with it means accurately diagnosing it; what has survived is therefore the product of correct information. We literally embody the union of truth and benefit though we hardly ever notice it. Language enables us to lie if we wish and seek profit thereby. But to lie, as distinct from being honestly mistaken, presupposes that we already know the truth which the lie obscures. Therefore falsehood can never, in principle or in practice, occupy the pinnacle of well-being, though it can and does thrive lower down.

From these high-flying thoughts we must descend to something rather more mundane, yet extremely important in connection with religion. This is the question of finding words for new discoveries, an issue that runs parallel to the earlier topic of making and thinking about such discoveries. How do we find new words? One way is to invent them from scratch, like quark, and evidently this is how all words originated. But within an existing language pure inventiveness has the problem of meaning nothing to anybody else, at least until the freshly contrived sound becomes familiar enough to make sense. This is usually an unacceptably slow process. The other option is to make new words out of old ones from our own language or by borrowing from another. So existing words, like existing knowledge, gives us a spring-board from which to advance into novelty and convert it linguistically into something familiar. And once again the personal is prominently involved, enabling us to speak of all sorts of things metaphorically and analogically on the model of human exist-ence. The trick here is to allow the practice to be informative without succumbing to its inherently distortive tendency.

And now, briefly, let us end this discussion of language with a few thoughts about an aspect mostly ignored by philosophers and theologians, namely the poetic and the sung word, so prevalent in life generally and in religion in particular. There are good reasons for that prevalence. Verse and song are remarkably versatile, exciting the mind, though obviously not in the detailed way possible with the spoken word and with prose, stirring the emotions, enriching the aesthetic sense and expressing those heights and depths of experience hinted at by the word spirit. They are wonderfully suited to corporate use while also giving great scope to individuals to express their deepest experiences of well-being or suffering, which are often poorly served by prose, better by poetic language, and best of all in song. Poetic and musical use of words can express, shape, deepen, preserve, intensify and satisfy the affective sense in a way that not even the finest prose or the spoken word can match. But whether it is the sung or spoken word that we examine, the point about both is surely clear, namely that very often they provide us with highly potent ways of furthering the quest for ever greater well-being.

Human finitude

It will not be necessary to spend much time dealing with our human limitations because they are experienced by each one of us every day. But although the fact of finitude is obvious, its implications for the anthropology being presented in this chapter are not, so they must be identified. Finitude in this context means that our desire for well-being is greater than the steps we can take to satisfy it. Every painful death is proof of that, every frustration confirms it. As the preceding portrayal of human existence shows, we are well equipped for the pursuit of our euonic goals, and the successes we have had in attaining them are considerable. But still the quest goes on. We solve one problem only to find others disturbing our hard-won relief, while few of the solutions are in any case perfect. Many pleasures once attained prove short-lived. These experiences only serve to goad us into further effort, as do our mistakes and failures in the battle against pain. Nor do we seem content with modest successes. Instead the drive is for ever-greater benefits, ever less suffering. Were our resources infinite we would maximise well-being at a stroke and there would be an end to our strivings. But as things are, with our finite resourcefulness, the campaign is an on-going one.

A central part of this finitude is cognitive. Ours is a condition of greater or lesser ignorance, never of omniscience or mental infallibility. We can never, personally or collectively, observe all that exists, so our perceptual equipment has obvious limitations. This forces us too into the hazards of inductive inference or conjectures to extend our knowledge – a sure sign of a finite mind. What we have to go by is thus made up of incomplete observations encrusted with theory, discarded hypotheses and as-yet unfalsified explanations. This is a tenuous cognitive grip on reality, but for all that it has borne plenty of fruit in the search for well-being. We must not, however, allow that to blind us to our intellectual limitations, mistaking our grasp of things for infallible truth and richly fertile guesses for absolute certainties.

Finitude means that demand exceeds supply on the euonic market. This generates an undercurrent of anxiety in us. We discover that despite every care failure is always possible and in any case death awaits us all, made worse by being unpredictable. We sense the gap between what we would like and what we can get, and recognise that existence is a flawed blessing because it is possible to imagine something better in which that gap is closed. So, for all its limitations, the mind comes to a climatic insight, namely that anxiety and suffering will disfigure every imaginable condition except one. The exception is the complete elimination of all pain. We learn that only a perfect remedy can completely heal and in that discovery we find a solitary, comfortless certainty: the existence we presently exemplify falls desperately far short of such a euonic paradise. The discovery is valid. Our anxiety is therefore perfectly natural, an inevitable experience in a being who can conceive of but not create a perfect, ultimate condition. Yet such is our resourcefulness that we do not collapse into inertia and self-pity at this discovery but make the best of the situation, exactly as implied by the drive to maximise well-being. And with this point about human finitude it is time to conclude our discussion of the general anthropological factor underlying religious phenomena. Let us review what has been presented so far. It is a picture of all human beings conducting a ceaseless campaign to diminish their sufferings and enhance the good things of life in a wider world which continually affects them, much of it invisible and obscure. To wrest well-being from such a context with any success depends firstly on finding out what will prosper and then doing it as effectively as possible. But being finite, our efforts of mind and muscle are necessarily experimental, prone to failure and never-ending. Thus the euonic quest yields its flawed harvests of beneficial knowledge and action, world-view and way of life. It is a constant feature of human existence. All of us strongly desire the experience of satisfaction; all of us must therefore discover the wisdom and undertake the practical steps to maximise it as best we can with our limited abilities. But what about the different systems of knowledge and life-style that are observable in the various human communities? To the reasons for these we must now proceed

FACTORS CAUSING THE REGIONAL
CHARACTERISTICS OF RELIGION

The explanation of regional religious differences is to be found in two related factors: the existence of a multitude of different geographical, cultural, social and historical contexts, and secondly their conditioning influence, moulding our minds and partly determining our behaviour. Human life has developed in separate and different places, often with little or no contact with other communities until modern times. Separation, isolation and physical diversity from one habitat to another ensure that a common human make-up will none the less issue in great cultural diversity. There will not be one pattern of belief and behaviour but many different kinds. Some contexts provide abundant rainfall, others are arid, one community is faced with high unemployment, the next struggles against endemic disease or oppressive rulers, and so on. The reason for saying that these variations of context lead to cultural and other differences is that survival is directly related to the characteristics of a given environment, like climate, the presence of hostile neighbouring communities and abundance or shortage of arable land. To survive a group of people must of course adapt to these characteristics, especially the physical ones, and this means concentrating their minds on its dominant problems and developing a life-style which makes the best possible use of its resources, as well as giving protection against its shortcomings. The resultant culture will be as closely contoured to the environment as the people in question can make it. Activated in relation to varied circumstances, the drive to maximise well-being necessarily gives rise to varied fruits, and dominant environmental features will be reflected in the imagery of those who live in close contact with them, like shepherds among the ancient Hebrews and the monsoon or Himalayas in Vedic India. A splendid example is provided by Sotho-Tswana culture in southern Africa, in which a central concept for all that is supremely desirable is *letsididi*, meaning moist coolness (Verryn 1981: 11). Anyone who has experienced the blistering sun of a highveld drought and the wondrous relief of the rains will know how perfectly the concept matches the felt reality of the area. But in temperate or frigid zones the idea would lose its power and relevance. Another good example comes from ancient Egypt (Baker 1971: 15). The people there regarded the Nile as a living being because their observations could offer no better explanation for its fluctuations, being limited to local conditions. Life in Egypt presents the regular spectacle of the river rising and falling but not of the tropical rains or melting snows in the Ethiopian mountains which feed its headwaters thousands of kilometres to the south, where no Egyptian had ever been. Hence the river seemed self-moving and therefore alive. Physical isolation conditioned the way the Nile was perceived, quite differently from our modern conception of the great river.

The geographical environment is thus a differentiating factor in the rise and development of cultures. And once a culture is established, it too plays a part in determining what people will think and do. Raised to accept without question a world-view and the corresponding way of life, most people will in all likelihood continue to accept them for the rest of their lives unless an external factor like contact with a new group holding other beliefs calls the native outlook in question. Our convictions, values and behavioural patterns depend much more on the accident of the cultural context in which we happen to be born than we often concede.

Historical change also helps to diversify human communities. The rise of Christianity contains a good example. Until the collapse of the Roman empire in the fifth century the Christian church had a markedly Mediterranean character. Then Rome fell to waves of Gothic and Vandal invaders from central Europe. This and the Islamic conquest of much of the Mediterranean basin turned the church into something it had never been before: a largely European phenomenon with Germanic, Celtic and Slavonic elements quite absent before, from the word Easter to Gothic architecture. The fir tree came to be a prominent symbol in a faith which once grew amongst the olive and the fig. Periodically dominant factors like wars, an economic recession, a series of capable and far-seeing rulers or the discovery of vast mineral wealth all influence us strongly, precisely because unless we adjust to them we will experience hardship. But sooner or later things change and a new set of historical factors looms in our lives. Those who were greatly affected by one kind of pressure may have trouble understanding the outlook and behaviour of a later generation facing different problems. German experience before and after World War II is a case in point. An implication of historical change is thus that peoples' minds and behaviours cannot be static. From day to day different specific concerns demand their attention, of course, but the more important point to emphasise is that entire world-views also change, though the pace can be so slow as to go largely unnoticed. And as this happens, the life-styles that correspond to them also change. Faced with the inevitability of such alterations, people soon find that it can be very painful to become too attached to transient things and naturally wonder if there is anything permanently worth-while on to which to hold. It is said that in the biological sphere evolution is a process of establishing resilient forms of life.

In connection with the affective sense history could correspond-ingly be seen as encouraging a search for enduring forms of satis-faction. Let us notice that if there are any they must transcend the changing fabric of human consciousness, from day-to-day priorities like the rising cost of food to those deeply-seated assumptions about the nature of things which we mostly take for granted and treat as secure truths. Naturally, long-lasting ideas that have held sway for many centuries offer better prospects in this regard than short-lived ones such as phlogiston. The problem we face is knowing in advance which is which. And can we ever transcend the inherent limitations of even our most venerable ideas?

Social factors also condition people, typically by means of the profound influence groups have on their members, for example pressure to conform to family or peer group expectations, dis-couragement of dissenting voices lest community values be under-mined and the sanctioning of a favoured ideology by politically or educationally dominant parties along with censorship of rival beliefs (Henslin 1975; Berger 1973). Factors like these play an immensely important part in setting our mental and behavioural agendas, and since they differ from community to community, the result is even greater human diversity. There is an additional social factor to bear in mind so far as the regional variations of religious belief are concerned, of utmost importance, namely the fact that social models like types of ruler and the structure of community life contribute to the stock of ideas from which thinkers can draw when they make their analogical conjectures in the course of developing fresh theories. We do not have to agree that religions are merely the product of social causes to appreciate that they can none the less be just as massively influenced by the social realities amidst which they form as by geographical and historical factors.

In general, then, context is a potent factor behind the diversity of human cultures. We have learnt not to think of ourselves as living at the centre of the cosmic onion but are none the less enveloped by layer after layer of impinging, conditioning factors: the intimate sphere of family and friends, the immediate physical environment, the further zones of society, nation and planet, with beyond them the ever more distant but still effective reaches of the solar system, the galaxy and the fringeless universe; and, in addition, whatever other powers seen and unseen may nudge, bully, tempt or lure us as we make our faltering way into the future. Thus contextuality is a major diversifying factor in human existence. We are not windowless monads untouched by the flow of forces and events around us. The first words we hear begin a long process of mental moulding to the verbal contours of a native culture, represented first by our parents and siblings, then by teachers and friends, then by whoever else utters the things we hear. The same is true of the physical context. Our bodies are proportioned to the earth's gravitational force and air pressure, even our pores are related in size and efficiency to the global range of relative humidity. Just as we verbalise the vocabulary of our native culture and scale our efforts to its values, so, quite literally, we embody the physical forces amongst which we live. To exist as we do is therefore to be a dependent member of a sustaining, sometimes menacing, always moulding matrix in a world where no two of them are ever the same.

It is clear, then, that although we human beings have a common hunger for well-being, the different environments in which per-force we look for ways to satisfy that hunger ensure that from-place to place there will be differences of belief, behaviour and value rather than a common mind or policy shared by everyone. Thus the deep structure of human existence, our common equipment for and participation in a euonic engagement with the forces of the enveloping, partly unseen cosmos, cannot fail to issue in a multitude of regionally different expressions of that engagement.

AGENT-SPECIFIC FACTORS

A final set of differentiating factors must now be identified, namely those which explain why the faith of each individual appears to be unique. There are four points to be kept in mind. Firstly, no matter how much a given society may discourage indi-vidualism, there is for everyone a unique set of particular circum-stances: the time and place of a person's life, who their immediate relatives are, their poverty or wealth, their personality, and so forth. Secondly, individual talents are uneven in distribution, kind and degree. Not everyone has an ear for music or nimble fingers with which to make intricate things, and among the talented some are more gifted than others. Thirdly, personal needs can vary. Some like to work in silence, others find it helpful to have rock music in the foreground. Finally there is the ability to choose at least some things for ourselves, to think, act and speak as we judge necessary and pleasing within the limits set by our context, thereby making possible a vast and maybe limitless range of personal differences. But even the oddest twirl in the brush-strike of a Salvador Dali is anchored in the affective sense which it pleases. Variation can be richly original without ceasing to express a common human desire for well-being. The undeniable evidence of regional and individual differences does not nullify the case made in this chapter for fundamental human unity in respect of the drive to maximise benefit, because the drive is activated in different geographical and personal situations and in relation to them necessarily produces varied fruits.

There are indications that the individualism alluded to in the previous paragraph has not been possible in all societies (Cornford 1957; Cobb 1967). Communities without much role-differentiation or in which collective patterns of belief and behaviour are very dominant, naturally give little scope for their members to develop different, personal interests in any significant sense. Historically, the first signs of change from societies with little or no individualism appear to have taken place no earlier than 1000 BCE in the great ancient civilisations and much later elsewhere. The relevance of this development, its location and date so far as religion is concerned will be made clearer in the next chapter when we consider the emergence of the first great religious leaders of history.

THE CREATION OF CULTURES AND THE TRANSCENDENTALIST OUTLOOK

The best way to draw together the many strands of the chapter thus far is by means of humanity's culture-creating activities all over the world. A culture may be defined as the total body of material and mental products and forms of behaviour developed and shared by a given group of people living in a particular set of circumstances and transmitted from generation to generation by other than biological means. It includes everything a people makes in their on-going interaction with the total environment, from plough to temple, warship to world-view. In the perspective of this book, a culture is the set of physical and conceptual tools we desire, design, produce, use and improve in order to maximise well-being. By fashioning them we externalise our questing, euonic selfhood in order to internalise the things we need.

Several implications of these remarks call for special emphasis. Firstly, the concept of culture embraces the humanly-made part of our existence as a whole. Secondly, the things people make include not only material objects but also patterns of behaviour, ways of organising social life, and all their intellectual creations such as literature, theories, beliefs, information systems and notions of how best to discover what reality is like and what we must do to obtain the greatest satisfaction. Thirdly, what a given society can produce depends on the resources the environment offers and on its peoples' level of knowledge and technical skill. Fourthly, the very existence of artifacts implies that people are both needful and creatively resourceful. Everything they have added to the face of the earth and the sky above is proof of the vulnerable inventiveness that is the core of the present view of culture, at once finite but also splendidly effective. Whatever their exact circumstances, people depend for their survival on an outside supply of sustenance: food, water, clothing and shelter; older, wiser and stronger fellows during childhood and youth, the esteem of peers and their cooperation in the middle years, support when old and frail, healing of illness and injury, knowledge of the sources of well-being, correction of error and harm-doing, comfort and successors when dying, and the means of coping with the grimmest of besetting problems. Without these we would perish. But we have not perished. Therefore needful-ness is only half the human reality. The other is the limited but effective creativity which turns seeds into harvests, guesses into theories, and pain into prayer. Culture is the name for all that creativity.

This is a broader view than the one held by some other theorists. Thus Clifford Geertz has written that a culture is 'a historically transmitted pattern of meanings embodied in symbols, a system of inherited conceptions expressed in symbolic forms by means of which men communicate, perpetuate and develop their knowledge about and attitudes towards life (in Banton 1966: 3). But to view the subject like this is to restrict it to mental activity and end with too narrow a view of human existence. Much more is involved than just mental activity, fundamental though it is. The broader definition given at the start of the present section is therefore preferable, and is also in line with the views of some other experts (Berger 1973; Malinowski 1977: 36). Given a euonic view of human existence, this amounts to the claim that culture is the elaboration of value. Driven by the need for well-being, we mentally engage the impinging milieu, sensing its prospects for good and ill, naming them, pondering them, experimenting with them, putting them to good effect as best we can. The result is an ongoing creativity that is no less marvellous for being often clumsy and misdirected, issuing in our scales of value, systems of knowledge, action patterns and linguistic achievements. Society itself is a human product (Berger 1973: 8). Thus we make a living of our drive to ameliorate the conditions around and within us, an existential farm to cultivate the crops of well-being by the thousand: ethical codes, rules, laws, customs and habits, all intended to enhance the yield of our actions; governments to institutionalise them; agriculture, mining and industry; the market and the ministry of commerce; magic and technology from mud bricks to Buckminster Fuller; entertainment empires, symphonies and De Chirico's art; Stonehenge and Enola Gay; propaganda to proclaim our professed values and budgets our real ones; names for insights and perceptions; world-views as intricate as a spider's web; wondrously ramified scientific theories; and somewhere in the busy fields a place also for Buchenwald and Bonhoeffer, Gandhi and Sharpeville.

This inventory of human inventiveness reminds us that our creativity comes to endlessly varied surface manifestations, because the scattered environments in which we live have different resources, problems and possibilities, as we saw in the previous sections. Cultural variation is consequently inevitable. The changes of design for something as simple as a table knife are seemingly without end; and the broad lesson of the things on display in the earth's museums of culture is that well-being can be pursued in a staggering variety of ways, with change rather than durability the norm. The rate of change is not of course the same for everything. Clothing fashions alter rapidly whereas the means of production change slowly. Slowest of all to change are our world-views, so slow, in fact, that they seem as secure as anything could be. But this is an illusion. Cultures are not random collections of assorted phenomena, like yard sales or parish bazaars, but flexibly structured totalities in which action, thoughts, products and institutions have a certain mutual coherence. Worldviews are thus wed to life-styles, shared, with room for internal variation, by whole populations. This naturally means that we cannot alter them with the alacrity of the fashion magazines. That, however, by no means exempts them from change. Yet within any culture there is also a natural pressure to conserve the things that have proved valuable, the warmest clothing and building materials in cold regions, precious weapon-making and tracking skills among hunters, types of conduct that stabilise communities, the healing arts, and the most efficient means of production. The strength of our affective sense naturally urges us to preserve these hard-won assets in the campaign against suffering. So we produce traditions as depositories for all that we think is worth keeping and handing on to our successors as they too take up the euonic quest. This is a sensible policy provided we remain ready at all times to relinquish inherited values which have ceased to yield experienceable benefits because of changed circumstances or improved alternatives. Seen in relation to the drive to maximise well-being, cultures are inherently fluid creations because everything we produce in our fallibility is open to improvement and should be kept only so long as a better substitute is not yet to hand. What is natural and normal on one part of our history can change drastically in another as we ourselves are shaped and reshaped by the energies of well-being. Cultures embody the results of the euonic quest. They are an index of how much benefit we are capable of supplying at any given time. In the nature of the case the benefit is never enough and the drive goes on, creating, preserving and demolishing in ceaseless rhythm, Brahma, Vishnu and Shiva, and back again to Brahma. As the creators of culture we externalise our needful selfhood so that we may internalise its euonic support. Thus human beings are physicians to their own infirmity. They bring to each event the deposit of prior experience and deploy a mentality capable of sensing the forces that favour them and a range of activities, spoken or otherwise, capable of tapping the sustaining resources of the total environment. To the extent that the venture has succeeded it is a euonic triumph, but while suffering remains the quest will go on, satisfiable only by perfect well-being. Humanity is not the helpless plaything or slave of outside forces, a tumbleweed rolling before the wind. Long ago people discovered that except in the rarest, fatal storms, it is the set of the sails and not the gales that determines where we shall go. Within certain not-ungenerous limits our circumstances are tractable, yielding to effort, above all effort rich with insight and hungry for well-being.

The implication is that human existence can be seen as moving through a series of overlapping cultural epochs or ages distinguished from one another by their world-views and life-styles and above all by the ways they conceive of, seek, obtain and use information in the quest for increased benefit. The reason for placing so much emphasis on information is that the cognitive process underlies our world-views in the first place and is crucial for success in the euonic adventure. Cultural anthropologists and others already distinguish several major stages of history on the basis of economic, physical or technological factors, recognising vast differences between the life-styles of hunter-gatherer societies, pastoral nomads and industrial communities, so the notion of dominant epochs is hardly novel. What is distinctive about this book is that these should be defined by means of the way knowledge is understood, sought and used. And so far as religion is concerned the cultural epoch which is of paramount importance is the one whose cosmology is based on belief in an unseen spiritual order which affects physical existence. It is sometimes referred to as animistic or mythological, but neither term has won general acceptance, partly because of pejorative connotations. But we do need a descriptive label for the historical and cultural age that most crucially affects religion, so I shall speak of it as the transcendentalist age or outlook in order to draw attention to its most important cognitive feature, namely deference to a supposed higher, spiritual realm for the most important kinds of knowledge and satisfaction. And, in line with the modern tendency, the phrase 'the transcendentalist paradigm' will also be used from time to time as an alternative expression for systems of existence and knowledge involving the concept of spiritual transcendence.

CONCLUSION

The purpose of this chapter was to identify the global, regional and agent-specific factors needed to construct an explanation of human religious existence. Now at the end it is helpful to summarise the main points that have been made. So far as the constant characteristics of faith are concerned, the explanation will be sought in the unfolding creativity of sentient, vulnerable, finite, but ever resourceful human beings, interacting with a larger, force-filled, changing and partly unseen cosmos of which they are part, in an on-going pursuit of well-being. Given certain specific circumstances which will be identified in the next chapter, our euonic creativity results inevitably in the formation of religion in its constant configuration or deep structure. And by means of the differentiating effects of geographical conditions, historical changes, cultural profiles and social pressures, together with the varieties of individual talent, circumstance, need and choice, we have in hand the means of explaining why the faiths of the human race exist in an immense but patterned variety of forms rather than as unchanging replicas of a standard pattern or as a formless mass of random variations. Such, then, is the cluster of factors required for the theory of religion set forth in the next chapter. And in every case, as undertaken, those factors can be experienced or inferentially validated by anybody in the ordinary course of life.

5 Religion as a Quest for Ultimate Well-Being

The previous chapters have brought us to the threshold of the promised account of religion by providing all but one of the necessary requirements. They have outlined the data, worked out an explanatory strategy and developed a set of global, regional and personal factors capable of revealing why people live religiously. The one item still to be produced comprises the initial conditions or activating circumstances in which the spiritual life emerges and develops historically. The first aim of this chapter is therefore to provide that remaining explanatory ingredient. The other aim is to combine all the relevant factors into a systematic theory capable of showing why some people are religious while others no less intelligent and moral repudiate that pattern of existence altogether, and why faith has the various global characteristics noted in Chapter 2.

Three activating circumstances affect the phenomenon of religion, each involving a profound human crisis. The first to happen was the need to identify the unseen powers of the cosmos which so massively and ceaselessly affect us all. Evidently it took place early in the history of human rational consciousness and although no documentary material exists to prove this contention yet we may be sure on logical grounds that it happened. The second of the initial conditions relates to the birth of the great axial faiths from about 1000 BCE onwards, a development that must count as the most important single change in religious history because of the unsurpassed spiritual energies it released. Here too there was a crisis, this time a sense of despair at the imprisoning quality of bodily existence, triggering a revolutionary change in the direction of the quest for greatest well-being. The third crisis is still with us, and is the undermining of traditional religious beliefs in a world of the spirit by the complex forces of the modern view of knowledge and the various secular life-styles that have become increasingly well established in recent times.

To explain these proposed initial conditions and develop the promised theory of religion it is best to continue the train of thought contained in the previous chapter, especially the theme of humanity's culture-creating activities. The result is a series of logical derivations from the relevant causal factors, whose adequacy as an explanatory theory must be judged by how closely they cover the facts of religion from the earliest known manifestations until the present. To complete the chapter the theory will be summarised, its threefold structure shown, the extent of the explanation discussed, and some general conclusions drawn about the religious future.

THE CREATION OF RELIGION

Religion in the forms of which there is historical and anthropological evidence takes shape in the emergence through human creativity of belief in an invisible, spiritual realm superior in power and value to the observable world. The name chosen in the previous chapter for the period of its dominance in our thoughts is, it will be recalled, the transcendentalist age. But why did our distant forebears produce this view of things? To find the answer we must relate the explanatory factors dealt with in chapter four to the first of the three activating circumstances relevant to religion. That circumstance involves an acute, fundamental problem arising once an awareness had formed that people are profoundly affected by strange forces whose workings they do not understand but whose power greatly surpasses their own. The problem is to find out what those forces are like, which of them are helpful and which bring harm, and how to react beneficially to their perceived character. We see here the operation of both the cosmological and anthropological factors. The wider world of partly unseen forces is experienced as both hurtful and beneficial, arousing fear and fascination, and the drive to maximise well-being impels people to do all they can to ward off the forces that injure while cultivating those that bring growth, healing and relief. The conditions in which these two factors produce a belief in spirits as the best account for those unseen forces are firstly gross ignorance about the nature of those forces and secondly a phase of mental development in which anthropomorphic projection would be natural and widely acceptable as the most fertile way of solving the problem. The predicament in question here is as severe as any we can face, bringing people to acknowledge the limits of known explanations and available remedies for suffering, and is an inevitable experience of growing human consciousness in the kind of cosmos we inhabit. The cosmos does indeed surpass us in scope, power and duration. Even now its workings are incompletely and perhaps minimally understood. And always it affects us both painfully and enjoyably, whatever we personally might wish to happen. Likewise, given the affective sense and the drive to maximise benefit, we have little choice but to fathom the deep, dark waters of the cosmic ocean, seeking for ourselves and our kind a favourable tide. We are not born with the necessary knowledge. But our cognitive equipment is enough to bring us by means of our senses and the stimulation of a causal awareness to consciousness of the enveloping world; secondly to alert us to its dual impact on the affective sense; thirdly, through our sense of finitude to create in us a recognition of its superior power and our relative weakness; generating fourthly a natural and well-placed anxiety, and thence, fifthly, leading to a creative attempt at improving things by finding out what goes on in the unseen parts of the cosmos and adjusting our behaviour accordingly, so that we might maximise benefit and minimise hardship. And the natural way to find the necessary knowledge is precisely by means of the analogical conjecture that those unseen forces are wielded by invisible beings with minds and wills like ours but much more powerful. We humans know that of all visible creatures we are paramount. As we ponder the mysterious, unseen forces which in turn exceed our powers, we are scarcely likely to conclude that they are the work of lesser beings than ourselves. Certainly some of the more awesome, crafty or fascinating animals and insects can offer vivid analogies in respect of functions where our own corresponding abilities are modest or for which we have none at all, like flying. Theriomorphism therefore has a real but limited fitness for the job of thinking up a likely account of the mysterious forces that exceed our own. But much the best known and most apt model is human activity freed of the obvious disqualifiers of weakness and visibility. The idea of a powerful directive agency, personal, intelligent but imperceptible, is a much more likely and plausible basis for what we would call a causal hypothesis about the unseen side of the cosmos than any other at the initial or early stages of knowledge (Hallpike 1979). It does not greatly matter whether this conjecture is made consciously as an attempt to correct an earlier hypothesis, now superseded and vanished, or, as is more likely, whether it is done half- or even unconsciously as a groping of the mind in the dawn of rational consciousness. What matters is that either way the spirit-hypothesis can be fully explained by means of mental processes which we still use; that it has been enormously persuasive, and that there was a time before rational life on this planet when it did not yet exist. Therefore at some stage it must have emerged. Obviously we have no documentary evidence to record its coming. But logical inference is clearly enough to establish that at some point it formed. As has just been shown, we know enough about our own cognitive processes to explain how and why this happened. Pin-pointing the hour and place of birth is irrelevant and unnecessary. This contention relates only to the genesis of those forms of religion concerning which we have historical or anthropological evidence. It is not another attempt to say what the original religion was, assuming that there is any sense in that concept, let alone a hint at an evolutionary view of spiritual development. (Burkill 1971)

On the basis of our cosmological and anthropological factors, and in conjunction with the need to identify the unseen forces affecting human well-being, we can thus account completely for the emergence of belief in spirits as powerful, invisible, intelligent agents causing those mysterious events for which no obvious or existing account was available. Nothing could be more natural than that beings like ourselves, prone to pain, hungry for relief, curious as to what could help and limited to analogical conjectures in order to find out, should form a concept of invisible personal causation to account for the unseen, mysterious aspects of the cosmos. Equally natural are the attitudes of fear and fascination in relation to the cosmos. Confronted by a looming external reality which menaces us, fear is inevitable and salutary. Soothed by the solace it gives at other times, for instance at the end of a drought, the positive attitudes of attraction and fascination are appropriate, particularly as the uncomprehended cosmos is precisely also a mysterious cosmos, evoking awe-tinged curiosity quite naturally from those who sense their own insignificance in comparison with its vastness, power and obscurity. The concept of mana and its equivalents, signifying a diffused potency responsible for all that is exceptional and mysterious, makes perfect sense when understood as a natural form of cosmic awareness in non-literate societies. And the religious experiences so influentially analysed by Rudolf Otto are also readily explicable by the present theory without the belief that they involve an independent sacred reality disclosed by a special religious mode of apprehension. Both the concept of the sacred and the alleged sense of the numinous are analysable into the more basic cosmic structures and mental processes identified by the present theory. Holiness, the awesome and fascinating mystery of Otto's famous book, is the face of the cosmos as seen by finite, groping, vulnerable beings living out their frail lives within its vastness and under its power to bless and destroy. Somewhere in it the probing mind rightly senses the presence of that fusion of the greatest value, power and mystery which is signified by the concept of the sacred. We do not need to suppose that in addition to the surrounding, naturally experienceable cosmos there is a further, independent reality called the holy without which the experiences so carefully investigated by Otto could not take place. It has just been shown that they can indeed be explained quite sufficiently without that supposition, which does not, of course, mean that no such realities exist. As for the assertion that we have a distinctive mental capability for sensing the holy, the present theory also shows that religious experience, even as defined by Otto, can be completely covered by the ordinary mental processes that were identified in chapter four. No special religious sense need be posited and none has in any case ever been shown to exist.

We are also in a position to explain the global religious concern with transcendence. Here too it is unnecessary to suppose that in addition to the ordinarily experienceable cosmos there exists another type of reality surpassing us in duration, power and importance. As with holiness, transcendence is the natural face of a mighty cosmos in the eyes of the fragile creature who gazes out into it, sees so little of its workings and yet must live in its power. To transcend means to surpass some other entity and its ability to comprehend. That is exactly what the cosmos is in relation to us. In some theological circles the concept of transcendence has been extended to the vivid but cognitively meaningless notion of 'the wholly other'. But whatever is wholly other will also be wholly unknown to us, since it must logically lack the slightest resemblance to or continuity with our own kind of existence, including our powers of apprehension. There may of course be such absolute unknowns, but on logical grounds they cannot possibly be part of human experience of any kind (Hinchliff and Young 1981: 28). Wholly otherness is a useful devotional hyperbole in the vocabulary of people who believe in a god of towering majesty but it is quite useless when taken at face value in a factual analysis of the spiritual life because it implies an outright self-contradiction, namely that the object of faith is such that it cannot possibly be the object of faith. So we are left with the other meaning of the concept, namely the property of surpassing something else. And the factors cited in this theory also explain the rise of our religious sense of transcendence quite sufficiently as a natural impression of the ordinarily experienceable cosmos: numbingly vast, largely obscure, massively powerful, and the source of the thing that matters most to us: our prospects for increased well-being. If this is not a paradigm of transcendence, it is hard to imagine what would constitute one.

Just as explicable is the global religious concern with finding benefit in what believers see as a powerful, transcendent, spiritual world. Our euonic make-up drives us in search of the greatest possible satisfaction. Obviously the search must extend to the unseen order lest there be an unprotected front of our existence at which the threat of injury and pain is acute. In fact the quest for well-being is especially pressing in relation to the unseen order because it is precisely there that our lack of control makes us most vulnerable. Such, at any rate, is the position with regard to cultures with very little knowledge or technology to increase their ability to control those outside forces. We will return to this theme of well-being later in the chapter because of its overwhelming importance in the religious life (Moberg 1979). Meanwhile, the wholehearted personal involvements known as religious faith are also explicable by the factors before us. Given the importance we attach to the quest for benefit and the great anxiety we are apt to feel in regard to the unknown, what else would we do but devote ourselves unreservedly to coping with them? Religion operates in the zones of greatest human vulnerability and apprehension. As such it will obviously not be conducted with levity or indifference. An interest as fundamental as this evokes and merits every available resource in those who are aware of it, giving us those intensities of thought, word and action so widely observable in terra religiosa. By the same logic all available resources in our cultural traditions will naturally be used to conduct the euonic quest. As finite, social beings we have no choice about employing ideas, terms, objects and behavioural patterns inherited from others, even if we modify them for our own use. Therefore no matter how distinctive our personal faiths may be they will none the less exhibit a more or less obvious family resemblance with those of other people from the same cultural background, also possessing a less easily detectable but still real resemblance with the thoughts and deeds revealed by other transcendentalist cultures. The characteristics of religious faith and the pervasive influence of traditions in the spiritual life are therefore both readily covered by the present explanation, just as it also accounts for the multiplicity of traditions by referring to geographical, and other differences between communities, and their conditioning effects on the people who live in them.

Thus the first known world-view to have been held all over the globe was a personified cosmos, the spiritual megatheory that has dominated human societies until modern times. It involves the belief that there exists a multitude of invisible beings of varying power, function and benevolence which can indwell and animate objects, animals and people or affect them externally (Eliade 1977: 11f). The speculations about the origins of this enormously widespread and influential world-view, sparked by E. B. Tyler's famous theory a century ago, need not detain us (1871; Phillips 1976: 26f). The important points are that the view has been so widely and lengthily held as to be a sign of something global and that its existence is entirely to be expected in view of our normal cognitive processes. Nothing could be more natural in ancient cultures especially than the belief that the unbidden changes in and around us, from sneezes to thunderstorms and falling rocks, are the work of invisible, individual beings with minds and wills of their own. We know enough now about the brain's powers to recognise that for a person convinced of this theory so deeply as to take it entirely for granted there can be experiences in which such beings are seen or heard with every semblance of an objective presence. Skilled hypnotists can induce visual experiences of this kind and the subject will be utterly convinced of the appearance though observers see nothing and television cameras record nothing. Such revelatory happenings may modify a belief in spiritual beings but they always presuppose it in the mind of the person who has the experience. Therefore they can never successfully explain the emergence of that belief. The answer would seem to lie in the natural conclusion to which the groping mind is led early in its quest for knowledge and benefit, namely a multi-personal cosmos. In any event the first great megatheory of which we have historical evidence is this essentially personal and social view of reality. In that the spirits are cited as responsible for happenings in human affairs and in nature, the belief is quite obviously a species of causal awareness, and since it offers an explanation for reality at large it just as obviously constitutes a megatheory, prone, like all theories, to supersession. Causal power is expressed by the idea of personal directive agency, yielding a social view of reality at large; the plurality and unequal strength of the forces in the cosmos is rendered as the multitude of spirits uneven in power; while a perception of an interacting field of forces issues in methods of relating the spirits to one another. A prominent way of doing this was to group them into families and pantheons. The relationship among the spirits was not always reckoned to be cordial, and reports of conflict among the gods are not unknown in the world's mythologies, a sort of warfare in the overworld. But even warfare is a relationship. The mystery of the cosmos is acknowledged because the spirits are unpredictable, and together they constitute a reality far transcending human existence in power and durability. Their very unpredictability enables them to be invoked as explanations of both benefit and harm, while the mythologies which narrate their origins or activities and the rituals carried out to honour, placate or manipulate them show that the spirit-megatheory, for all its mystery, none the less sets forth a picture of reality which gives scope for comprehension and encourages people to tap its powers in their own interests. Finally, since the theory is extensible to everything, it clearly qualifies as a genuine world-view. Thus our awareness of the cosmos comes to expression mythologically through the perfectly natural conjecture that things are through and through personal. It turns out that the spirit theory is none other than what we might call mythological naturalism because it explains present events by means of spiritual causes, the product not so much of priests or prophets but simply of humanity in the early days of the search for knowledge and benefit. Einstein and Darwin, and not just Billy Graham or the Dalai Lama, have mythographers in their ancestry. Could it be, then, that the linear cultural descendents of Moses or Gotama are not necessarily the rabbis and priests but Nietzsche, E. O. Wilson and Jacob Bronowski? Whatever the answer, the point is that for much of history religion is not something that can be detached from the rest of life. It was not the special preoccupation of only some people but the everyday business of all. Homo religiosus and homo sapiens are identical; religion is culture and culture is religion. (Van der Leeuw 1938: 679, footnote 1)

RELIGION AND ULTIMATE WELL-BEING

A central thesis of this book can now be stated. Religion is human effort tapping the euonic possibilities in the unseen part of the cosmos in one or other form of the spiritual world-view and its accompanying way of life, coming into being at the frontier of available knowledge and beneficial activity. Our need and desire for increased well-being quickly exceed our own ability, mental and physical, to satisfy them. The circumstance which calls religion into existence – the initial condition called for by explanation theory – is therefore the discovery that true and total satisfaction, the thing that matters most to us, is beyond the limits of our own minds and ability to ensure as finite, mortal, physical beings, dependent as we are on strange forces that surpass our comprehension and control. Human finitude is crucial in this theory, so that the ontological reality on which faith rests is the fact that what happens in the cosmos exceeds greatly what we know and can control. This inability is a constant feature of human existence, in the sense that despite all the undoubted success at solving countless theoretical and practical problems we still are ignorant and helpless about many others. The kind of inability changes as the drive to maximise well-being works away at the vulnerabilities that worry us, but for all human life there is always something which nobody understands and controls, but which none the less profoundly affects us. In distant phases of the transcendentalist epoch the problems included the causes of rainfall, victory in battle, the germination of seeds, the movements of the sun and moon, the powers of fire and fertility and the seasonal cycles. They were the unsolved yet critically important riddles of the earth itself and of human fortune. Nowadays science has given convincing answers to most or even all of those ancient perplexities, but let us not forget that there was a time when they were complete mysteries, yet profoundly affected people. The result was the deepest anxiety at the precariousness of the available grip on things that had such power to hurt or help, an entirely realistic and natural reaction, for that was precisely what the situation was like.

At that frontier of human insight and ability one of history's marvels unfolds, namely the genesis of religion. The drive to maximise well-being responds not with resignation and self-pity, except perhaps in some people, but with a venturesome resourcefulness that is almost breathtaking. It puts out feelers into the dark zones beyond the limits of the familiar, in the inevitable and natural form of the supposition that the mysterious forces operating from there and affecting human life so deeply are wielded by invisible personal agents. The advance hereby made is immense because it implies that the dark zone is not absolutely obscure, an endless well of random intrusions into human existence that are in principle unfathomable, unpredictable and uncontrollable. The implication is that the dark zone is only dark to us in our ignorance but in itself is luminous and patterned, the place of intelligent beings whose power clearly exceeds all human effort but is none the less in principle a controlled, potentially scrutable power. Even the most flint-souled latter day materialist must surely do homage to the achievement of our mythological forebears at that frontier of available ability, and acknowledge in the birth of religion the birth not only of mythology but of all our large-scale attempts to decipher the nature of things, science included.

To be religious is thus to reap harvests that none of us has sown, to advance creatively beyond our own abilities and certainties into resources greater than our own, understanding those harvests as the result of invisible spiritual agencies, techniques or powers. For the obvious lesson of the survival and flourishing of religion is that there are such resources waiting to be reaped, that the supposition of a tractable spirit-world, however symbolic, results in the garnering of real benefits, real satisfactions, real successes in the struggle with suffering. It is inconceivable that such pragmatic beings as ourselves would have persisted with a conception of reality and its accompanying life-style if they were not yielding experienceable benefits. In view of the way we humans function and of our setting in the force-filled, partly unseen cosmos, it was inevitable that some day people would stumble their way to an absolutely vital question, namely what affects us most, what is chiefly relevant to the well-being we supremely desire? And no less inevitable was the fertile supposition that invisible personal beings held the answer. The limits of that supposition lie in literalising the analogy with the human, and science has latterly given us additional ways of thinking. But its strengths include the implication that the forces of the cosmos are not chaotic but controlled and amenable to discovery. This part at least of the spirit theory remains in full force. In this very special sense, mostly overlooked, everybody is religious.

The process of probing beyond the limits of available insight and ability brings us to the concept of the ultimate in connection with religion. It somes from the Latin words *ultra*, meaning beyond, and its superlative form *ultimus*, that which is furthest beyond, and is thus an apt expression for the phenomenon just described (Glare 1982: 2085). But faith is the quest for ultimate well-being in two other senses as well, both of them directly related to the one just mentioned. It is subjectively ultimate by being the search for whatever matters most to a given people at a given time within the framework of spiritual belief. In this subjective sense ultimate means whatever people think is the supremely important reality affecting their existence. Given the shifts of insight that characterise the growth of knowledge, such conceptions are apt to change with deepening awareness, and notions of ultimacy in one period or place will differ from those held elsewhere. But in addition there is an objective meaning, according to which the ultimate is that which cannot be surpassed, the final, uttermost reality on which any prospect of complete or perfect well-being depends. The subjective notions of ultimacy held from time to time are approximations to this objective, formal consideration and until it is realised, assuming that such a development could ever happen, the drive to improve things will go on as the pressure for complete satisfaction relentlessly sets up and then undermines its conjectures at whatever really is ultimate, and experiments with life-styles tailored to test those guesses in daily experience. We cannot be permanently comfortable with flawed systems of existence, and so are constituted as to be able to seek a philosophy of ultimate insight that would yield an existence of ultimate benefit. Whether in the last resort things are such as to thwart that quest or, as the religions of the earth uniformly allege, to realise it, is not as yet a question anyone can settle. The principle involved is however perfectly clear: only a perfect remedy can produce a complete cure of the anxieties foisted on us by our sentient, finite vulnerability and by the cosmic forces that affect us so ceaselessly.

MYTHOLOGICAL NATURALISM

From these comments about the nature of religion in general we must return to the topic of mythological naturalism in order to emphasize some very important points and deal with its main manifestations. In devising the concept of a spiritual realm people are prompted by the pressure placed on them by the unseen part of reality. Neither the world around us nor our own experiences are self-explanatory. For example, it is not always clear why we undergo inner conflicts or feel torn by different loyalties. It is not clear, at least to pre-scientific minds, why sudden periods of cold weather arrive bringing illness and damaging crops, livestock and property. It is not clear why the seasons come and go regularly or why other people should sometimes harm us. Yet in every case we are involved willy-nilly, are often hurt by them and driven to seek ways of lessening that vulnerability. Since there is no chance of a complete bodily escape from the situation, a promising policy will be to ameliorate it. Belief in spirits does just that by offering people a purported causal explanation of the obscure, unseen side of things. Accordingly, mythological naturalism asserts that there is a superior spiritual level of realities and yet at the same time also focusses its ameliorative explanations on this present world of everyday experience. After all, it is precisely here that the original problem of unseen, unavoidable and potentially hurtful forces is experienced. That is why it is permissible to think of belief in causally active spirits as a species of naturalism, at least in pre-scientific cultures. In any event, no rigid separation of body and spirit is implied; instead, it is held that a higher, more potent type of reality invisibly acts upon and within a lower, visible, less potent type, producing experienceable effects there. Rain or storm gods, spirits occupying bubbling streams or gloomy forests, deities of sea, sun or fertile earth all exemplify this pattern of operation, extending the model of human causal agency into the things that cannot be seen. In due course we shall find that the axial religions depart strikingly from the greater interest in this world shown by mythological naturalists, and in modern, materialistic forms of naturalism the spirit hypothesis is of course entirely rejected.

For the moment, however, we must concentrate on further aspects of mythological cultures. Of great importance is the way they vary without deviating from an underlying causal logic. The reason is, of course, contextual variation. If the spirit hypothesis forms in a region dominated by agricultural realities then it will deal with sunshine, rain, drought and soil fertility. But in a territory occupied by hunters the concept of spiritual causation will be used in connection with the movements of game, physical strength, courage, skill and the importance of hunting at the right time. Consequently the multitude of separate human settlements in different environments yields a splendidly speciated crop of mythological naturalisms. In cultures with time and talent for elaborate ramifications of the basic model, detailed spiritual personalities will gradually crystallise because of the pressure on us always to improve our knowledge; the spirits will receive names and characters to match the phenomena they affect. Where the graphic arts are sufficiently developed, pictorial expressions of the belief will be produced. The invention of writing opens up further possibilities for embellishing the personalities of the spiritual powers. There is a well established practice of speaking about the detailed, ramified versions of mythological naturalism as polytheism or monotheism and of the more modest kinds, found mostly in non-literate societies, as animism. The distinction is useful and valid so long as the underlying similarity of all three types is kept in mind. Each of them is essentially a belief in personal, spiritual beings which exercise significant powers over events on earth or in human life, whether by entering and indwelling the relevant phenomena or by exerting effects on them from outside.

The concept of the gods

It follows from the preceding argument that the concept of the gods as directive spirits is the central explanatory notion in the experience and thinking of mythological naturalists, quite apart from also being the focus of their faith. Nowadays many theists are apt to forget that before the rise of science people looked to the heavens, as it were, for the causes of earthly problems for which no other explanation was to hand. Natural phenomena like the daily passage of the sun or the coming and going of rain and drought were ascribed to divine causation in the same way that some contemporary believers attribute events they cannot other-wise account for to the hand of God. Fulfilling cognitive and devotional functions of such magnitude, the concept of the gods is obviously one of the most important in history, so it is necessary to consider it in some detail at this stage of the discussion.

The word god generally refers to a supposedly invisible, personal spirit with great power directing some or all aspects of nature and human affairs. It does not matter much whether a given community actually spoke of these causal agencies as gods or not. The important consideration is the belief that things happen because invisible personal beings are making them happen, from ancestral spirits bringing illness to a descendent in order to signify displeasure at neglect of tribal custom, to Baal causing rain in ancient Canaan or St. Peter asserting that it was his god who had raised the crucified Jesus to life (Acts 2: 32). From society to society conceptions of these unseen, personal powers differed greatly, ranging from the most stream-bound Greek nymph to the omnipotent lords of creation spoken of by the Semitic prophets, but all these variations are logically within the category of spiritual beings as understood by those who believe in them. Often people reserve the word god for the loftier, more powerful kind and speak of the lesser ones as spirits. This has the unfortunate and misleading effect of suggesting that there is a known way of establishing where the one type ends and the next begins, but no such dividing line can in fact be drawn. We simply do not have a spiritual litmus test for differentiating between deities and lesser spirits. The important step is to see past the peculiarities of language to the world-wide religious phenomenon of belief in a plurality of invisible, personal beings with their own minds and wills and with the ability to cause things to happen in the world and in human life, some of them quite modest in power while others are thought to be toweringly mighty beings. But despite the common ground between these versions of the spirit hypothesis, their mutual differences are still great enough to warrant separate treatments for polytheism and monotheism.

When the concept of spiritual powers forms in an area with several prominent characteristics all affecting its inhabitants in important ways, a natural tendency will be to believe that for each of those characteristics there is a spiritual overlord. The result is the pluralistic view of causation known to us as polytheism, especially when those overlords are conceived with definite personalities and histories of their own. If a physical phenomenon like the sun in Egypt or a pronounced interest in warfare dominates a society there is likely to be a corresponding elevation of the relevant deity to a position of prominence and even seniority among the gods and goddesses. Rudimentary perceptions of cosmic order lead to the concept of a divinity who bestows it, or to attempts at relating the deities to one another as families, rivals or members of a pantheon. To do this requires imaginative skill, and since that tends to take time and affluence to produce, ramified polytheisms tend to be found in relatively developed circumstances like those provided by the great ancient civilisations of Egypt, Greece and the Indus valley. In any case, the concept of distinct, divine beings invisibly at the several levers of power is an impressive cognitive and euonic achievement. The deities are an assurance of at least some cosmic control. Even better, they are potentially approachable provided the right methods are known. The way thus opens for a proliferation of experts in the arts of divine communication. Peoples' dealings with earthly superiors are indispensable models on which to build, and those who derive benefit from bowing to chieftains and kings will soon also bow before their gods. Mythological naturalism becomes heavily ritualised, serviced by priesthoods who possess the all-important cultic expertise of how to relate beneficially to the gods.

There is much, in other words, to make intelligible the appeal of polytheism to the many who believed in it during the heyday of the ancient civilisations. As an explanation for the unseen forces it had an obvious plausibility because of the evident aptness of the personal model of causation. The cosmos does indeed comprise a plurality of powers and their workings can readily enough at the apprioriate stage of mental development be ascribed to the direction of separate, divine overlords on the analogy of human authorities and the way they work, severally presiding over separate areas of jurisdiction. Ritual activities would cement this impression by providing avenues of participation for the ordinary person, led and guided by echelons of priests. And when cultic acts failed to bring desired benefits it would always be acceptable to conclude that the gods had seen fit to withhold their favour, as was their right. Therein, precisely, is the resilience of personal causation. Changes of the divine mind are always possible and can then be invoked to explain anything that happens.

On the other hand the polytheistic solution to the problem posed by the unseen order also has inherent shortcomings, affecting its devotional and intellectual appeal alike. To explain everything is in fact to explain nothing, in the sense of enabling us to predict events. When a recognition forms of the inter-connectedness of natural phenomena, increasing strain is placed on the credibility of so divided and piecemeal an explanatory conception, with its plurality of petty divine princelings but no real sovereign. For the devotee there is the practical problem of pleasing rival deities. How does one live out a pledge of loyalty to both the god of war and the god of peace? And how much inspiration can people in any case draw from such severely limited beings? Finally, as with all theories, the same facts can always in principle be explained by an alternative proposal. Inevitably there will be people who detect shortcomings in a prevailing theory and search for an improvement. So far as polytheism is concerned, this can take one of two basic directions: either by looking for a superior type of spiritual world-view or by exploring non-mythological alternatives. The search for a unitary religious philosophy hinted at in the later Vedic hymns and the rise of Greek philosophy are cases in point, and polytheism has in fact proved to be an unstable form of religion, yielding on one flank to monism and monotheism and on the other to the classical naturalism of Greek and Latin materialist thinkers from Thales onwards.

There are also situations which incline people to focus attention and loyalty on particular gods rather than on many. For example, if a group is very much involved in warfare its members' obvious interest is to pay maximum attention to the war god. And if their history were to have a sustained and victorious connection with battle to the virtual exclusion of other concerns, then their faith will come to be greatly dominated by that deity. Should the community also find itself struggling to retain an identity amidst polytheistic neighbours, what better way could there be for it to distinguish itself than by continued loyalty to the god who had aided it previously? We have already seen how natural it is to persevere with measures that brought success in the past. Faith is no exception to this tendency. Another situation encouraging devotion to single deities is occupational. People who make a living from a specialised craft or trade have every reason to reserve their worship mainly for a patron god or goddess. The principle is once more that of having a dominant concern. The plain consequence is to incline such people towards an incipiently monotheistic or at least monolatrous faith, better suited to their needs than any other, while still working entirely within the causal pattern of mythological naturalism. Instead of having to deal with a range of problems they find their lives bound up with one major issue. This would not lead to doubts about the existence of the other gods but merely to a lack of interest in them. Polytheism makes it possible for believers to react like this because the deities are all limited to particular spheres of jurisdiction. Naturally, then, those who never enter a particular god's territory, so to speak, have no great need or obligation to pay homage to that god.

Once taken up the monotheistic path will not be quickly abandoned because the concept of a single, superior deity more powerful than any others has great potential for expansion. It can be enlarged sideways and upwards, so to speak; the sideways expansion being a potentially limitless increase of jurisdiction since there are no real divine rivals anyway in the eyes of relevant believers, while the upward expansion involves an increased majesty along with a lessened connection with purely local functions like causing rain in Palestine. Given such scope for improvement, the concept is sure to attract the energies of the euonic quest, interested as it always is in the richest, most adequate and most satisfying beliefs. Powerful, questing minds will sense here an extraordinarily evocative concept and find great personal refreshment in devoting their mental explorations to it, lured by the prospect of a unitary explanation for everything. Moreover the retention of a personal model of causation also has advantages. Monarchs can change their minds just as readily as petty princelings. On the other hand, more subtle explanations for events contrary to the perceived character of God, like disobedience, could also be found in the logic of the new view. Truly powerful sovereigns are able to permit a measure of real freedom to their subjects, some of whom will sooner or later try to go their own way. People living in or familiar with great empires ruled by mighty kings, especially wise and tolerant ones, will find in that socio-political milieu a suggestive analogy for their developing theistic conceptions. So contextual conditioning adds its force to the logical potential of the concept. And thus is born the idea of a divine monarch, majestic without being remote, able to inspire awe without killing attraction. Compared to polytheism the one deity of the monotheist is impressively lofty while still being relevant to human needs on earth. His devotees continue to believe in divine control over events in nature and history and in a divine creation of the world. So we find that the present theory also accounts for the development of incipient monotheism into what has been called universalist monotheism, because nothing less will satisfy a theist's desire for maximum well-being. And in this concept of a heavenly king who created and rules the world mythological naturalism finds its most ambitious expression.

Next we must consider the functions theism fulfills. There are two main ones, cognitive and euonic, though a sharp separation would be contrary to the anthropology worked out in chapter four. In connection with both of them, for example, no puzzle is as important to us as what finally governs our well-being, since other factors are involved as well as our own efforts. Theism in all its forms has had a mighty historical influence by supplying a highly satisfying answer. An instance of a distinctly cognitive function is the immense pre-occupation with explaining the origins of things that we find in the world's mythologies. The Hebrew creation myths in Genesis are an obvious example. Interestingly, the Winnebago Indians of Wisconsin believed that there was an earthmaker who created the world by wishing and thinking and then made a being like himself from a piece of earth, enabling it to speak and reply by breathing into its mouth. Those accustomed to thinking of the Hebrew scriptures as unique and divinely revealed will be especially interested in this parallel (Eliade 1977: 83f). Comparable examples have been found in many other parts of the earth. Some modern commentators on the book of Genesis have proposed allegorical and other kinds of non-literal interpretations of the aetiological myths in it, seeing in them symbolic accounts of the human condition and its endemic alienations. They seem willing to countenance anything except the conclusion that the material in Genesis was at least partly intended as a factual account of how the universe began, using mythological categories. It is a prime example of the theory of spiritual causation, whatever else subsequent Hebrew redactors may have used it to accomplish (cf Westermann 1974: 5, 11).

The euonic function of belief in one or more gods will not be disputed by many. For one thing it simply helps the believer to develop a sense of belonging to an orderly totality. Having a world-view is an integral part of the experience of well-being, as we saw in the previous chapter. Then there is the more specific benefit of the way theism combats not just the ignorance of its exponents but also the common human problem of anxious vulnerability. The gods are antidotes not just to uncertainty but especially to suffering. And as we noted in chapter four, there is extra security in thinking that everything is under divine control. To think like this is to suppose that we have the answers to the ultimate question about reality and know who or what is strongest among the cosmic forces. We dislike the unknown because we fear that hurtful agencies may lurk in its shadows. It soothes us to know what is what, because we can come to terms with the known, however unpalatable it may at first sight seem. Theism, with its claim of being able to identify and create bonds with the governing powers of the cosmos, fulfils precisely this euonic function. It is small wonder, then, that some custodians of this potent concept should be unwilling to undertake a rigorous inspection of their belief and where it comes from. To probe here is to probe the conceptual cornerstone of an entire cultural epoch. Those who live in it have reason to resist anything that might undermine a system of existence in which they experience the greatest benefit.

Be that as it may. The evidence contained in religions all over the world is that people think explicitly of their deities as providers of benefit. This can be illustrated by the god Bunjil of the south-east Australian Kulin Aborigine people, who is spoken of as benign, by Leza in Zambia, Ndjambi-Karunga in Namibia and Raluvhimba among the Venda, each of which is thought of as compassionate or provident, and by comparable views held in many other regions (Eliade 1977: 3–73). But arguably the greatest euonic function of theism is not these explicit conceptions of benevolent deities so much as the broad implication of any kind of theism. The possibility of sheer, unmitigated cosmic chaos is nightmarish, far worse than an evil spirit. The former involves the complete absence of order and control. The latter spells harm but it is a purposeful, controlled kind of harm against which steps could in principle be taken. Theism of all kinds repudiates the former and soothes its adherents accordingly.

The concept of causally active spirits has a further function that is of great importance though it is seldom associated with the word god. This is the explanation of misfortune, harm, wrongdoing and outright malevolence. There is a dark side to things known in theological language as evil. An entire province of human experience concerns this phenomenon and the fear, suffering and anxiety it brings. Here if anywhere the euonic quest must be effective in providing firstly an account of evil and secondly ways of diminishing its power. And just as the spirit hypothesis gave people ways of understanding natural phenomena, as we would call them, so too it provides them with an explanation of evil. Here too there are invisible beings at work, manifesting themselves in terrifying forms of human behaviour, in temptations to do wrong and in some forms of ill-fortune, so giving us the religious belief in demons and devils. To conceive of evil in this way is extremely helpful to many people because evil spirits, like human wrong-doers, can in principle be opposed, restrained or even defeated. Sheer, mindless, inscrutable evil would be a much more fearsome adversary.

As is well known, the gods are seen in a multitude of specific, local variations and functions. For example, a role filled in one society by a goddess is filled in another by a god. The ancient Egyptians are a case in point. They had an earth-god, Geb, and a sky-goddess, Nut, sometimes depicting them as lovers with the prone diety overarched by his consort. But in most other places it is the earth that is female while the sky deities are male. This can be illustrated from societies as far apart as ancient Canaan with Baal and Anath and the Maoris of New Zealand with their mythology of Papa and Rangi (Larousse 1959: 468). Why is there this departure from rule in Egypt? It is difficult to resist an environmental explanation. In Egypt as in hardly any other country the fertilising waters, male by human analogy, come from the earth by means of the Nile, not from the sky. Regional variations in the way the deities are visualised and understood can thus, in principle, be quite satisfactorily accounted for by local physical characteristics of landscape, climate and life-style. Different territories produce pantheons made in their own image. This verdict fits perfectly the differentiating factors proposed in Chapter 4 and also flows logically from the present interpretation of the spiritual hypothesis, which sees the gods as causal explanations for the various phenomena encountered in ordinary experience. To function like this they must relate very closely to those phenomena. The violent storms of the Indian monsoon season call for a tempestuous male rather than a retiring maiden as their cause and, in the figure of Indra, Vedic mythology supplies just that. We need look no further than environmental profiles and anthropomorphic projection to explain the many variations of detail within the broad framework of theistic conceptions. Thus, concerning an Australian Aborigine society, a commentator has written that when their supernatural being makes himself visible 'it is in the form of an old man of the Australian race' (Eliade 1977: 5). There may even be a physiological aspect to this phenomenon, there being evidence that our brain programs are such as to yield personified conceptions of the divine (Young 1978: 254). The dominant characteristics of an environment and life-style would then determine what function these personal spirits will fulfil. Why else should there be no snow-god in the Egyptian pantheon, or the sea-faring Greeks be so impressed with Poseidon?

Human nature in mythological naturalism

Of great interest is the way people subscribing to a doctrine of spiritual causation will see themselves. The different kinds of mythological naturalists make for variations of anthropology, but there are none the less some important connecting threads. The main one is the belief that people themselves are a prime instance of this supposed phenomenon. They comprise bodies animated by souls, as well as being influenced by independent spiritual activity from outside, like demon oppression and visitations by angels or ancestral spirits. As an anthropological theory this notion offers answers to some recurring human problems. What makes us living beings? What happens at death? What are dreams? Why do we sometimes think we have a divided self, as when struggling against temptation or with a dilemma? What is meant by conscience? Why do we sometimes let ourselves down or say that we have surpassed ourselves? It would be incredible for people who thought of the unseen causes of external phenomena as spirits or gods not to apply the same thinking to human existence. The widespread and entirely natural result is to view people as comprising bodies animated by an invisible component commonly known as the soul.

A second prominent anthropological theme applies mainly to polytheism. As people's concepts of the gods become more imposing there is a natural and related sense of increased human dependence on them. Those whose forebears created the spirit-hypothesis and developed it in imperceptibly slow but steadily accumulating stages over the centuries come to see themselves as the products and underlings of divine overlords. The human origins of the concept are entirely forgotten, if they were ever consciously acknowledged, which is extremely unlikely. Questions about the origins of human life receive the answer that the gods created it, a perfectly logical reply within the framework of spiritual causation. So the ancient religious conception of human beings as divinely-created, soul-infused dependents of the gods takes shape as a perfectly natural component of the spiritual world-view. And from here it is a short further step to an interest in what happens at death. In fact there is no logical alternative to some or other belief in an after-life, however short or shadowy, for people holding a belief in human souls. If we are animated bodies and death is the event at which the soul leaves the body, then obviously people will ask where the souls go. Several answers are possible. One is that they go a place occupied by such previously embodied souls, perhaps itself presided over by a spiritual overlord (or underlord). Another is that they reanimate new bodies, human or animal. And it is always possible to be honestly unsure and entertain only a vague notion about the after-life, possibly tinged with the gloominess that many of us feel at such a thought.

But although mythological naturalism leads logically to concepts of an after-life, there is a more human reason for the subject to receive attention and indeed for it to be given some optimistic touches. Death is usually a devastating blow to those whom it bereaves and a source of great apprehension for many who contemplate its inevitability in their own lives. Here above all the desire for happiness and reassurance is severely tested. But the drive to maximise well-being has resources with which to counter and soften the problem, none more effective than to make death itself a euonic asset. This can take several forms. An agreeable after-life, perhaps hinging on good deeds or a well-placed faith on earth, is one possibility. Bodily reconstitution for continued but improved existence in this world is another. Being in the bountiful presence of the gods is a third. And there are others. But since they relate to the axial faiths we must leave them till later. For the moment it is enough to note that in terms of the present theory, belief in an afterlife of some kind is a corollary of belief in spiritual causation, augmented by the need we all feel for reassurance about death and the unsettling prospect of our own absolute cessation as beings. And this means that we can explain the emergence, continuation and optimistic component of doctrines about an after-life quite readily in terms of the unfolding logic of the present theory. Furthermore, revelatory experiences of the gods or ancestral spirits, a phenomenon already referred to in this chapter, will greatly strengthen belief in spiritual immortality for those who undergo them. What else would one expect of people entirely convinced that they have heard or seen someone they know to be dead or who never lived anyway?

The dimensions of mythological religion

In chapter four a picture of human existence was given in which certain prominent facets of the self were distinguished. The present theory of religion can be further clarified by expressing mythological naturalism in terms of those facets, starting with mental characteristics. The religious mind can then be seen as functioning according to the ordinary processes shared by all people, (Hick 1974) except that the relevant world-view is of course based on the notion of spiritual causation. In other words the unseen forces of the cosmos which affect us all are thought of as beings like ourselves but much more powerful and durable, mighty, invisible agents with minds and wills of their own. As beings they resemble us but as forces that give and take life and happiness they transcend us by far. So deeply is this personal interpretation imbedded in the minds of people with a mythological outlook that it can issue in visual experiences in which the spirits and deities appear to the subject with convincing vividness. The evidence of such visual and also auditory experiences is very strong and need not be doubted (Laski 1961; Tart 1975; Maslow 1976; Loder 1981; Greeley 1982: 21, 35). Nor should the enquirer deny that to the person concerned the experience is entirely convincing, more so than any ordinary experience (Hardy, 1979). That it is possible for one person to be convinced of seeing or hearing a personal presence while another is aware of nothing unusual is an established fact and has been demonstrated on television, for example on BBC 2 in a programme shown on 27 September 1982. The enquirer, examining the iconographic evidence of religions in various parts of the earth, will notice that Zulus depict the deity quite differently from the ancient Egyptians or Canaanites, each one seeing the spiritual beings in the human forms and even clothing with which they are familiar. The verdict of unconscious projection is very hard to resist as an explanation, and applied to experiences of seeing or hearing the spirits it is entirely justified to conclude that the explanation lies in the perceiver and that we do not need to posit objectively real spirits to account for the claims that some people have seen or heard them, though they may of course be objectively real. Once the belief in spirits is implanted, visual and auditory experiences are possible that will have every semblance of objective authenticity. The problem is to explain how the belief arose in the first place if not as the result of the self-manifestation of such beings. The present theory, invoking only known, natural, mental processes, provides a way of doing so through the mechanism of unconscious, anthropomorphic projection. In this respect it follows suggestions first made by Schleiermacher but developed by later thinkers like Feuerbach and Freud, though without the fatal subjective reductionism that undermines the work of the second and third of these theorists.

The point to grasp is that in principle if not always in practice a belief in spiritual beings is detachable from the encounter with cosmic forces in which it is seemingly vindicated. This is excellently demonstrated by one of William James' informants, who wrote as follows: '. . . as I was walking in a thick grove, unspeakable glory seemed to open to the apprehension of my soul. I do not mean any external brightness, nor any imagination of a body of light, but it was a new inward apprehension or view that I had of God, such as I never had before. . .' (1902: 213). James himself commented that in the minds of Christians this 'sense of enveloping friendliness becomes most personal and definite' (p. 275). His informant has done the study of religion an immense service by providing this report, which so clearly enables us to see that a powerful, inner event was thought of as a view of God. Others have had comparable illuminations without the same theistic apperception, a fact which is easily explicable in terms of the present theory. In theistic circles revelatory experiences will be seen intuitively as disclosures of the deity. For a non-theist other interpretations will come spontaneously to mind, from hallucination to a shortage of serotonin in the brain (Hooper 1981: 81). The question of supposedly special divine revelations is, however, sufficiently prominent in some faiths to warrant further assessment. This will be given when we come to discuss the axial religions because that is where revelation is said to be fundamental so far as theism is concerned.

In sum, then, the religious mind in mythological cultures serves the quest for ultimate well-being by offering a way of understanding the forces on which success in the quest mostly depends as one or more spiritual beings, which is one of the most evocative and successful concepts ever devised. It provides a way in which human minds from the lowliest to the most gifted and trained can focus attention, combining intelligibility with mystery and accessibility with distance, and it permits the countless local permutations we have noticed. But perhaps its greatest strength is the way the god-hypothesis enables people to find in a luminous symbol that fusion of the deepest truth, loftiest power and greatest value the experience of which is the aspiration not just of all faith but indeed of all human existence.

Turning next to linguistic expressions of the spiritual worldview, it is at once clear why the most prevalent form should be mythology, the narratives that tell of the activities of the gods (Cassirer 1946; Kramer 1961: 7f). This is the spoken and written counterpart of the believer's visualisable notion of spiritual beings, and just as the graphic religious art of the epoch abounds in depictions of heavenly and chthonic figures, all recognisably modelled on people or occasionally on animals, so its discourse revolves around power-denoting agent nouns – the creators, kings, rulers, lords, warriors, shepherds, judges, potters, mothers and fathers that we all know so well. It is even possible that the generic word for deity in the Semitic languages, namely *ēl*, has connotations of power in its meaning, (Pope 1955) just as the Greek word *kyrios* (English: lord) also means one who has power.

But mythology involves more than just a set of power-denoting agent nouns. It also has descriptions and narratives to express the characteristics and activities of the gods. These reflect prevailing human analogues. What better models of power were available in those ancient societies than those of king, warrior, judge and fertile mother?

In metaphysical modes of discourse, considered as the elaboration of abstract rather than pictorial models of thinking, theism has a further linguistic medium, partly complementing but partly superseding mythology as a way to speak of the processes and forces that affect us. Both give expression to a belief that reality is dynamic, orderly and ultimately beneficial. Mythology maps it pictorially and speaks of it narratively, while metaphysics maps it conceptually and speaks of it philosophically. The earthmaker who fashions people out of clay and breathes life into them in the former is the prime mover of the latter. One is best for vividness and impact; the other for precision and conceptual elaboration. Each is a linguistic means of generating benefit. And each, of course, is humanly created, however sublime the messages it conveys.

The language of ritual is at least as important as the language of creed and doctrine, and probably more so for a great many devotees. Here the theist typically uses styles of utterance fitted to an attitude of deference and sometimes one of intimacy, depending on how the gods are understood. Praise, thanksgiving, declarations of loyalty, admissions of wrong-doing, requests for forgiveness and the restoration of a disturbed relationship are natural modes of speech in religions focussed on spiritual beings. We saw in Chapter 4 how valuable poetry and song are in this connection. The point of these varieties of liturgical utterance is not just that they show a logical dependence on the concept of divine overlordship but that they give people many ways of verbalising their hunger for the help and favour of those overlords. Musical instruments, dancing, incense, the atmosphere of sanctity inside a temple or shrine, the wearing of special robes, the voicing of themes lying deep in our consciousness, all help create in the devotee a sense of the profound reality of the gods and their potential as helpers. It is easy to see behind this marvellous tapestry of linguistic ritual activity the creative, questing energies of the drive to maximise well-being. Pondering the remains of ancient temples we investigators become vividly aware that resourceful but deeply vulnerable and groping beings, like our-selves, laboured there long ago to raise those crumbling walls and long-dead chants to the gods, unfurling the sails of the soul lest there blow a favourable divine wind.

The remaining dimension to be considered here is activity, both ritual and socio-ethical. It is at once clear why theistic rituals are dominated by attitudes and postures of deference. This is the natural counterpart of a world-view which visualises people as dependent on the deities for the main blessings of life. What is more likely than that such pragmatic beings as humans should seek the favour of the gods on the model of their relationships with earthly superiors? The gestures of respect, obeisance humility and all the rest are due enactments of the demands of a subservient position and, as all thoughtful subordinates know, they work (Berger 1973: 49; Geertz 1966: 28). Among some theisms a second type of ritual attitude dominates, that of intimacy and loyalty stemming from a sense of divine support, succour and closeness rather than dominance, expressed in the great traditional images of divine mother and father, guide and friend.

It would be a grave mistake to regard ritual activity as merely an echo of something more real and important making its chief impact elsewhere. The indications are that cultic practices are themselves charged with the power of the divine for those who take part; indeed, that is their main function. They are done because they make divine power available, transforming and uplifting the devotee as nothing else can (Smart 1972: 44; 1973: 71). Conversely, behind every lapsed worshipper and defunct rite there is a sad tale of the wells of inspiration drying up and frustration or emptiness being felt where satisfaction and inspira-tion are required. Ritual is, as it were, the point at which the devotee can be plugged into the spiritual circuitry, and once contact is made he or she will be aglow within and without from the power received. Compared to the transforming effects of such experiences, most academic seminars are dull affairs indeed.

Ethical codes are another conspicuous facet of theistic religion. They prescribe how people should behave towards one another in order to conform to the supposed wishes of the gods and spirits. We have already seen enough of the workings of religion to know that those wishes will be interpreted in accordance with the perceived character of the divine being. What that will be seen as depends in the last resort on the values that confer greatest benefit according to the collective experience and wisdom of the people concerned. Among the ancient Israelites it was adherence to law. A strong judicial character therefore pervades their concept of deity, though other themes were also present. So the conception of Yahweh synthesises into a lustrous symbol the central, benefit-giving value distilled by ancient Jewish experience. The doctrine of God becomes a condensed transcript of a people's mind and soul, crystallising the euonic lessons of a long struggle for better days.

The device that specifies desired patterns of behaviour is the rule, and this enables us to understand religious ethics and taboos as the regulated behaviour of a spiritual community hinging on its dominant values, which will be whatever it has found most productive in the search for well-being. Rules are of course indispensable in social existence, for no corporate life can flourish if the people do as they please. Rules temper individuality in order to harvest collective good, by force if need be. Their contribution to social and individual well-being is therefore obvious. Small wonder that they should also play a part in prescribing how to behave towards the gods in the form of ritual codes and prohibitions. And in view of the power of the divine, it is no surprise either that many who believe in spiritual causation maintain that their rules of behaviour are god-given or pleasing to the spirits. The notion strongly reinforces them, yielding the added social benefit of strict observance lest there be divine retribution. It is not a matter of naturalistically evolving an ethic and then craftily alleging that the gods in fact authored it. What happens is that theists actually experience life as divinely governed so that when an unexcused failure to fulfil religious duties is followed by sudden misfortune, the person experiences the trouble as divine displeasure quite uncontrivedly.

While considering the activities typical of this kind of mythological religion it is important to include the functionaries who service it, the priests and priestesses, prophets, augurers, soothsayers, spirit mediums, sacred kings, healers, shamans and diviners whom we find in all faiths of this kind. There is a common purpose here, and that is to facilitate the flow of euonic energies from the spiritual realm to its earthly dependents. The cultus must be regulated, due sacrifice made, the mind of the gods must be declared, advice and healing channelled, problems detected and corrected and in general a bridge kept open between deity and devotee. The evidence shows that spiritual functionaries have at times played an immensely prominent part in certain faiths, Thebes being the best-known example in the ancient world. As would-be helpers the prevalence of these functionaries fits perfectly into the present view of religion.

The example of southern San religion

A concrete illustration of these somewhat abstract contentions will be helpful. It comes from the southern San people who once lived in parts of southern Africa before the advent of black and white migrants with larger numbers and superior means of warfare, and whose wondrous rock-art survives in caves and shelters as an exquisite but fragile monument to their vanishing culture (Lewis-Williams 1980, 1981). Theirs was a hunter-gatherer way of life with a spiritual world-view. The dominant, day-to-day problem facing them was to hunt antelope successfully. How would we expect them to deal with this problem? Obviously by perfecting the art of making bows, arrows and poisons, of stalking the game with consummate skill and using the meat as efficiently as possible. All this they did within the limits imposed by the available raw materials and their own knowledge. But even the best hunters, and the San were arguably among the very best, can and do fail. They could not control the movements of the antelope herds in the first place, nor their relative scarcity or abundance, nor the sudden changes of wind direction which can wreck the most careful approach. So they learned quickly and painfully that there were factors affecting their existence over which they had no control. But driven by the pressure to relieve hunger, ways of alleviating this vulnerability were sought and found. According to the present theory, one was to form an idea of what controls those external factors. No visible explanation was apparent, so perforce their theorising equipment will have come into play, unconsciously giving rise to the belief that the responsible agent was an invisible person, or several of them. In any event, the southern San people believed in such beings. The plain evidence of the most important issue in their existence was that the invisible agent affecting the hunt with its highly uncertain outcome was unpredictable and capricious, which gives us the character of

Kaggen, the trickster creator-spirit believed in by the San. Mythology functions here in an entirely rational way as the accepted explanatory supposition about the causes of a significant aspect of experience, which then appears to be confirmed by events because of its close fit with them. A conception of Kaggen as straightforwardly and unfailingly bountiful would not survive many unsuccessful hunting expeditions, though the student of religion soon forms a healthy respect for the resilience of the spirit-hypothesis in the face of evidence that might seem to refute it.

Another step taken in order to ease the problem of human vulnerability in southern San society would be to develop a set of practical measures related to the mythology and undertaken to order to compensate for the deity's trickiness which, after all, was the root of their problem as they saw it. Personal analogies manifestly encourage the hope that spiritual beings are amenable to persuasion in the humanly productive way of giving people what they desire in order to get the things we want from them. Praise, respect, thanksgiving, donations, all solemnised by ritual, thus offer practical avenues of euonic effort, undertaken with the realism that they deserve in those pressing circumstances. As with all our experience, these ritual enactments are part of an experiment in living, a way to maximise benefit in circumstances of numbing vulnerability. In the outlook and effort of the San people we can identify fundamental human experiences. We must find food and depend greatly on the hunt to do so. But the presiding spirit could choose to thwart us. So we acknowledge openly our dependence on his favour, praising him, promising loyalty or service and sacrificing to him gifts valuable to ourselves as pledges of our subservient declarations. Then the hunt is mounted. Suppose it is successful. This will tend to confirm the preparatory rites as conducive to success and will be repeated next time. Failure, on the other hand, has many possible explanations within the logic of the belief-system. Maybe we neglected to admit to previous disrespect, maybe the sacrifice was done incorrectly; maybe we overdid the accolades, and maybe the deity was simply enjoying a trick at our expense, hurtful but not fatal. In a surviving culture the mishaps are by definition not fatal and the controlling spirit will quite plausibly be seen as prankish or admonitory rather than as plain nasty. It is essential to grasp, then, that once a supposition about the cause of things and its attendent ritual pattern have coincided with enough euonic success to seem effective in engendering that success, the sheer importance of the issues involved – the pains of hunger and the anxiety that starvation may be looming – will make it exceedingly difficult to dislodge them. Given this connection with the affective sense, the mythico-ritual complex and those who service it will be virtually immune to challenge from within so long as the system works tolerably well for its members.

Early western explorers left accounts of San culture which distorted and derided their beliefs (cf Lewis-Williams 1981: 117f). A wider interest than spiritual or physical imperialism shows just how beautifully southern San mythology conforms to our global humanness in the time and place concerned. With an exquisite conceptual touch those beliefs were moulded to the hard, harsh contours of experience, and human limitation became the springboard for a venture into the mysterious, force-filled cosmos that is not to be thought of as cognitively primitive because other forces, chiefly gunpower and imported disease, have all but wiped it from the earth.

Strengths and rivals of mythological naturalism

Despite the fate of the San and their world-view, mythological naturalism has had a tenacious hold on people, sometimes lasting for thousands of years, a durability that can also be explained by means of the present theory. For one thing belief in spiritual causation is logically immune to empirical falsification because any event can be squared with it. This means it can seem to work perfectly to believers no matter what happens. Being modelled on humans, the spirits are usually seen as changeable, even capricious, so any turn of event contrary to expectation is compatible with the theory. The spirit allegedly in control of the rains is no less effective for causing a drought, and being invisible is added protection against the corroding potential of humanity's natural critical ability. The theory has other ways of persisting too. Since it asserts the existence of a plurality of spirits, unexpected turns of events can always be regarded as interference by a rival spirit, and because most of them are finite, some things can plausibly be said to exceed even their superhuman abilities. So, the cognitive principles worked out in chapter four can account for the rise, persistence and prevalence of the personified cosmos. Why it has been so widely, though not wholly, eclipsed is also explicable in terms of those principles. We touched briefly on them in connection with polytheism. Spirit-causation can be countered on one flank by materialistic alternatives. With the stirring of Greek philosophy in the sixth century BCE but especially with the rise of modern science this is exactly what has happened, in one of the most jolting quantum shifts of all time. As a way of accounting for what we now like to call natural phenomena, spirit-causation has been completely displaced by science with its non-personal modes of explanation. Instead of believing in personal intelligences at the levers of power, the search has been for regular processes capable of being stated as laws of nature (Dampier 1977: ch 1). We shall consider the relationship between science and religion in the modern world later in this chapter. In the meantime it is the other vulnerable flank of mythological naturalism that must be explained, namely its extensive replacement by a more recent form of spirituality.

THE OTHER-WORLDLY HYPOTHESIS

Our picture of religion would be without its most distinctive development were it left in the form so far described. Given our drive to maximise well-being, we cannot be content with anything but the greatest possible satisfaction, so we inevitably also direct our ameliorative powers to religion itself, sensing scope for improvements and translating them into fresh systems of spiritual existence through our creative capacities. Above many minor advances one stands out as the quintessentially religious refinement, and this is what might be called the other-worldly hypothesis, the contention that true and perfect well-being can never be realised on this earth but only in a radically different order of reality, the world of the spirit, entirely shut off to our physical senses but accessible to special mental and spiritual techniques or mediations. If one great sector of the faith of the transcendentalist epoch is orientated to this world, the new development is just as clearly directed to another one. The former looks to the spirits and gods as controlling powers for earthly phenomena, evidently content with a basically unitary view of things. Deity and devotee, spirit and stone are interacting parts of a single spectrum of existence, like electricity warming a home or powering a computer. Those who gave us the other-worldly hypothesis saw another reality beyond space and time, beyond the physical cosmos altogether, though mysteriously impinging on it, and directed the euonic quest to it.

The activating situation that gives rise to this massively influential development is an insight of awesome power both to unsettle and to inspire. It is a radical critique of spatio-temporality as such, ending in the verdict that the yearning for perfect, imperishable well-being is forever unrealisable here on earth. The insight forms that bodily existence is itself the problem, possible only through a sentience which cannot operate without the polarities of pain and happiness, so that it can never yield abiding peace. The effect on some is the deepest pessimism about embodied forms of existence, which must always frustrate the yearnings to which they give rise. Corporeality is found to give survival at the price of incomplete satisfaction, forever goading us into renewed efforts to eliminate that incompleteness, but never actually achieving it (Shutte 1976). The spatio-temporal order is itself seen to be hopelessly shot through with problems. It changes, is finite, is clogged by the pain-prone, sin-riddled encumbrance of bodily existence. The earth as the beloved mother of ceaseless bounty, benevolent even in her harshness, yields to the vision of physical bondage, of matter as inherently imprisoning the life it bears, of the present life as shackled by original sin.

As ever, the drive for maximised benefit does not bow in resignation at this insight. Here too it reacts to anxiety with creative resourcefulness, countering a sense of the exhausted euonic potential of this world with the other-worldly hypothesis, and asserting that transcendental satisfaction is available when all mundane hopes have gone. Ultimate well-being, the peace that passes all understanding and all words, is declared possible and found fulfilling as an orientation, but only through liberation from the provisional type of existence to which flesh and blood belong. What was a campaign against worldly anxiety, ignorance or inability and for worldly benefit in mythological naturalism here becomes a quest for release from worldly existence as such. The problem is not to improve the earth and mortal existence but to leave them behind. If the gods are to survive this development it can only be by a change of function and status from the alleged causes of what are now seen to be merely physical events to the ultimate powers of liberation from our present material existence in its entirety. Naturalistic explanation is transformed into supernaturalistic salvation. Thus the euonic quest becomes the otherworldly orientation which has come to dominate many of the faiths of humanity. The earlier conception of things, mythological naturalism, reaches a euonic ceiling and the conviction forms that there can be no more improvement within that conception, so a paradigm shift or quantum leap is made to a new horizon of the spirit.

The earliest known signs of this development took place somewhere around 1000 BCE and the idea has grown into the main form of religion all over the earth. This indicates that it has been a euonic success, delivering to its adherents sufficient confirmatory satisfaction in the form of increased conditions of well-being to establish and maintain plausibility. The implications of this point are very important. Other-worldly faith, as we may also call it, can hardly have held sway on such a scale with beings restlessly hungry for benefit were it merely an hypothesis, merely another inductive guess fired into the dark. To have become the dominant form of spirituality for so long the hypothesis must also be fertile and bear fruit for its upholders, who continue to probe critically the euonic merits of proffered world-views and lifestyles, experimenting and accepting whatever works best. It is reasonable to suppose that as a philosophy it satisfied all available criteria of plausibility and as a practice was found beneficial. Ritual activity is one obvious test of its merits, and the available evidence of meditation and prayerful communion strongly suggests that experiences are available by these means which in fact deliver to the believer a sense of supreme well-being utterly surpassing all forms of merely physical gratification. For the devotee concerned this would obviously tend to confirm the other-worldly hypothesis with its contention that ultimate well-being is not available in the divisions, changes and alienations of spatio-temporality. The indications, moreover, are that these confirmatory benefits are not just found in peak experiences but ripple outward into moral judgements, philosophy, literature and civilising concepts, as well as giving physical and emotional healing and yielding social benefits in the form of new compassionate forms of community and life-style. These in turn add to the new vision's already great appeal and further cement its hold on people. Such is the fundamental character of this epoch-making development. Now we must account for its main sub-divisions.

Spiritual monism and transcendentalist monotheism

The specific concepts in which the new faith comes to expression depend mainly on the kind of idea that already circulates in the culture where the insight dawns. Germinating in an animistic or polytheistic context with a relatively low sense of individuality and its value, the effect is a dismissal of the gods as themselves part of the problem of existence, followed by penetration to a form of transcendental, non-personal spirituality. The reason is the supposed unimportance of individual existence, the limited power of the gods and their earthbound functions, whereas a desire for infinite blessing in a transcendent world of the spirit can only be satisfied by something that is itself infinite and other-worldly. A sudden conceptual leap from finite, localised deities who make things happen on earth to an infinite divine saviour is too drastic to be likely. A more promising tactic would be for other-worldly visionaries to abandon belief in individual spirits to those whom it still satisfies and explore the euonic potential of the realm of spirit as such, purging it, as it were, of the encumbrance of individuality. In any situation where there is a well-entrenched polytheism, scope for alternative views and people who diagnose the human predicament as a malaise caused by bodily and therefore separate and finite forms of existence, the search for ultimate well-being will result in a desire for access to an all-embracing, undifferentiated spiritual reality. Spatio-temporality or the world of change can then be seen in one of two ways: either as a lower tier of existence, giving us a dualist world-view, or by being deemed less real than the realm of spirit, a delusion which the skilled mind recognises for what it is. This gives us spiritual monism. Both forms relativise the physical, leading logically to an attitude of detachment from it. An impression that salvation requires self-liberation rather than dependence on the gods is entirely natural in this way of seeing things. In a well-developed monotheism where individual existence is logically valued, the tendency will however be to refine the concept of god even further rather than transcend it, so retaining it in the service of the other-worldly hypothesis. Monotheists already see their god as the final

188 Religion and Ultimate Well-Being

reality. Enhanced euonic insight will thus lead to conceptual
revision rather than to the supersession which happens to polytheistic thought. The result is a rarefied monotheism in which
God will be regarded as the ultimate reality, not only the
sovereign power over nature and history but the fountainhead
and goal of all finite being, the reality than which a greater
cannot even be thought to exist. And whereas monistic spirituality emphasises self-effort in the path to salvation, transcendental monotheism will have an opposite effect, magnifying the
believer's feeling of littleness into a sense of absolute dependence
on divine grace. Divine action will be understood more in terms of
saving people by giving them access to heaven than just in terms
of making things happen on earth, because the main focus of
religion has now moved away from worldly benefits. Thus is born
the concept of an absolute divine sovereign and redeemer, a
magnificently successful notion that has come to dominate the
faiths of a majority of believers throughout the world. And once
established it can provide surviving polytheists who hear of it with
another option than just monism when they too discover the low
euonic ceiling of their native belief. That there is a limit to the
refinement possible in the logic of anthropomorphic theistic
notions appears to be indicated by some kinds of philosophical
theology, in which God is thought of as pure actuality or Being-
itself rather than as a being, however majestic. The internal
refinement of monotheism is in any case only to be expected in
view of our critical powers. But for the moment the main point is
that the initial expression of the other-worldly hypothesis involves
conditioning by ideas prevalent when it appears and that its
tendency is to subvert polytheism and animism but refine monotheism. There is thus a cultural factor affecting other-worldly
concepts, and once again we see the importance of localised,
differentiating causes in the explanation of religion. There could
of course be other natural factors as well, such as right- or left-
brain dominance. But cultural circumstances are certainly
operative in giving rise to the two other-worldly forms of transcendentalist religion (Tillich 1955). In short, the desire for supreme
well-being in a realm of the spirit can be pursued in one of two
main ways: either by dissolving individuality and the need for
relationships which it implies, or by perfecting them and retaining a personal world-view.

The emergence of these two variations of other-worldly religion coupled with the mythological naturalism which preceded them implies that the earth's religions can be assigned to a total of three basic categories, a conclusion very similar to the typology suggested by John Hutchison (1975). The first type includes all the faiths which make use of spiritual causation to explain the mysteries of this world. The euonic thrust of these religions is largely if not wholly to ameliorate things here on earth; immortality if anything is automatic and natural. There is of course a higher, unseen realm of the spirit but the world of everyday experience is still prized and affirmed. In this book the term mythological naturalism has been used for faiths like these; Hutchison calls them cosmic religions. The second type is the polar opposite of the first because it includes all the faiths whose other-worldly orientation is so strong that matter is deemed a mere appearance. The terms spiritual monism and monistic spirituality have been used in preceding paragraphs as labels for them. Hutchison speaks neatly of its members as acosmic religions. The third type covers the transcendentalist monotheisms we have been considering. In them the concept of god is developed in an other-worldly direction but without abandoning interest in this one, which after all is itself the result of divine creation and operates under an ultimate divine control. We see here the presence of an interest in this world in conjunction with a stronger interest in the realm of spirit. The term chosen by Hutchison for this third category is the historical faiths. Real though the differences separating these types are, we should not lose sight of their common account of reality as comprising a spiritual tier which is superior to physical existence in at least some respects. This shared subordination of the physical is the reason for saying that all religion hitherto has involved a transcendentalist outlook. The appropriate strategies for greatest benefit are thus to seek the help of spiritual beings in struggling with the problems of our present existence; to seek final liberation from the prison of matter with its distressing separations, alienations and illusions; or to cast oneself absolutely on the saving power of an utterly sovereign Lord. In each case the richest blessings are thought to depend on a realm of the spirit for their fruition. We are also now in a position to account for the fact that the transcendent is seen in one of two ways, either personally or non-personally, by believers, as was noted in chapter two when the global characteristics of religion were identified. The non-personalists correspond mainly to what Hutchison would call adherents of acosmic religions, while the personalists are those who believe in gods and spirits, whether as mythological naturalists or as transcendental monotheists. The operative factor behind this bifurcation of belief is, let it be said again, the conditioning effect of prevailing circumstances when the other-worldly hypothesis forms, such that animism and polytheism are by-passed but monotheism retained and refined.

Objections to the present view of theism

There are believers in God for whom this interpretation will be unwelcome because it ascribes the concept of the divine to human inventiveness. It should of course be clearly understood that the present theory is in no way subjectively reductionist. It does not regard the concept of the divine as a piece of mythological or metaphysical fiction, standing for no objective reality whatsoever. On the contrary, theism is evoked because of the experienced effects of objectively real but mysterious cosmic forces, like the sudden shift of wind that carries the San hunters' scent to the antelope they had stalked so carefully or the one that parted the waters of the Red Sea for the children of Israel. According to the present theory, belief in one or more gods definitely has an objective referent in the unknown causes of the forces that people experience in their struggle for well-being. Nobody invented these. The human contribution is firstly to discover causal connections and then to create the supposition that the best way to think of them is on the model of human agency. But even though this contention is not another piece of subjective reductionism it will still be resisted by some theists. Consequently several further points need to be made by way of defence and clarification.

The main reason why some believers resist explanations like the present one is their conviction that special divine self-revelations have happened, injected, as it were, into the stream of earthly events from on high and therefore uncontaminated by merely human ideas. Nothing in this theory rules such a contention out as absurd or impossible in connection with the causing of any proven events which genuinely cannot be squared with the workings of nature. In cases like that divine causation is certainly a possible explanation, though it involves very serious problems of identification. This is something we will return to in connection with religion in the modern world, but the core of the difficulty is that divine causation by definition operates imperceptibly, making it impossible for anyone to verify or falsify the proposal empirically. To rule empirical validation or refutation out is, however, to make it impossible to know whether divine causation actually happens or not. None the less, it remains a logical possibility in connection with proven events contrary to the workings of the cosmos or human life. But the present account of theism definitely makes divine actions superfluous in explaining the emergence, major modifications and diversifications of belief in one or more gods because no conflicts with cosmic or human nature are involved. The ordinary workings of the cosmos and human life as set out in the previous chapter are capable of accounting fully for these developments, as we are now seeing, including the theist's belief that they arose because of supernatural interventions. It has already been explained in connection with mythological naturalism that once belief in spiritual beings has taken root in people's minds, it conditions their experiences, including those significant moments of profound insight which sometimes come when people wrestle with problems that deeply concern them. A convinced theist with no knowledge of the way our preconceptions shape experience will quite naturally see at least some of those illuminating moments as god-given; that is exactly what the spirit-hypothesis is all about as a causal account of the mysterious. So once theism is established as a belief there is no problem about accounting naturally for subsequent illuminatory events which believers are sure have a divine cause. The problem is how theistic belief arises in the first place. This book contends that it arose naturally as a direct consequence of the impact on our affective sense of a largely unseen, forceful cosmos, our ignorance about it, the euonic pressure to make the best of our situation by probing its nature and literally feeling our way ahead, and by using our built-in cognitive equipment in which human models constitute a virtually inevitable basis for trying to solve the riddle of the unknown by means of analogical conjecture and projection. This proposal makes use of established cognitive processes and their logical implications and is manifestly consistent with the evidence of religious experience. Opposed to it is the assertion that belief in the divine has for its originating cause an act of direct divine revelation. For several decisive reasons this assertion must, however, be rejected. The first one is the global range of evidence. Many believers know little of that evidence, being familiar instead with their native tradition only. But the widened perspective made possible by a planetary range of information creates a very different view of theism. The investigator is confronted not by a seemingly unique theistic tradition claiming a divine source for itself, but with evidence that all societies have had a belief in spiritual beings under some or other name, that all of them invoke their gods and spirits for help or blessing and as causal explanations for why things happen when no obvious reason is to hand, that all of them describe the gods anthropomorphically, with variations of detail tailored to known physical and cultural phenomena. The investigator also finds that many and perhaps all of the world's theistic traditions also report revelatory experiences in which their deity or deities appear, speak or in some other way disclose themselves, with several of them claiming to possess the ultimate or final truth.

To contend that all this has a supernatural explanation involves severe difficulties, none of them capable of being squared with the central doctrines of any existing theistic tradition. For one thing none of those traditions in its classical statements of belief even acknowledges the global data just mentioned, let alone accounts satisfactorily for them. And it does not seem possible to devise such an account within the logic of those forms of supernaturalist thought. Monotheists are obliged to suppose that their deity either caused all the world's theisms, or some, or just the one to which they belong. If he originated all the world's theisms, why did he not ensure a uniform picture of himself, at least regarding essentials? Why, if he (or she) is infinitely good, wise and powerful, as virtually all monotheists maintain, would the deity cause one culture to be polytheistic and its neighbour monotheistic, or impress on one his justice but on another his love? Why are some divine images male and others female? Mere human effort in the sciences has created a global consensus about the composition of water, the orbits of the planets and the formula for hydrochloric acid. If a single omnipotent and benign deity really were the author of all the world's theisms, why are the results so varied and, at times mutually inconsistent? Confusion in the product is not a very promising basis for asserting a perfect single producer. Worse still, why did the deity neglect to reveal himself to earnestly questing non-theists of immense influence like the Buddha or Lao Tzu; of even to less influential ones from Bertrand Russell to Chairman Mao?

To retort that one's god caused only some of the world's theisms fares no better. It smacks of unfair dealing, and it means that the less favoured cultures either had to manage without theism or invented it on their own, single-handedly creating a set of concepts so similar to the ones the deity is alleged to have authored as to cast unfavourable aspersions on his work. Neither of these implications will square with the doctrines of divine goodness and perfection insisted upon by virtually all monotheists. Even less tenable is the claim that the deity caused only one's own religion, while all the others are human creations. This is impossible on the part of a god of universal love and goodness. It is simply unbelievable that such a being would bestow the priceless gift of his favour on only one of his children, or bestow it in varying quantities. If there are favourite children in the divine household, then it cannot be the place of a perfectly good and loving householder. Monotheists thus face insurmountable problems in the attempt to assert a divine cause for the world's many theisms or even for any one of them, unless they relinquish their belief in absolute divine competence and goodness. That would betray the heart of theism. It would be much better to give up altogether the attempt to deny a human source for all the world's theistic conceptions. The logical problems facing a polytheistic account are somewhat less formidable, but they have other difficulties to contend with. The main one is to explain the error of monotheism, for error it must be to a convinced polytheist. If Baal really did control the rains in ancient Palestine and his consort the soil's fertility, why didn't they make this clear to the Israelites with their stubborn monotheistic delusions? Indeed why does nobody in that region today still believe in Baal? As these remarks show, the polytheistic case is difficult to take seriously at least until we are offered something more resilient than the vanished polytheisms of antiquity.

There is another decisive objection, this time on logical grounds. Direct divine self-revelation or theophany is an inherently tricky, not to say self-cancelling concept. If the event in which it is supposed to happen really is of God then it cannot be perceivable because the deity, being pure spirit, cannot in principle be perceived in any way. Conversely, any being who really is seen or heard cannot necessitate the conclusion that he or she is in fact a pure spirit. Nor will we get far with the assertion that the concept of the divine is innate, implanted in us through creation by a god. The evidence is that people are taught that concept just as they are taught the languages that express it. In any case, if further evidence on this score were needed, the few grim cases of children raised in the wild from infancy give no confirmation at all for alleging that belief in divine beings is something we are born with. Only one way of asserting that there is a supernatural revelation at the fountainhead of theism remains to be considered, and that is an original, direct divine implant into some people's minds without using their normal cognitive channels. Could this happen? In theory yes, though one is entitled to ask why a perfect creator would need to by-pass learning processes he (or she) had provided in the first place. But in practice the claim fails because we could either not identify such an implant or it would make no sense. To be intelligible to the recipient the message would have to fit into existing knowledge and thought-forms and thus be more or less continuous with them. But in that case it will be impossible to tell exactly where the older, merely human notions end and the new, divinely-caused ones begin. Like theophany, the message must be delivered in a way that we could identify and understand, but then its very accessibility would obscure its supposed divine origins. If, on the other hand, the message could be clearly distinguished from all human notions then it would also have to be completely different from them. But then it would make no sense, like hearing an entirely foreign language, only worse. And if it makes absolutely no sense it could never be seen as a source of knowledge.

All in all the case for a natural, human basis for the concept of the gods is a much better prospect. It makes more sense of the global evidence and does not involve the manifest circularity of appealing to belief in the supernatural to explain itself. Another advantage of such a theory is that it accords perfectly with the known procedures of human cognition. Best of all so far as believers are concerned, it involves no assumption that because theism arises from the minds of people it must be false. It is perfectly possible that our theistic guesswork, for such it must be according to this theory, is none the less closest to the mark and gives us, when all is said and done, the best approximation available to the mysterious forces that ultimately affect our existence and well-being. Theism is not made false by being a human product, though it is made provisional. The present theory is not an attack on or defence of the validity of belief in God or any other form of the spirit hypothesis. It is an account of the concept in ordinary, experiential terms made mandatory by the logical incoherence and poor empirical basis of the alternatives. Believers wishing to stand up for the truth of their theism are not placed under any pressure on that front by the present interpretation. What is rejected is any allegation that the world-wide phenomenon of belief in God can be coherently explained within the logic of any of the world's existing forms of theistic religion.

In returning from these remarks about the justification of the present approach to the theme of the other-worldly faiths we must consider next how the theory accounts for the phenomenon of spiritual genius, when the twin forces of individual talent and transcendentalist vision fused to produce the greatest religious drama the world has yet seen, namely the wondrous creativity of the axial faiths.

The great luminaries

We do not know who originated the other-worldly hypothesis. What is known, however, is that a handful of spiritual masters made it a global force of millenial durability, converting this deeply private and personal moment of profound insight into ways of faith for entire civilisations. So we come to consider the great luminaries of religious history from Moses to Gotama and Muhammed, whose influence has literally reshaped the spiritual landscape. A full euonic portrayal of these figures has yet to be written and may never come, for how shall we calibrate the magnitude of their achievement? But, however falteringly, something must be said.

In terms of the present theory, the great luminaries are to be seen as those whose spiritual perception penetrated to the richest reservoirs of well-being ever tapped, and who found ways of unexcelled efficiency to channel them to others. It is as if they discovered the mother lode of individual and social benefit and opened its seemingly inexhaustible richness to all. Evidently it takes an unfettered selfhood to accomplish such things, and the indications are that for these giants of faith individual talent made aglow with the energy of transcendental insight, led not to solitude but to service. Theirs was height of euonic vision coupled with breadth of euonic concern for others, a blend of insight, love, compassion and transforming action the like of which we have scarcely seen again. How else are we to explain the discipleship and devotion these figures have evoked in circumstances so remote from their own as to be unrecognisable, if not by the responsiveness, coiled in many of us like a tight spring, waiting for that triggering influence which only the most inspiring truth can release? Moses, Gotama, the nameless Isaiah of the exile, Jesus of Nazareth, Muhammed, these and a few others are the people who have mediated the sublimest well-being in human history, couching their messages in terms that meet needs felt deeply by people from cultures radically unlike their own but without ceasing to be intelligible and inspiring to their contemporaries. This blend of immediacy and yet duration of impact involves a communications efficiency that has yet to be fully understood, but whatever the formula it certainly is an astonishing success. One factor in it is the use of vivid local imagery that is also current elsewhere, to convey a message potentially global in content, touching on euonic realities common to all human experience anywhere. Such a message will then in principle be endlessly restatable without essential change of content, again and again meeting people's deepest needs and hopes in terms they readily understand. Another is the availability of the written word to preserve and spread their teachings and help form the world's great scriptures.

So far as the content of their message is concerned, the central requirement for the kind of following these great figures have generated is a world-view with a euonic core but not contrary to prevailing critical norms or to realistic experience. One way or another theirs is a plausible declaration of the benign nature of ultimate reality, how it relates to the discordant realm of everyday experience and how to be transformed from the one to the other. A doctrine of this kind commits itself to practical vindication, so once again we find the analysis of religion forcing us to recognise that the great spiritual masters of history cannot be seen solely as purveyors of a theoretical message of the greatest good news to suffering humanity. At the very least they also provided tangible evidence in the form of mental liberation, moral growth, fellowship, healing, a sense of purpose, cosmic bearings, feelings of peace and the deepest joy, sometimes with such intensity as to elicit the revealing metaphor of rebirth and the symbolic gestures of name-changing, shaven heads and experiments in alternative life-styles. The nature of the benefit can vary as long as it is felt, so that the philosophy of ultimate well-being translates into the beginnings of a new system of euonic existence whose portals are mercifully present in this life but whose banquet-hall is in another world where there is no more sorrow, and where the former things are done away. Quite possibly the strongest practical vindication of other-worldly doctrines came from the founding, directly or indirectly, of new kinds of social life defined not by collective self-interest, greed or aggression but by service, a sort of euonic fellowship governed by the principle that the well-being of all must necessarily be the well-being of each, whether consciously stated or not.

Acceptance and discipleship on the scale of the axial religions thus depends upon a cluster of factors all amounting to the provision of an incomparable well-being hinging on the vision of another, better, unsurpassable world which is none the less accessible in this one. The glowing prophet, seer or incarnate deity must enable others to shine too or fail them in their need. Whence their saving power is a difficult question for the mere investigator to answer, for there is a limit to what can be known of the summit by gazing upward from the valleys. But one or two major clues are visible. Firstly there is the huge mental energy released by the dawning of the other-worldly hypothesis, which opens to the euonic search the possibility of a limitless goodness unfettered by bodily confinements. The attraction of such a prospect is surely obvious. Then there is the fact of human individuality, of variations in giftedness occasionally producing the genius and the prodigy whose attainments by definition far transcend those of their fellows (cf. Cobb 1967: ch. 5). Thirdly there is the enormous power of a globally relevant concept, simultaneously illuminating, placing in perspective and transforming the concrete particularities of anybody's experience. The great axial metaphors of divine fatherhood, the wheel of life and human fellowship all appear to have or imply this characteristic. These three factors alone make a potent combination, bringing to an historical high-point the quest to maximise well-being, but others are doubtless waiting to be detected as well.

There are, however, further considerations affecting our understanding of the great luminaries that must also be mentioned. They appeared in mutual isolation, separated by great distances, language barriers, cultures and time, though a handful lived very close to the year 500 BCE. Whether this fact severely affects the validity of their doctrines is another question, but it remains true that Gotama and Jeremiah were ignorant of each other, and the New Testament does not refer to the Upanishads or the Bhagavadgita, though Jesus of Nazareth clearly attached great importance to his great axial predecessor, the author of the part of Isaiah beginning at chapter forty. The next consideration is the involvement of these great figures in the cultures and thought-forms of their own day, and the fact that even such a peerless spiritual vision as theirs can never be entirely free, so far as verbal expression is concerned, of the conditioning effects of that involvement. In the contemporary interaction of the world's religions this question is sure to be high on the agenda sooner or later. But in terms of the present theory it will be clear that no message is ever entirely free of local colour, even these. In any case it would be an outright self-contradiction to say that a given set of doctrines perfectly expresses for all time an ultimate truth which one elsewhere says is ineffable or mysterious. The next issue is the related fact that in every case the great axial masters of faith inherited and retained the spiritual world-view so typical of transcendentalist cultures. All of them from Moses to Muhammed produced highly significant modifications to that outlook, but none appears to have questioned its essentials, namely the belief in a spiritual realm of some kind, superior to earthly existence. Moses and the classical Hebrew prophets are nowhere recorded as justifying this belief. To them the reality of the divine seems to have been as self-evident as to any of their contemporaries and theistic successors today. The problem was to find the correct kind of spiritual belief, not the correctness of spiritual belief as such, which they took for granted. The same appears to have been the policy of Jesus of Nazareth, the writers of the Bhadavadgita and Muhammed, the other major theistic luminaries of the axial faiths. In today's world, where the adequacy of the spirit-theory is widely doubted even among some of the devout this may seem a strange assumption. The present theory helps us to understand why it was made. In the axial period the spiritual world-view was everywhere an accepted account of experience. Having passed all available critical tests, it had long been completely embedded in human consciousness in the ways described in chapter four. The sure sign of a successful world-view is precisely unobtrusiveness in the thinking of its acceptors. The anamolies that have led some to reject this ancient way of seeing things had yet to make themselves significantly felt in the axial period. It was a time for refining, not replacing, the accepted spiritual view of reality. The same holds of the non-theistic axial luminaries like the Buddha, Lao Tzu and Confucius or the writers of the Upanishads. Admittedly most of them broke with animistic and polytheistic ways of believing, but none repudiated the underlying concept of a higher, non-material reality like Brahman. From the China Sea to the Aegean they reshaped the textures of human belief but always within the accepted spiritual view of things. In fact their great contribution, the perfecting and publicising of the other-worldly hypothesis, could not have happened in any form but such a view. If materiality is a prison or the earth a place of sin, and if salvation is indeed possible, then it must necessarily involve another world of a spiritual kind.

We are now in a position to account for the importance of a few decisive events in some of the axial faiths and for the formation of the great scriptures. Events, however dramatic, seldom reveal much in themselves. It takes the eye of an interpreter to see in them a profound truth. Several of the figures who dominate world religious history exercised precisely this function, for example the second Isaiah in connection with the Jewish exile of the sixth century BCE or St Paul and the death of Jesus. Once we have extended the theory to the great luminaries and their closest associates it is a small further step to explain why a few of the faiths make so much of certain particular events. Naturally the event must lend itself to a euonic interpretation, but without the discerning eye of the seer or visionary it will remain mute and unexplored. And in any case it is only to be expected that the drive to maximise well-being will probe any major happening involving many people or a notable turn of events for ways of relating it to the concept of supreme blessing. In other words, we would not have these great religious events if we did not also have people who could see meanings hidden to ordinary minds in them.

As for the great scriptures, their formation became possible when literacy and spiritual genius coincided, the former supplying the medium and the latter the message. The drive to maximise well-being enlists the written word in the service of those who have done most to satisfy it, making their contributions available to an immensely bigger and longer lasting spiritual community than ever the merely spoken word. Would it be going too far to suggest that the convergence of literacy and the axial luminaries is the single most influential synthesis in human history? In any event the fundamental point is surely clear, namely that once written records became available it was inevitable that people would use them to preserve and spread the benefits of their greatest religious leaders. What better way was there of doing so than in books until the invention of modern electronic methods of information storage and transmission?

This is a convenient point to explain why the other-worldly hypothesis formed only in some regions and not all over the earth like mythological naturalism. Once again the answer lies in prevailing circumstances. The decisive factor is the existence of scope for exceptional individual creativity. This in turn depends partly on a relatively high degree of economic and technological specialisation. Only when people begin to do different things instead of all following the same daily pattern of activity is a significant sense of individuality likely to form and toleration of divergent ideas and behaviours likely to be forthcoming. Another factor is the availability of enough surplus wealth for some people to live on while giving their attention mainly to reflection and mental explorations. And for these to achieve high standards of sophistication there must also be a well-developed cultural context. Literacy and education thus constitute a third factor, making it possible for pioneering insights to be preserved accurately, handed on to disciples and refined. This enables cooperative individualism to make itself felt, so maximising the contributions of a series of skilled thinkers and visionaries. Where these requirements are met the conditions for exceptional religious creativity will be highly favourable, typically in or near the riverine civilisations of antiquity. But in economically precarious and heavily communal societies the conditions are entirely unfavourable. The urgency of satisfying basic physical needs militates against both the emergence and the toleration of spiritual prodigies with new ideas, and in any case mythological naturalism will still be highly functional in that kind of situation, with its this-worldly focus. But in the circumstances identified above and given sufficient time, sooner or later the natural occurrence of exceptional individual giftedness will issue in the equally exceptional doctrines of the great axial luminaries, their predecessors and their successors.

The dimensions of other-worldly religion

As for the mythico-ritual matrix of axial religion and its ethical and social dimensions, these are just as thoroughly revolutionised as the doctrines we have been considering. Gross anthropomorphism is an early casualty, because the more the gods resemble us the less likely they are to be able to help us, needing salvation themselves instead. The direction of thought in the other-worldly hypothesis inevitably puts strains on all but the most symbolic understandings of transcendental personalism, since to be a being of any kind is to exemplify finitude, a fatal disqualifier in the search for boundless well-being. In this process of overhauling and reinterpreting mythological material the devotee, with an eye on the Beyond – as some have called the other-worldly ultimate – is immensely helped by conceptual and metaphysical methods of thinking or speaking. The loss in vividness and impact is considerable but the gains are greater, because it becomes possible to transform the images of pictorial theism, which are strictly incapable of doing other-worldly business on account of their manifestly this-worldly nature, into the marvellous philosophical subtleties of a Shankara or an Aquinas. This will not be a Sunday School winner but that is not where the victories are needed. The superlatively penetrative spiritual thinker is the one who needs this equipment and where it has been available in philosophically developed cultures, it has been extensively used to elaborate the transcendental vision. This brings us to explain the emergence of intellectually sophisticated forms of belief such as doctrinal language. It emerges when members of a religious tradition subject their beliefs to intellectual reworking, evident in the technical vocabulary and attempts at logical coherence discernible in doctrinal formulations. Doctrines are thus the thinker's rendering of a religious belief. For those seeking crisper definitions and tighter arguments this is a decided benefit, permitting conceptual refinement of notions which might otherwise be of doubtful adequacy.

Much depends on the culture in question. If it prizes this sort of thing and possesses philosophical resources, mythology will issue in doctrine, otherwise not. Since metaphysically sophisticated cultures are a more recent development than the other-worldly hypothesis itself, religious doctrines of a technical kind tend to be a characteristic only of some axial faiths. Christianity, Buddhism and parts of Hinduism have emphasised it but other faiths less so and some not at all. Apparently, doctrinal formulators have used both imagerial and abstract modes of discourse. The Nicene Creed in Christianity is a good example, asserting that Jesus Christ is of the same substance (which is an abstract notion) as God the Father (a mythological image).

At the same time the very nature of the exercise outstrips the capacities of any words for adequate expression. Language has evolved as a spatio-temporal device of magnificent efficiency in its native context. At high levels of abstraction and in the best poetry it offers some scope for the articulation of transcendentalist insight, but the scope is limited, though it greatly surpasses the capacity of literalist mythological language for precision or evocation. The focus of faith is now an ultimate reality utterly free of all bounds and flaws, beyond all polarities and the tensions that go with them, a pure and absolute suchness, the one beyond which there is no other. The contrast with mundane realities, where language works admirably, is too great to encourage confidence in mere words, or so the sages say. The point is made in all the other-worldly faiths, though the best known formulation is in the *Tao Te Ching*: 'Those who know don't say and those who say don't know.'

Inevitably, such a focus of the spiritual life has less use for wordy kinds of worship than for the rituals of silence, except as preparations for inner discipline or for the multitudes who labour upon the cultic foothills. Sacrifice makes sense in some heavily anthropomorphic types of this-worldly theism, but is offensive to the faith of many other-worldly believers, for whom inner fitness or the pure and contrite heart are what really matter. Similarly, the role of religious specialists tends to change, with much greater importance attaching to the teacher and visionary than before. The day of the guru and the rabbi comes as never previously. Behavioural precepts also change. An action is good if it conduces to ultimate liberation, and the patterns of earthly life come to be judged by a heavenly perspective. Above all, physical gratification is censured as the enemy par excellence of spiritual purification. The ascetic ideal becomes embodied in the hermit and the holy recluse, sometimes denouncing the run of society from the fringes of the wilderness. Priestly roles take on the added, indispensable dimension of exemplifying in sanctuary and slum a holiness that overcomes the world.

The prevalence of these and other religious figures in this new kind of religion must now be explained. They neither sow nor reap yet others who do these things willingly support them. This can scarcely be disinterested charity because it happens even in economically marginal societies with too little surplus wealth to squander. Nor will it suffice to say simplistically that the world's priesthoods have beguiled a captive audience with promises of a blessed afterlife in exchange for this-worldly cash. There have doubtless been dishonourably motivated manipulators in the history of religion. But the evidence also tells of the rich, the powerful and the learned giving of their substance to maintain chaplains and monastries. The caricature of a rapacious clergy swindling an ingenuous and docile yokelry, popular in some circles, is wide of the facts. Humble peasants indeed gave their labour to build Salisbury or Cologne cathedrals. But the funds also came from people with no earthly reason to bow to the bishops. The present theory offers a better explanation than either pure charity or rank greed, namely the importance to all concerned of a steady flow of this-worldly benefit and satisfaction, strong enough to warrant investment in seemingly unproductive personnel and buildings. To put the point bluntly: people support cultic functionaries if they provide them with what they desire: instruction, encouragement, respect for authority, alms, healing, inspiration, balm for the deepest psychic wounds, a sense of purpose, joy, acceptance and, sometimes, the key to wealth and power. There is, we may venture to suggest, a direct correlation between public contributions to religious coffers and religious contributions to public and personal well-being in the broadest sense. The balance is, however, favourable to the clergy because the benefits they channel are so deeply important in a theistic society. Secular communities are rather different, since by definition they have, so to speak, devalued the shekel. But where its value is intact there is no doubt that ritual and other religious personnel share the euonic powers they channel, and wield immense authority. When this ceases to be matched by the

flow of well-being, dissatisfaction will sooner or later set in, as
religious reformers sometimes demonstrate. The drive to maximise benefit has unseated more than one abbot, with others,
doubtless to follow. And between the ebb of priestly effectiveness
and the spring tide of revolt there can be long periods when
powerful clergy, Theban to the core, obstruct the flow of euonic
energy they are supposed to promote. In any case the reason why
people, often in great poverty, give funds and support to officials
and buildings of no overt economic value can be identified. They
do so because the recipients are brokers for a supremely desirable
commodity in their eyes: that sense of fundamental well-being
without which much else including material prosperity can swiftly
seem pointless, absurd or psychologically incapacitating. 'For
what shall is profit a man,' asked a great spiritual leader, 'if he
gain the whole world but lose his own soul?'

Human nature in the light of the other-worldly hypothesis

A revolutionary change of religious orientation like the axial faiths
can scarcely fail to bring about equally major changes in the way
human existence is understood. If the present theory is sound we
would expect them to be as follows. The ancient emphasis on the
spirit will increase significantly and take on a fresh character.
Whereas mythological naturalists use the concept to explain and
ameliorate this-worldly problems the axial faiths invoke it mainly
as a basis for salvation from the sins and sufferings of bodily life.
The besetting problem of existence is no longer to understand the
unseen order but to find liberation in it. Axial humanity sees itself
as a prisoner needing help or release, so that the practical priority
of life is to find a key or a keyholder to unlock the door to ultimate
blessing. The entire thrust of the other-worldly hypothesis is that
such blessing can never be enjoyed in this life. On its own a
picture of human nature as imprisoned in matter or engulfed by
sin would be a sombre one. But underlying it is the immensely
heartening vision of a transcendental world of perfect well-being,
adding the reassuring theme that people can find the necessary
key or keyholder and reach that ideal condition. It is thus
fundamentally an anthropology of hope, sustained by that other-
worldly vision and the spiritual experiences it engenders in those
who meditate, worship, pray and reflect. Earthly existence may

be hopelessly problematical but what does that matter if the superior realm of spirit contains a solution?

Given this transcendentalist orientation with its accompanying devaluation of the present life, the ancient belief in spiritual immortality will obviously continue to be entirely plausible but its character must also change. For example, there can be no desire to retain a doctrine of reincarnation because it merely perpetuates our intermittent but still imprisoning connection with the physical world. And in the monistic version of the axial faiths the goal of spiritual striving must obviously be to leave personality itself behind. Only so can imprisonment be absolutely abolished, for there will then be nothing to capture or be captured. According to this view, words themselves become obsolete because there is nothing to name or qualify. It is only in a world of separate entities that naming and qualifying are possible. Accordingly, true, limitless well-being is realised when it no longer makes sense to think of it as being well. It simply is.

For monotheists, on the other hand, the details are different. Bodily life is of course just as much subordinated to the spirit but the logic of salvation changes. The specific problem of human existence is not how to transcend personality but how to enjoy forever the presence of the perfect person. At this point the two versions of axial religion differ most sharply. One group's members must work out their own salvation because according to its vision of ultimate reality there is nobody else to do so. The other group must look to the saving grace of God or some other redeemer for help, because the corollary of absolute divine sovereignty is clearly absolute human dependence. So axial religion bifurcates anthropologically and soteriologically just as much as in its ways of seeing the ultimate reality, while still showing a common, other-worldly orientation in the quest for perfect well-being, giving us the two great spiritual strands that were mentioned in chapter two as a major feature of religion, one of them autosoteric, the other heterosoteric, salvation being either through one's own efforts or through the help of another being.

In view of these anthropological changes, religious experience also modifies. Faith takes on its classical link with salvation rather than explanation, becoming an all-absorbing concern because the believer is now confronted with an issue of unsurpassable importance, namely the offer of a way to ultimate well-being. This is the pearl of great price for which the merchant sells everything else. The euonic quest is here offered the richest conceivable satisfaction, and as long as the concept of spirit holds sway there is no way it can fail to respond. Aglow with the light of this brightest spiritual sunrise, the responding soul will sometimes experience a richness of insight for which no words are adequately luminous. The mystic and the visionary make their advent. In theistic traditions eschatological prophets will come to declare the final victory of the spirit, summoned by an inner voice that cannot be stilled. And when – exceedingly rarely – the vision unfolded and the message announced by these prophets has an impact so overpowering as to radically change the believer's life, then the logic of spiritual causation will offer no better interpretations than those of supreme divine messenger or even god incarnate. Axial spirituality opens to theistic believers the unprecedented experience that these are justified superlatives. To feel and think and speak like this is to encounter a euonic power strong enough to override even the fear of death. The strength of the drive to maximise well-being can perhaps be gauged when we notice what it does with the worst terrors, making the arena, the flames and the gallows the symbols of its triumph.

'

Strengths and criticisms of the other-worldly hypothesis

To enable people to face agony and death willingly religion must obviously wield enormous power. What does the present theory offer by way of explanation of this fact? Why have the axial faiths in particular been so immensely persuasive for nearly three millenia? Several factors can be cited. To start with there is the power of belief in the transcendentalist euonic vision. To be utterly convinced that there is a better world than this one and that we can enter it at death and have a foretaste of it now is already to possess something more potent than the worst bodily problems. Once people believe in the spirit theory they are in a position to relativise drastically the problems of physical existence and therefore cope better with them. In the axial faiths this belief had long since been completely accepted all over the world, to the extent of being taken entirely for granted. Its origins and its cognitive status as a provisional, humanly devised theory about the unseen side of things were everywhere unrecognised.

Therefore it had all the force of an accepted truth, made even stronger by the supremely comforting picture it paints of reality. It is hard to imagine what would be more desirable to the affective sense than this. So the present explanation shows that axial religion is a large-scale instance of the well-known phenomenon that the very act of fully believing something releases great power over our behaviour. In fact it is so great that the power is released even in situations where the belief in question is in fact poorly grounded. Being cured of an ailment by what we think is a genuine medicine but is in fact only coloured water is a trivial yet revealing demonstration of this phenomenon. What counts most is plausibility and acceptance; this is the faith that removes mountains. And whatever doubts some people may have about the spiritual world-view, it is by far not just a doctrinal form of coloured water. The position is very much more complicated than that, as will be shown in a moment.

A second reason for the success of the other-worldly hypothesis is the limitless hope its sweeping euonic vision encourages people to feel. To have grounds for hope is to be able to act effectively; to have none often spells the withering of even the will to live. We all know from our own experience what hope can do. A recent book goes as far as making the interesting proposal that religion itself is a product of the need for it (Greeley 1982). But why would we hope for something if not because we deem it desirable? It thus seems best to regard hope as a consequence of the desire for well-being and to root religion in the latter. In any case the importance and power of hope are acknowledged by all. A euonic theory of religion is in a position not only to make use of this power but to explain hope itself.

Both belief and hope depend for their continued effectiveness on another factor. This is the continued plausibility of the other-worldly hypothesis. Nobody's life is going to be changed by a doctrine that does not ring true. So a third reason for the success of the axial faiths is their realism in the eyes of believers. The imperfections of this life are squarely faced while the unseen order which confronts us all is explained in a way that long ago passed all available critical tests, in the form of the spiritual hypothesis. Realism about the visible world and a convincing account of the invisible one are all that is needed to vouchsafe the continued acceptance of the world-view, ensuring that the power of belief and hope will remain available. The absence of any serious rival philosophy until modern times has naturally helped spiritual transcendentalism to maintain its persuasiveness. Deeply satisfying mystical or ritual experiences, improvements in day-to-day living engendered by the new optimism and the growth of highly sophisticated systems of doctrinal support all add their weight to an already powerful case. To cap them there is the further fact that the other-worldly hypothesis, just like spirit causation, is in principle resilient to falsification by empirical means. God or the Beyond are never accessible to our senses, and nothing on earth can ever conclusively refute the supposition that they exist and invisibly affect mundane events. As theists say, quite logically on their own terms, God moves in mysterious ways. Believers might expect their god to help them solve a problem but if help is not forthcoming the conclusion is not that there is no god after all but that the deity knows best. They are not being perverse when they react like this, merely honouring the logic of their faith. But although falsification by empirical means is impossible, seemingly confirmatory experiences can and do happen. If nothing that occurs counts against a belief, then everything can be seen to count for it. In this way the spiritual view of things is self-perpetuating on its own terms, inviting and receiving immense internal sophistication whose effect is to deepen conviction within the fold. The internally logical move of saying that the focus of faith – God, the Tao or Nirvana – is beyond the capacity of words, transcending definition, makes the belief even more resilient. Vagueness is thus spiritually proper and presents the combative sceptic with something too conceptually elusive to pin down and dissect. It does not require much imagination to see how little impact sceptical linguistic analysis will make on a faith whose last word is that there is no last word.

Despite the clearly transcendental orientation of the axial faiths, and with full acknowledgement of the satisfaction believers experience through it, we must none the less recognise that the only direct evidence we have about this kind of religion is entirely in this world. There may of course be another realm superior to this one and perfect well-being may indeed await us there. This is always a possibility. But the philosophies that assert this claim, the life-styles that embody it and the satisfactions which seem to confirm it are all without exception earthly phenomena, announced, lived and felt here in this life. Part, at least, of the power of heaven is the peace it can bring on earth. That power can be every bit as real as believers say without necessarily being best describable in the terms they use or without having the transcendental source they allege for it. In short, the argument that religious experience establishes the reality of such a source is false. But it may point in the right direction. All that we can know with certainty is that there is no need to posit a supernatural order of reality to account for the axial faiths. Mundane explanatory factors are sufficient. And yet this, in its turn, must not be seen as establishing the truth of materialistic naturalism. In the circumstances there appears to be no better policy than the open-ended approach adopted in this book, with this-worldly factors being allowed all the sway for which their explanatory power fits them but without falling into the dogma of asserting that there can be no other kind of reality.

Thus the present theory implies that not even these superlative world-views are immune to criticism, correction and replacement. Three major issues give cause for concern in this regard. Firstly, the adequacy of the spiritual account of causation. Secondly, the moral neglect of this world that is made possible by a life-style whose real interest is elsewhere. And thirdly, there are the sharply divergent accounts given by monists and monotheists about what is presumably the same, ultimate, spiritual reality; one seeing it impersonally while the other sees it as a person, a divergence which some critics regard as amounting to mutual incompatibility. Are these two historical strands of the greatest spiritual insight not telling us that the selfsame, supreme reality is, so to speak, both round and square?

The other-worldly faiths, their strengths and their problems are thus covered by the explanatory factors set forth in chapter four. They beautifully exemplify the operation of the drive to maximise well-being; on their own terms they bring that drive to fulfilment in the only objectively possible way: by universalising its goal and perfecting it in the concept of the ultimate condition, the heaven, nirvana and pure land of the axial faiths. They evince the euonic mentality of criticising suspect ideas and practices, creating improvements of wondrous sophistication, providing confirmatory experiences through increased benefit and opening the way to large-scale acceptance of the new ways of being religious. They draw plenteously from the euonic reservoirs of the cosmos and account for its workings in a manner entirely plausible to the believer, using the idiom either of perfected

personal existence, as in theism, or of a perfection beyond personality itself, as in monism. Their diversification into the
Semitic, Indian and Chinese traditions is a consequence of a
package of differentiating factors as identified in chapter four:
local world-views, whether polytheistic or incipiently monotheistic, geographical separation, historical change, culture, logical
options, socio-political models, favourable intellectual conditions, literacy and above all sheer spiritual genius drawing from
the cosmic ocean to refresh the thirsty spiritual landscape with a
timely rain.

RELIGION IN THE MODERN WORLD

Many centuries have passed since the axial faiths were launched.
During that time they made their way into most parts of the
world, winning countless converts from every one of the remaining animist and polytheist cultures which they encountered,
though seldom having much impact on one another. This golden
age of other-worldly spirituality has lasted upward of 2000 years.
Meanwhile the drive to maximise well-being has continued to
work at the slow improvement of physical life, exactly as we would
expect. Bodily pain and pleasure do not cease to be felt by
other-worldly believers, however much they are relativised. The
transcendentalist orientation of the axial faiths is however, likely
to have retarded material progress because we cannot be maxi-
mally effective with worldly problems when our main energies are
directed heaven-ward. Even in axial religions with a strong historical connection or social ethic the emphasis is still on the
demands and rewards of the spirit, so that here too the healing of
physical wounds cannot have quite the prominence of spiritual
well-being. How else are we to explain the appalling complicity of
believers in slavery, apartheid and nuclear destruction? And this,
precisely, is the soft underbelly, the exposed flank, the worrisome
shortcoming of axial religion. The drive to maximise well-being
means that people will not be content merely to endure physical
suffering out of confidence in spiritual benefits, but will look for
ways to prevent and eliminate it as far as possible. This might of
course receive some indirect encouragement from any axial faith

with an emphasis on compassion, for all its other-worldly priorities. For a measure of just how strong the desire for physical gratification is, let us notice that it is in the sphere of Christianity, with its harsh words about the rich, that the greatest wealth has accumulated. But to maximise material well-being we must have the best possible understanding of material things, including the parts we cannot see. This in turn means that prevailing views of causation must be critically reassessed and if necessary replaced. And to do that the primary requirement is to examine physical phenomena ever more carefully and critically for divergences from established theories, especially if there are already doubts about the adequacy of those theories. For example, careful observation shows that there is a drop in temperature associated with rainfall. A natural alternative to the rain spirit begins to suggest itself. Tests follow and are successful. We find we can convert steam back to water in the laboratory by cooling it and the same thing happens every time. The new view works spectacularly, beyond the wildest dreams of the most extravagantly-minded shaman, druid and diviner. The alleged rain spirits play no detectable part in the process. This does not disprove their existence but it does deprive them of an explanatory function. Since that was the basis of belief in them to start with, its loss is still apt to be a blow to continued belief in them. The intellectual revolution installing the new method in the sciences is all but complete. The drive to maximise well-being impells us always to look for the best and world-views are no exception. They are born of our constructive mental power, hold sway through our capacity for acceptance and perish or are retired from office when our critical ability and hunger for improvement find them deficient. So the roman numerals of cosmology are displaced by arabic and binary modes of representation. The turn-over of world-views is certainly slow but for a being who starts out in ignorance, is never perfectly informed, and whose learning depends on fallible mental processes, they are inevitable. The euonic quest is interested only in satisfaction, not in permanent attachments with the transiently useful things our minds and hands produce in order to help it along. In this sense the present view of religion corresponds closely with the Mahayana Buddhist understanding of religious ideas and actions as strictly provisional aids to increased insight, a notion summarised in the concept of skilful means or *upaya* (Pye

1978). In any event, the present theory makes the rise of science fully intelligible by means of the same factors that produced religion, portraying it as itself an expression of the drive to maximise well-being focussing its powers on physical phenomena. The quest eventually produces enough increased wealth to finance the search for better instruments and equipment and to provide some people with time for patient observation. Tycho Brahe, the pioneering Danish astronomical observer, is a splendid example. But the truly revolutionary quality of science is not the explosion of tested knowledge so much as the method that has produced it, which is radically opposed to the cognitive profile of theism and to most other versions of transcendentalist religion. In science people are the finders and makers of knowledge and know that this is so. Their observations, meticulous and exhaustive, their theory-building, their conjectures, measurements and rigorous testings have given us the exponential increase in our grasp of things that is a mental mainspring of the modern period. Science rests on personal investigation, imagination and scepticism, with the person who uses these methods becoming a conscious creator of knowledge, the physical senses playing a vital part in the process. The most important discovery in history is thus how to discover and control knowledge, the greatest quantum leap yet made. Theism, by contrast, regards trustful acceptance of the words of the gods as the ultimate key to knowledge, by whatever means they happen to be channelled, such as sacred writings, the words of the prophets or the diviners' reading of signs. And there is a further, equally radical contrast between the scientific method and any version of other-worldly religion. The latter subordinates and devalues physical existence, considering the main truths and powers to be inaccessibly hidden to sensory detection in the realm of spirit. Human life on earth depends on help from above or needs release from what is seen as the prison of bodily life or gross, sinful confusion. Scientific method counters cognitive dependence on the gods with reliance on one's own intellectual efforts and the devaluing of the physical with a demonstration of its awesome power.

The new view of knowledge

The result is a sweeping change in our view of knowledge. The inherent uncertainty of all theorising, especially cosmology, and the theory-laden character of ordinary perception have been revealed, facts which are belied, incidentally, as much by dogmatic materialists as by dogmatic religionists. Conceptual relativity is now widely recognised for the pervasive reality that it is, enabling us to see that our thoughts are not timeless mental tokens negotiable everywhere but the products of specific contexts which they partly reflect, which necessarily denies universal currency to them. Like physical tools they can and do become obsolete. Traditional believers who regard their concept of the divine as absolutely valid find this is a thorny problem but on the other hand it fits perfectly the religious ideal of maximum well-being through unimpeded growth for all. Such an ideal is not helped by being tied forever to any particular set of concepts. Fixed notions merely hinder evolving insight. Another characteristic of modern knowledge is the value it has found in unrestricted criticism. We saw in chapter four that this is a natural human talent, indispensable for sifting the promising from the suspect in the euonic quest. In recent centuries it has come into its own as never before, so that Immanuel Kant could write in the preface to the *Critique of Pure Reason* in 1781 that 'the present age is in especial degree an age of criticism, and to criticism everything must submit' (Kant 1933: 9, note a). Even our understanding of causation is changing from the famous push-pull model of classical thought to modern forms of field theory emphasising the inter-connectedness of things (Hanson 1969: 271ff). Generally it is found that scepticism is a much more productive cognitive policy than credulity.

The life-style that corresponds to the new cognitive paradigm is secularity. Here the model of human existence implied by the scientific method is lived out. The possibilities of this world are given priority; matter is seen as tractable and therefore capable of being shaped to human interest instead of being regarded as an inert prison best left behind. Such a life-style may be absolutised into the dogma that there is no other reality than the present one, often called materialism or secularism, but it need not be. Open-ended attitudes can just as readily be held, so it is important to use another word than secularism to refer to the policy of giving priority to the challenges and opportunities of spatio-temporal existence. Giving priority is not the same as denying any other kind of existence. The word secularity appears to be the obvious choice (Geering 1980).

Implications for religion

What happens to traditional forms of religion in this new age of science, secularity and scepticism? The characteristic religious interest in finding the greatest well-being is itself unaffected. As a fundamental feature of our human make-up, the desire for ever greater benefit remains as potent as before. The new, secular world-view is after all a change of outlook and not an alteration of human nature itself. Therefore the connection between faith and the quest for increased well-being is untouched by recent conceptual upheavals in science. Instead it is the spiritual understanding of reality, with which the religious quest for ultimate well-being has hitherto been virtually identified, that is called in question by the implications of the new paradigm. Those implications vary from negligible in the case of faiths with a very strong other-worldly orientation to drastic for mythological naturalism. Hybrid religions combining an interest in physical existence with a stronger emphasis on the spirit fall between these two extremes. But before looking at each of them in more detail we must first identify the underlying logic of the situation before us. Two points stand out clearly. Firstly, those who accept the new, empirical approach to knowledge cannot deny that there is a spiritual reality quite different to physical existence without themselves departing from that approach. Their way of seeking knowledge by means of observation or other empirical methods does not of itself provide a basis for pronouncements about the nature of reality as a whole. That is not science but metaphysics. So believers who confine their faith strictly to other-worldly things are logically immune to the new outlook, though they can legitimately be asked to justify their belief in a spiritual realm as a true account of the unseen order, or at least as the best account. The second point is that any religious assertion about this world and how it works is much affected by the scientific method and its results because both the believer and the empiricist are now talking about the same phenomena for which the latter has in many cases produced vastly superior explanations. In short, the concept of spirit as a causal theory about anything observable or directly related to observation is now called in question by a highly, though not wholly, successful rival. On the basis of these two fundamental points we can now deduce the implications of the secular paradigm for the three main types of religion: mythological naturalism, transcendental monism and transcendental monotheism.

Those who define matter as a mere appearance – not just the surface but the entire substance of matter, so to speak – and direct their faith to a way of release focussed entirely on the realm of spirit are the least affected because they can assign the new developments to a level of things which makes no real difference to them, though it is extremely unlikely that their attitude will be shared by others around them who are less adept at disciplining the body and more affected by the cycles of pleasure and pain. The Theravadin parts of Buddhism, for instance, while squaring with the secular view of human self-reliance, repudiate its sense of the importance of physical existence. At the far end of the spectrum are the surviving forms of mythological naturalism. Here the new paradigm is a direct rival because it provides an alternative, superior account of causation. Thus science, which in Newton's day included the concept of God as an operative cosmic factor, (Attfield 1978: 60, 70ff) now proceeds along entirely demythologised lines, though its explanatory concepts are of course in exactly the same provisional epistemological category as those of spirit-causation. But so far as content is concerned, the new view is revolutionary. Regular, natural forces replace the gods, an extension after nearly two millenia of the classical naturalism of Epicurus and Lucretius. The gods were present in their world-view but played no part in the workings of the cosmos. As Lucretius wrote, 'nature is free and uncontrolled by proud masters and runs the universe herself without the aid of gods' (1976: 92). In any event, mythological and scientific naturalism are at base alternatives, not compatibles. The Egyptian sun is not powered across the sky by the god Ra; the winter rains in the Levant are produced by condensation at the cooler, higher elevations of the mountains running parallel to the coast, not by the good pleasure of Baal. Where such forms of mythological naturalism survive they do so only by the incomplete extension of the new approach. It began, ironically, with the heavens and has completely taken over what we now call the physical and biological sciences, but its passage through the social sciences and humanities is incomplete. If Baal vanishes in favour of meteorology, what will happen to Yahwistic causation if history and ethics are given convincing naturalistic renderings by scientific methods? The resurrection of Christ could then be seen as a real event but with a very different explanation to the ones currently held in Christian thought.

Between these extremes of immunity and acute vulnerability lie the remaining forms of transcendentalist religion. Ethical monotheism is gravely at risk whenever divine action in the world is asserted. Thus Aubrey Moore is quoted as saying that a 'theory of occasional intervention implies as its correlative a theory of ordinary absence' (in Vidler 1968: 121). This calls in question the coherence of two pillars of historical theism, the doctrines of divine revelation and miracles. P. Nowell-Smith has summarised the difficulty as follows: 'The supernatural is either so different from the natural that we are unable to investigate it at all or it is not. If it is not, then it can hardly have the momentous significance that (the traditional theist) claims for it; and if it is it cannot be invoked as an explanation of the unusual' (Rowe and Wainwright 1973: 400). These words indicate that a dualism of body and spirit or between natural and supernatural entities may safeguard the other-worldly hypothesis at the expense of this-worldly relevance or even intelligibility. That would not bother anyone who has little interest in this world anyway, but it is a problem for the hybrid faiths which try to hold rationally together the earthly and the heavenly. But perhaps the severest problem faced by adherents of those faiths is, as we saw earlier in this chapter, how to identify an alleged instance of spiritual causation (Flew 1974: 30). The realm of spirit is defined by believers as incapable of being detected by the senses, so we can never observe its operations no matter how much we refine our instruments. This means that spirit must operate undetectably in matter, but if it is absolutely undetectable how can it ever be identified? Undetectable operations are indistinguishable from non-operations. As was pointed out earlier in this chapter, the spirit-hypothesis is immune to refutation but it can be made redundant by rival theories or shown to be cognitively vacuous.

The scientific approach to knowledge cannot enlighten us about the behaviours that would qualify us for the spiritual realm, if such there be, because it operates only with data that can be observed or directly related to observations. But to the extent that other-worldly forms of religion de-emphasise life on earth, the new outlook is given ample scope to develop a secular morality. Here the most vulnerable party is once again historical theism because it claims to involve the earth but directs its faith heavenward. Secularist ethical critics have been quick to sense scope for attack on historical theism, because it has a mixed record as a source of this-worldly transformation. On one hand there are impressive fosterings of education, art, medicine and social welfare. On the other there is the ability to co-exist, even encourage, phenomena like slavery, slums, nuclear weapons, imperialist exploitation and apartheid by whatever euphemism it is called. Secular morality asks how these can be squared with a faith like Christianity whose founder prayed that the divine kingdom should come on earth and whose gospel declares that God loved the world so much as to save it through his only son. Religions which appear to regard the sanctuary not as a way to transform the slum but as more important than the slum are apt to court the deepest resentment of slum-dwellers and others, and enhance the appeal of secular movements vowing to eliminate the conditions that produce them.

Such then are the main characteristics and implications of the new paradigms of knowledge and human existence brought about by the rise of science. The response of the hybrid faiths like monotheism is vigorous, varied and as yet unsettled. It has taken place mainly in the industrialised Christian societies of the west over the past centuries but is rapidly becoming a global religious phenomenon of our times as well. According to the view of religion developed in this book the main reactions of these faiths to science and secularity will be resistance, adaptation and a search for new spiritual beginnings. The following examination of these three reactions was written before Peter Berger's much longer treatment of the question came to hand (1980: 60ff). While very similar to his in various ways it is still different enough in others to warrant retention in its original form. The religions covered in it are the theistic axial faiths only, because mythological naturalism is simply obsolete in the present context and transcendental, spiritual monism is not directly challenged by the new paradigm.

Religious resistance

Underlying the policy of those who refuse to yield anything from traditional religion to science and secularity is a conviction that their faith is in fact untouched by them. We have seen this to be a likely reaction on the part of people who define religion in such strongly transcendental terms as not to be bothered by worldly science or life-styles. It is made even more likely by belief in the truth of the ancient faiths, for when one has the truth any new development (so called) will, if valid, merely confirm it and, if different, be false. Either way the old doctrines are unaffected.

Resistance to the new paradigm and the knowledge it produces can take various forms. An obvious one is to absolutise traditional beliefs and discourage contact between devotees and modernists. Dogma becomes the serum against data, helped by quarantine. A study of the syllabuses taught at the world's seminaries and theological faculties will show just how much in vogue this policy has been. It is entirely understandable. An education featuring free access to Lucretius, Hume, Flew or even Schleiermacher is unlikely to produce transcendentalist zealots. But there may be a fearsome price to pay in the end. If religious beliefs are in fact as much prone to improvement as anything else then the greatest disservice is done to faith by blocking its growth in this way. What is sincerely thought to be the service of the living God would then in fact be the slow strangulation of any prospect of enriched spirituality. The serum turns out to be embalming fluid. Naturally, the truth must be defended and cherished; just as naturally it is harmful to religion, as to all else, to freeze the imperfect. The agonising question facing many believers today is how to decide which horn of this dilemma the retention of the old faith is, in fact, involving.

A second way to resist the new age is by compartmentalising faith and reason. It can be done in all sorts of ways, from classical dualism where the inner eye sees heaven while the outer eye observes the earth, to the theory that science deals with how-questions while religion gives us answers to why-questions. Prominent here is the assertion that religious faith involves a special path of knowledge linking the spiritual realm and the believing soul, a path that has its own mysterious processes, including miraculous, divine self-disclosure. The traditionalist therefore counters the secularist with what amounts to an alleged revelatory by-pass of ordinary human knowing. The seeming neatness and ease of this tactic makes it likely to be popular but here too there is a problem, namely how such dissimilar realities can interact. In the form of the mind-body problem this is an ancient philosophical puzzle and it is not clear how much gain there can be in trying to resist the new paradigm with so problematic a ploy, whose difficulties were outlined earlier in the chapter (Miles 1972: 45f).

Then there is the notion of derived autonomy in the physical universe. Believers in divine creation who are impressed by the success of scientists in accounting for phenomena without spirit causation might find this a promising way to have the best of both worlds, as we say. God or Allah bestows on his creation the ability to operate on its own, which accounts for the scientists' naturalistic findings without harming theistic doctrine. When urgently needed, the deity can always perform special actions in the form of miracles. A variant of this option is to distinguish between spiritual and material causation, discerning the former with the eye of faith as mysteriously present in the latter. This has been ingeniously developed into a theory of primary and secondary causation by some theistic philosophers, notably neo-Thomists (Owen 1971: 9). Sceptics have found it uncomfortably reminiscent of the tale about the emperor's new clothes, which were of course also mysteriously present. Despite such misgivings, the idea cannot be logically refuted by any conceivable scientific advance, exactly like Kaggen in southern San mythology. The problem is not refutation but being overtaken by one's rivals and robbed of followers, though this can sometimes be prevented by discouraging or even forbidding those followers to acquaint themselves independently and thoroughly with the opposition.

The appeal to paradox is yet another possible avenue of resistance. Apparent contradictions between the new knowledge and the old or between different parts of traditional doctrine can be regarded as paradoxical and thus made acceptable. There is a crass form of this tactic which is merely a retreat from reason, but the move has a sophisticated variant as well based on the modern recognition of just how provisional all our theorising is. This being the case our analogical guesses will sometimes fit rather uneasily together, but are the best we can do. After all, even physicists have to make do with an odd fusion of wave and particle views of light, so we must expect even odder couples when laboratory and pulpit meet. The appeal to paradox is at its most effective in the service of theistic claims that the realm of spirit is wholly other than physical existence, an extreme dualism much favoured by hyper-transcendental fideists in the Barthian mould, but one which causes conceptual agony to rationalists because in their eyes it exacerbates the problem of identifying divine action to breaking point. If the deity is indeed absolutely unlike us or anything else, then his (or her) alleged dealings with us must be indiscernible. And if they are in fact discernible then God cannot logically be wholly other than we.

The traditionalist can of course counter-attack by exploiting the grave problems of modern existence, especially the horrors made possible by science in the form of nuclear weapons and the environmental sullying of the earth. Secular thinkers have not been shy about castigating the moral failures of believers, real and imagined. But the tables can just as easily be turned. In fact there is every indication that the contemporary anxiety caused by the abuse of modern technology will give traditional religion immense scope for growth. There is a sense in which the appeal of heaven is so much stronger when the earth is wretched and afraid. Such a flourish of the ancient faiths would be very much helped by an alliance with nationalism, that other great secular force of our time. (Smart 1981: 208ff) And if all this fails there is still the possibility of resisting modernism by exorcising it. Demonology may yet prove a major asset to some of the mytho-logically devout. As these points imply, there is every likelihood that traditional theistic religion will continue to thrive. The state of its rivals alone makes that a virtual certainty. None the less, the present theory also means that continued success will ultimately depend on how successfully the character of the new age can be ignored, obscured or rationalised, because objectively there is an obvious divergence between mythological and scientific attitudes to the sources and methods of knowledge and therefore also to their respective views of human existence. Traditional theistic religion cannot make peace with the contemporary secular paradigm without losing its soul. But it is well equipped to hold the new situation at bay. And as for the resultant sense of alienation from the world, this is exactly what every committed traditionalist thinks should happen anyway. To be truly devoted to God is to be in the world but not of it, as such people often say. Alienation is therefore a mark of spiritual success, not something to deplore.

Religious adaptation

In any religion like Christianity which makes factual claims about the world a second type of attitude towards the new cognitive paradigm is to be expected, and this is to look for ways of adapting the old world-view to the new. The underlying conviction here is that some traditional religious beliefs and practices are indeed affected by the new picture of reality, so that restatement is called for in the interests of the truth and of religion itself. It is a reaction which is available only to believers who have come to think that their inherited doctrines are, in part at least, less than perfect. Those who reject such a view will see this second reaction as a betrayal of the truth through a misguided and fatal beguilement by the new paradigm. People who disagree with religion altogether will often see it as a watering-down of the old ideas in an attempt to have a foot in both camps or as a process of ingenious but futile epicycling done to save an obsolete world-view. But for those who follow this second, adaptational path, there simply is no other option. They are convinced by the new scientific knowledge and they are also sure, through personal experience of the transforming power of faith, that religious doctrines in some sense remain essentially valid. This obliges them to rethink the nature of religion in order to accommodate that double persuasion.

Here too several strategies are available, of which a couple stand out as particularly important. One of them is to distinguish between two categories of religious belief: a core of eternal truths about which there can be no negotiation and an outer zone of secondary ideas which are merely the provisional elaborations and interpretations of the first category. The former are divinely given but the latter are the products of human effort and can be freely adjusted or even replaced in the light of scientific progress or historical discovery. It is interesting to record here the opinion of Alister Hardy in view of his combination of scientific training and research into religious experience. He wrote that theology, 'still based upon the thoughts of men of more than a thousand years ago, is unlikely to remain what it was; part of it, a large part of it, may well be as much in error as was the optical illusion of the sun going round the earth' (1966: 228f). And William James was even harsher in his judgement of the philosophical parts of traditional monotheism, declaring them to be a 'metaphysical monster' and 'an absolutely worthless invention of the scholarly mind' (1902: 447). The strategy in question has a natural appropriateness in any historical religion combining elements of mythological naturalism with the other-worldly hypothesis, its discernment of an inner sanctum and an outer courtyard of belief lining up neatly with the perceived structure of faith. The difficulty, however, is to give reliable criteria for the sorting of beliefs into two piles, one negotiable and the other one fixed, because none is objectively to hand. Doctrines are not die-stamped 'made in heaven' and 'made in Rome' respectively. Subjective criteria then have the field to themselves, and one person's inner sanctum is the next one's market of ideas. Notwithstanding this problem, the strategy makes for great creativity and renewal, not just in response to science but also to other religions and to social insights such as those developed in feminist thought. Apparent contradictions in traditional belief asserting, for instance, that God both absolutely predestines our actions and is also perfectly just when he punishes the sinner or saves the elect, can also be assigned to the negotiable pile of beliefs and reworked or set aside. A major issue currently pressing for attention is religious pluralism, with believers brought up in one tradition sometimes coming to appreciate the spiritual depths and the doctrinal quality of others. Traditionalists who resist the scientific paradigm as making no difference to their doctrines will think that they are just as little affected by other faiths, especially if their own doctrines already define them as inferior or false. But anyone with an inclination towards reformulation or whose attitude towards other faiths is determined by experiential evidence rather than inherited doctrine will feel obliged to do some extensive rethinking of those inherited beliefs after making contact with people from other sophisticated faiths. Exclusivist or elitist doctrines of salvation are likely to be the first to be reformulated, but the process will not stop there. In the end, as resistance-minded theists always say, the reformulations are likely to be very extensive indeed, and may even prove so sweeping as to lead to the radical policy of seeking fresh spiritual beginnings altogether. The reason is simple: the issues placed on the reformulator's agenda by religious pluralism include the concept of God, because some faiths manage without it or relativise it, advaitic Hinduism being one. And this is to place in question what theistic traditionalists correctly see as the core of their religion.

But even without the added pressure of religious pluralism the concept of God is perforce being more or less extensively reconsidered in theologically liberal circles. We have seen that the new paradigm leads to doubts about the crucial doctrine of divine action in the world and to this issue it matters not one whit that several religions teach that doctrine. In fact, for those who are seriously rethinking their faith, religious pluralism is ultimately a much less severe problem than the secular paradigm because the latter calls in question the validity of the single most fundamental concept in any and all traditional religion, namely the concept of spirit. The debate about world faiths is a debate about different forms of that concept; the new picture of human knowledge and existence question the concept in any form. Therefore it is the more serious problem. In any case the process of adapting traditional beliefs will certainly be dominated by discussion of the doctrine of God. The contemporary context of that adaptation means, however, that the really important task will be to rethink the meaning of theism and its place in religion. As John Hick has said, the issue is 'whether religion should be defined in terms of God, as man's varying responses to a real supernatural Being, or whether God should be defined in terms of religion, as one of the basic symbols with which religion works' (1974: 162). Clearly the central issue here is that of meaning. For those so engaged the older debate about the existence of God, which presupposes that the question of meaning is settled to the satisfaction of the contending parties, must be suspended while the newer question rises to the top of the agenda.

A second adaptive strategy for religious liberals is to create a conceptual synthesis of old and new rather than adjusting pro-blematical parts of the husk of belief. This is an ambitious exercise in imaginative restatement. Ancient beliefs are lined up with new knowledge and a fresh set of concepts is invented and systematised in order to fuse them. The assumption governing such a tactic is that beliefs can be restated without essential loss of meaning, and is a desirable option for those wishing to retain most of the old doctrines while also accepting a great deal of new knowledge. It differs from resistance to doctrinal change by declaring that the essential message of religion is variously expres-sible, and calls for much greater conceptual creativity than merely reformulating peripheral beliefs. Criticism of this tactic is apt to come from believers anxious that even the ancient wording of faith be honoured and from reformulators who dislike such wholesale restatement. Elaborate systems cannot really be accepted piecemeal, and not every adaptively-minded believer will favour the all-or-nothing terms on which this strategy usually operates because of its fondness for systematic expression. Another sign of this approach to the problem of adaptation is the novel terminology that must necessarily be developed to carry out the proposed synthesis. Given these options the policy of adapting old doctrines to new discoveries will continue to provide for the needs of people attracted to both traditional religion and the new knowledge. But because the two are in key respects incompatible, quite apart from the acute problem of determining exactly where the process of doctrinal adaptation must stop, this second reaction to the secular paradigm will ultimately prove frustrating and transient. And that brings us to the next reaction.

Creating a new religious future

We come now to a third kind of religious response to the scientific age and its secular, sceptical implications, the response of people who think that even the main, traditional, spiritual beliefs are now obsolete but do not become agnostics or materialists, interpreting the situation instead as an unsurpassed opportunity for radical religious renewal. To them the new age is the graveyard of inherited beliefs but not of faith, which they think can find fresh expression in terms and lifestyles consistent with the changed paradigm of human existence. In the language of the present theory, these are people who have washed their hands completely of the transcendentalist age and are now at the frontier of a religious quantum leap into a new age of faith, whereas in their eyes the other two responses involve either a wholesale or a partial continuation of transcendentalist religion in a global culture fundamentally at odds with it. To radicals these two policies turn religion into a mortuary or a hospice just when the need for complete regeneration is greatest.

Once again there are various methods of conducting this type of response to modernism. Some go eastward from theism to Zen, attracted by its autosoteric naturalism, meditative sophistication and philosophical freshness after the scriptural or syllogistic grind of the abandoned mentality. New mysticisms flourish in the sudden demand for a spirituality without dogma or obscurantism, encouraged by the resilience of ultimate silence. Innovate religious movements spiring up like wild flowers in a neglected graveyard, their adherents sometimes wiring themselves for sacra-

mental gadgetry, sometimes contemplating the cosmos as a galac-
tic guru, and sometimes just withering away. But there are others
who seek faith not in the east or in electronics but in new forms of
personal creativity far surpassing a mere reformulating of the old
faith or the project of devising fresh marketing strategies to put
across an unchanged religious product. Implicit here is a view of
religion, pioneered by the young Schleiermacher, which
relativises all belief, actions and ritual so that although faith will
always engender them it is never tied to any particular ones. This
makes doctrinal creativity a condition of religious growth, while
something other than belief must then be seen as the axle around
which the wheel of faith revolves (Prozesky 1981).

Specifying what that axle or core element is presents problems,
and there is no way of knowing in advance exactly what a new
generation of spiritual creativity will decide. But the present
theory has definite implications about the broad character of any
successful creativity. If there is to be a new religious future it can
only be because something fundamental in the religious past is
still valid and important enough to attract the wholehearted,
unstinting dedication of faith. But if the new scientific paradigm
of human existence is correct, as radicals believe, then they
cannot logically identify that abidingly valid religious datum as a
set of supposedly eternal truths. On their terms that is precisely
what dooms traditional religion. Therefore the new generation of
religious teachings must be deemed provisional and experimental.
This however immediately raises a fresh question: for exactly
what purpose are those provisional ideas developed? The present
theory provides a clue: they will be experiments in understanding
the powers that make for the greatest well-being even in an age of
science, secularity and scepticism. By centralising the euonic
venture of all the earth, the new version of faith would at least
base its intellectual explorations and practical experiments on the
bedrock of human striving all along, while simultaneously working
with rather than against the modern view of knowledge with its
relativity, critical attitudes, creativity, openness to new data and
radical uncertainty about answering ultimate questions. The
scope for moral action would be limitless. A religious philosophy
in the service of such a faith could be developed yielding a rebirth
of meaning for old symbols and old activities, above all the concepts of spirit and deity. One example is Mordecai Kaplan's vision
of the divine as an inherent force in the universe which enables

people to achieve satisfaction (1957: 316f). The traditional debate about the existence of God becomes entirely meaningless in such a perspective, like asking where the edge of the earth is. Instead the main questions become whether the concept of God as a purely human construct adequately or inadequately symbolises the cumulative experience and wisdom of all the earth, whether the powers that make for growth, joy, wholeness and peace are best understood in natural or supernatural terms, or whether that polarity even makes sense any more. Such a policy might come to see Hume and Feuerbach as modern heroes of faith along with the prophets and visionaries of the axial age. In principle there would be no reason for the new radicals to regard the spirit-hypothesis, in whatever form, as any more the last word on the way of the cosmos than roman numerals are in mathematics. But above all any venture of this kind must relate realistically to the secular perception of the cosmos. There is no agreed statement of that perception but for many its main characteristics could be summarised as follows: It changes through the interplay of forces, but the changes seem orderly rather than random, and the orderliness is flexible rather than rigid; it is severely hurtful but also at least partly remediable; amenable to effort, especially to intelligent and determined effort; a source of grave concern but also of some hope, with great possibilities of well-being though absolutely no guarantees; apt to foster illusions because of its harshness and confusion because of its complexity, but also to reward realism and courage; wasteful in its propagation of life; exceedingly slow-moving; and quite unsentimental in its dealings with the individual.

Clearly the difficulties facing this response to the new age are formidable. Believers in the conservative and liberal camps will regard it as gross over-reaction at best and outright capitulation at worst. Dogmatic materialists will dislike being challenged by the new paradigm of faith, though they badly need a thorough-going exposure of their own betrayal of the inherently non-dogmatic method of science, and are thus unlikely to look with much favour on a revival of religion using cognitive methods they have come to see as exclusively theirs. Then there is the absence of a coherent conceptual system with which to articulate the new venture, though followers of Whitehead might contend that his thought provides one. Finally, the politics of the venture are scarcely likely to be smooth and cordial, at least in places dominated by transcendentalist zealots. The new radicals will need all the tactical skill they can muster, plus friends in the right places. Severe as these difficulties are, they are unlikely to deter those who have experienced deep personal transformation in religion, have sensed the full impact of the new age but despair at finding fresh resources in the ancient patterns of spiritual belief. For them the only option is to create the religious future they want for a desperately needful world, redefining the human predicament, refathoming the cosmic ocean, recharting the sources of well-being, and activating a fresh surge of saving power in a world more vulnerable than ever but grown wary of promises and sceptical about final solutions. The prospect of such a policy in the global terms now possible is likely to prove irresistible to pioneering radicals. And, paradoxically, it could be inherently better equipped to pursue the classical religious ideal of complete fulfilment than its theistic alternatives, in which only the deity will enjoy infinite selfhood for ever, an ultimately subordinationist view in which perfect well-being is not universalisable. In a way closed to transcendentalists and materialists alike, the radicals could champion the cause of comprehensive, this-worldly well-being without denying that other realms of existence could await us. But given the metaphysical agnosticism of the new age they would have to emphasise the direction of the healing path and its present benefits, rather than trying to define ultimate destinations. It is precisely our inability to do this successfully that the new cognitive paradigm emphasises. The ancient religious metaphor of the way could then once again mean exactly what it says. People will be offered a healing path now, not perfect health later. As for the prospects of such a position, much will depend on boldness of imagination, tactical skill and especially depth of commitment to the euonic quest. Poised at a new frontier of ignorance and inability, the radicals find themselves returning to the historic, activating situation of traditional, transcendentalist religion, except that this time their task is not to create the spiritual hypothesis but to replace it for the sake of faith, the new humanity and its endangered planet. In the earlier situation the bold use of available resources led to a marvel of history to which all who have ever lived and will live are massively indebted. Today the available resources are staggeringly improved, and above all people have discovered that it is they who create knowledge, including the old idea that they do not create it but receive it from on high. In ancient times, of immense ignorance and technical crudity, it was realistic to interpret experience in terms of massive dependence on the whim of outside forces. Nowadays the new interpretation makes much better sense to many people. The result is not necessarily to jettison traditional religious concepts but it definitely involves a fundamental change in the way they are perceived and handled. The old concept of spirit comes to be seen as a stained glass window and not as the light that has illuminated it these many millenia, an interpretation created by fallible people as they sought to fathom with their minds the unseen powers that affected them, rather than the powers themselves. Human life needs both for its fullness though it is not the window that endures but the light.

CONCLUSION

At the end of chapter three a list was given of the criteria for satisfactory theory-building. Subjecting the present proposals to them and assessing their merits in relation to other explanations of religion are tasks best left to independent, expert critics. It should however be clear that every effort has been made to honour those criteria and to use as explanatory factors only such items as are part of the ordinary experience of any person. As for the global characteristics of religion, or the five questions about it which were also posed in that chapter, the present theory has yielded answers to them in the long main section of this one. In view of that length and to encourage critical evaluation, it will be helpful to summarise the unfolding explanation of religion as part of the conclusion to this book.

The explanation summarised

Our cosmic setting implies that there is a natural, unseen, transcendent reality comprising the forces we neither understand nor control but whose power we none the less feel for good and ill. The drive to maximise well-being and the qualities of vulnerability, finitude, curiosity and creativity that go with it mean, next, that people will inevitably seek benefit in their cosmic context by means of knowledge and action, tested by the satisfaction or discomfort they bring. Being finite, our measures are always provisional. Human cultural evolution is therefore an immense, euonic experiment, successively proposing, exploring, testing, correcting and replacing the world-views and lifestyles by which we try to map a mysterious, transcendent cosmos in order to mine its beneficial resources. In the slow passage from total ignorance to steadily improving knowledge a stage must arrive when people become dimly aware of their immense lack of understanding and consequent vulnerability, anxiously sensing the flimsiness of their lives and thoughts before the mysterious, transcendent powers that affect them and acknowledging the painfully limited steps they can take on their own to maximise well-being. This is the first activating situation in the history of religion. Progress will now depend on transcending those limitations by attempting to discover what the unseen forces really are and why they act as they do. And the only humanly available method at this stage is to form an unconscious conjecture about them on the basis of analogies with things already known and to test it in practice. No analogy is more likely or suitable at an early phase of intellectual development than a model of human causation, giving rise to belief in spirits as the invisible, personal beings responsible for the mysterious things that happen to us and around us. It is an enormously significant step, producing the transcendentalist outlook that has gripped people's minds for thousands of years.

Because this outlook initially has the characteristic of belief in spiritual beings causing events on earth, including what we would now call purely physical events, it amounts in the first instance to mythological naturalism, though the concept of spirit need not be used for this purpose. Geographical, historical, cultural and developmental differences between communities and physical separations cause this globally human reaction to be modified locally into many regional variations, the most influential being ancient polytheism and especially monotheism. The latter forms when a community's experiences focus lengthily and extensively on a single, major and successful interest and therefore also on the god who controls it. In every case, however, these variations must be seen as simultaneously religious and cultural. The modern concept of faith as something separable from the rest of our concerns had not yet arisen. What we nowadays distinguish as religious belief and scientific knowledge were still a single, unified concern.

Impressive though its qualities are, mythological naturalism is of course a provisional, conjectural attempt at mapping the unseen order. The drive to maximise well-being implies that sooner or later its inadequacies as a causal hypothesis for physical phenomena and even as a world-view will be detected in the relentless search for improvement. Then a rival hypothesis forms. The first known instance of such a development happened in ancient Greece when philosophers like Thales declared, significantly, that everything is water or some other material element. But the refinement and testing of this conceptual experiment were interrupted by the advent of another, immensely powerful interpretation of the unseen order and of our existence in relation to it. This was the other-worldly hypothesis. The drive to maximise benefit sooner or later induces in us the concept of perfect, imperishable well-being, but common experience at once shows that it is unrealisable in our physical form of existence. If it exists it must therefore be in the spiritual realm. For those to whom these thoughts occurred the purpose of our present existence becomes a search for the way to that ultimate condition by leaving behind bodily life and its woes. The human experiment modifies itself in the service of this ideal possibility, a challenge which gives us the second activating circumstance in the history of religion. And as with mythological naturalism, the other-worldly hypothesis comes to expression in different forms according to circumstance. There are two main ones. In polytheistic or animistic cultures with a relatively low sense and evaluation of individual existence, as implied for instance by belief in reincarnation, the supreme goal of religious striving will logically be seen as an undifferentiated, ultimate reality where personal distinctions no longer exist. Spiritual monism is a prime example. Physical existence is naturally interpreted very negatively as a prison from which we need to liberate ourselves by using the saving techniques of bodily subjection and spiritual upliftment.

On the other hand monotheists with a higher sense and valuation of personal existence and a determination to remain loyal to their god will interpret the other-worldly hypothesis as an infinite divine kingdom ruled by an absolute divine sovereign who alone can save us. In either monistic or monotheistic form the new vision offers the believer a limitless blessing in the world of the spirit, an obviously magnetic prospect for suffering, finite beings. The inherent power of the belief itself is massively enhanced in practice by a set of further developments, namely the invention of writing to preserve and spread ideas, the emergence of scope for individualism after the long age of intensive social dominance and collective behaviour, and the natural occurrence of sheer genius. Just as music has its Mozart and literature its Shakespeare so religion also has its outstandingly gifted figures with an effect no less powerful on others less penetrative and commanding. So the great founding and reforming figures of the axial faiths take over the spiritual stage, people with the ability to interpret the saving significance of special events, to communicate the new vision to others beyond number as an effective message, life-style and ritual practice, and to inspire written collections of their thoughts and deeds. Added to mythological naturalism, these two forms of axial spirituality give us three basic types of religion, one affirming the earth, the second devaluing it altogether and the third assigning to it a subordinate status.

Enormous though the satisfaction of axial faith undoubtedly is, here too we are in the ranks of conceptual imperfection, as with any human proposal. Meanwhile the drive to maximise well-being continues its search for improvements. Its most likely next area of operation is the physical, an area open to neglect in any religion which emphasises the spiritual realm as the truly important reality. The consequence is the resumption of the naturalistic experiment begun in ancient Greece, namely to explain phenomena in terms of orderly natural forces rather than as the work of spirits. Science makes its triumphant cognitive debut leading to an unprecedented transformation of knowledge and physical existence and encouraging the development of a secular outlook in contrast to the transcendentalist orientation of all religion hitherto. We have here the third activating circumstance affecting the spiritual life. In this modern situation mythological naturalism is obsolete. Believers who care nothing for physical existence are unmoved. But members of faiths like monotheism which retain an element of this-worldly interest alongside their main emphasis on the spirit are very much affected whenever they assert anything about the physical realities so successfully explained by science. Among them there are some who define their doctrines as perfect truths. They cannot make doctrinal concessions to science and secularity without committing spiritual suicide, so their only course of action is to resist these new ideas on any matter where there appears to be mutual contradiction. But there are also believers who see their marginal doctrines as open to improvement and who follow a policy of accommodation to the new knowledge concerning them. Finally, there are yet others who hold that the central, traditional religious concept of the spirit has now been made redundant even in matters of faith, but that religion itself is larger than any of the concepts it uses, no matter how hallowed by time and acceptance. Their response to science, secularity and any other unavoidable challenge like contact with other great religions must be to experiment afresh in quest of a radically new kind of faith. And if we add to this already very diversified picture of religion the ways in which each person can fashion a distinctive spirituality, for example through choice, differences of immediate need, opportunity and circumstance, then it will be clear why religion should be uniquely personal at the level of individuals.

A three-part euonic model of religion

According to the present theory the crux of religion hitherto is the belief that our welfare depends in the last resort on a transcendental reality. This means that the life of faith is best understood as comprising countless benefit-giving engagements with what the needful believer takes to be that higher reality, conceiving it after the fashion prevalent in his or her culture and being transformed thereby from a condition of distress to one of relief. These transforming moments resolve themselves logically into three constituents: needful, vulnerable but resourceful believers; salutary powers, as we might call whatever it is that aids such people; and, by the effect of the latter on the former, a resultant experience of increased satisfaction, seen in the axial faiths as part of a bigger transformation to an ultimate spiritual condition of perfect and imperishable well-being. It is a dynamic, three-fold pattern repeatedly evidenced in all provinces of terra religiosa: the ancient Israelite caught between the pharoah's army and the Red Sea, the strong east wind that Yahweh is said to have caused to blow in order to part the waters, and the resultant deliverance of the chosen people; the Canaanite farmer of those distant days, desperate because of drought and therefore making sacrifice to

Baal, lord of the rains, and sooner or later rejoicing at the coming of the rain; or a Sri Lankan monk seeking release from the cycle of rebirths, applying the liberating force of the dhamma, and, as a final consequence, attaining the boundlessness of nirvana.

The same three-part structure can be found in any of the key experiences which shape and empower the religious life. Zen meditation produces in the person who practices it a remarkable mental transformation from the scattering of ordinary conscious- ness and its anxieties to a crowning sense of peace and an inclu- sive insight into the ultimate oneness or emptiness of reality. The threefold pattern described above is readily apparent in the medi- tator desiring to penetrate the stressful appearances of the sensory manifold, the transforming power of the meditative technique and its associated disciplines, and the attainment of supreme insight or satori. The Hindu devotees of Mariamma noted earlier in this book exemplify the same process. Beset by the fear of illness they participate in temple rituals which are believed capable of inducing the goddess to protect them. Having done so, they are at once reassured that an important step has been taken in the interests of their own well-being and that of their children. This is not proof of immunity to disease but it certainly is an extremely real psychological benefit. And then, thirdly, there is the benefit-giving power of the mythico-ritual complex associated with the goddess. The investigator need neither affirm nor deny the reality of the goddess to recognise that in fact a desired transformation has been effected in the devotee. And exactly the same pattern is evident in the experiences of the convert to Christ in evangelical Christianity, the penitent emerging from the confessional, or the disciple Tzu-kung being much helped, and vast numbers of other Chinese also, when Confucius recommend- ed that the one saying by which people could always act is 'Never do to others what you would not like them to do to you' (Analects XV: 23; Waley 1938).

In view of all this it should now be clear exactly how religion as hitherto practised differs from secular existence. All people, according to the present theory, desire the great possible well- being and all are involved in the power of an unseen order of reality which transcends their ability to understand or control. But whereas the believer regards that unseen, transcendent order as a realm of spirit in which perfect well-being is possible, the non- religious person either holds that we cannot know about such things in view of our limited intellects and manages with a non-spiritual interpretation of the unseen order, or outrightly rejects the concept of spirit. In either case such people will not expect to achieve a complete and perfect solution to all that distresses and disfigures our existence, unlike believers, though they are quite justified in working for the enrichment of life in this world so far as possible.

The theory evolved in this book can now be summarised in a formal statement. The religions of the earth are a set of provisional, culturally conditioned and regionally differentiated human constructs created by people themselves in order to maximise benefit through the salutary power of a transcendentally orientated system of existence, understood hitherto as involving a realm of spirit from which assistance in dealing with present problems may be obtained and in which ultimate well-being is thought by some believers to be possible, but not necessarily tied to this spiritual conceptuality or to any other; produced because finite physical beings cannot satisfy all their needs on their own or in spatio-temporal conditions; devised, maintained and modified in on-going interaction with the forces of a mysterious, transcendent cosmos, often under the influence of exceptional luminaries, events and scriptures; and finding expression in locally conditioned, personally distinctive systems of belief, ritual, behaviour and institution. So, in religion, people become physicians to their own deepest needfulness, using healing powers latent in themselves and mediating others from outside to pursue and have a foretaste of the conditions in which there would be ultimate well-being and an end to sorrow.

The extent of the explanation

Now, at the end of the book, there is one question left to answer, namely how much the theory succeeds in explaining, assuming that it survives the critical evaluations of competent judges. It should be clear that the religions of the earth would in all essentials of belief, behaviour and development as set forth in chapter two be accounted for by the factors that have been proposed, chiefly the promptings of a mysterious cosmic context and our own powerful desire to maximise well-being. These religious essentials at least can be covered by wholly immanent factors, making the concept of special supernatural interventions and revelations superfluous to the explanation of religion. The structure of the cosmos and our own make-up would be sufficient to have produced it in all the respects dealt with in this book without such occasional spiritual promptings. The euonic quest should not and will not be deterred by the conceptual upheaval such a finding is apt to cause in some devout circles; its purpose is to enrich our experience, not to perpetuate our conjectures. Nor should this finding be misconstrued as a rejection of the existence of a transcendent, spiritual reality, which it clearly does not imply. But it does imply that the nature and workings of any spiritual reality which might in fact exist have in some major respects been imperfectly, even minimally, understood by at least some of our traditional religions.

There are of course additional questions which this book has not tried to answer: Why is the cosmos as it is? Why do we have an affective sense? Whence the forces that help and harm us? Is there any event that we can justifiably regard as genuinely incompatible with the workings of the cosmos or human life itself? These go beyond anybody's present knowledge. They are the province for the time being of metaphysical speculation, opinion, dogma and personal faith, all of which fall short of constituting knowledge in the time-honoured sense of justified true belief. But it would none the less seem, according to the view of things developed in this book, that there are two possible answers to them. Either they involve the brute facts of nature or they involve spiritual forces as yet very blurred in our vision, glimmerings of transcendence seen through a glass darkly, as St Paul once said, by our traditional religions. Those who think that finite reality is the cherished handiwork of a mysterious personal deity inviting it to fellowship and blessing through a long process of growth could perhaps see in the present theory an account of the activities and mental forms by which people gropingly come to faith in that deity. But it repudiates any allegation that those forms are perfect or permanent truths. Conceptual absolutism of this kind is an outright cognitive mistake, however psychologically comforting it may be for some.

Such, then, are the possibilities. To settle between them we ourselves have only those fallible but still fertile techniques of mental and practical experiment with which the drive to maximise well-being functions. Either we are at the twilight of the spiritual age and the triumph of materialistic naturalism, or we are at the daybreak of a revolutionary new age of faith beside which all existing doctrines will seem like roman numerals. Some there will be who out of desire for discovery and love of their fellows will experiment with their own lives to probe these options, perhaps finding in the end that they are one and the same and their apparent difference yet another confusion caused by the conditioning effect of inherited but faulty concepts. And in the meantime the search for true satisfaction will continue, a durable characteristic of human existence amidst the fading of former dreams.

Bibliography

Adams Brown, W., 'Salvation, Saviour', in J. Hastings (ed.), *A Dictionary of the Bible* (Edinburgh: T. & T. Clark, 1902) 357ff.

Aleksander, Igor, 'Artoo-Detoo, See-Threepio and the Mathematical Explanation of Living Things', in *The Times Higher Educational Supplement*, 17 April 1981.

Arberry, A. J., *The Koran Interpreted* (London: George Allen & Unwin, 1955 and 1980).

Attfield, R., *God and the Secular: a Philosophical Assessment of Secular Reasoning from Bacon to Kant* (University College Cardiff Press, 1978).

Aulén, Gustaf, *Jesus in Contemporary Research* (London: SPCK, 1976).

Baker, John Austin, *The Foolishness of God* (London: Darton, Longman & Todd, 1971).

Banton, Michael, *Anthropological Approaches to the Study of Religion* (London: Tavistock, 1966).

Barash, David, *Sociobiology: the Whisperings Within* (London: Souvenir Press, 1979).

Barbour, Ian G., *Myths, Models and Paradigms: the Nature of Scientific and Religious Language* (London: SCM, 1974).

Barr, James, 'An Aspect of Salvation in the Old Testament', in Eric J. Sharpe & John Hinnells, *Man and His Salvation: Studies in Honour of S. G. F. Brandon* (Manchester University Press, 1973) 39-52.

Becker, Gary S., *The Economic Approach to Human Behavior* (Chicago & London: University of Chicago Press, 1976).

Berger, Peter L., *The Social Reality of Religion* (Penguin Books, 1973).

——, *The Heretical Imperative: Contemporary Possibilities of Religious Affirmation* (London: Collins, 1980).

Bornkamm, Günther, *Jesus of Nazareth* (London: Hodder & Stoughton, 1960).

Boulding, Kenneth E., *The Image: Knowledge in Life and Society* (Ann Arbor, Michigan: The University of Michigan Press, 1956 and 1982).

Brand, Gerd, *The Essential Wittgenstein*, trs and with an intro. by Robert E. Innis (New York: Basic Books, Inc., 1979).

Brandon, S. G. F., *Man and His Destiny in the Great Religions* (Manchester University Press, 1962).

——, (ed.), *The Saviour God: Comparative Studies in the Concept of Salvation Presented to Edwin Oliver James* (Manchester University Press, 1963).

Brodbeck, May (ed.), *Readings in the Philosophy of the Social Sciences* (New York: The Macmillan Company, 1968).

——, 'Explanation, Prediction and "Imperfect Knowledge",' in Brodbeck, May (ed.), *Readings in the Philosophy of the Social Sciences* (New York: The Macmillan Co, 1968) pp 363ff.

Bronowski, Jacob, *The Origins of Knowledge and Imagination* (New Haven and London: Yale University Press, 1978).

Bruce, F. F., '"Our God and Saviour": a recurring Biblical pattern', in S. G. F. Brandon (ed.), *The Saviour God: Comparative Studies in the Concept of Salvation Presented to Edwin Oliver James* (Manchester University Press, 1963).

Buddhist Services and Gathas for Children (Depts of Sunday School of Buddhist Churches of America and Honpa Hongwanyi Mission of Hawaii).

Buddhist Service Book (San Francisco: Buddhist Churches of America, Bureau of Buddhist Education, 1967).

Buijs, G., 'The Role of the Mother-Goddess Mariamma in Natal', in *Religion in Southern Africa*, vol. 1, no. 1 (1980) 1ff.

Bullock, Alan and Stallybrass, Oliver (eds), *The Fontana Dictionary of Modern Thought* (London: Fontana/Collins, 1979).

Burkill, T. A., *Faith, Knowledge and Cosmopolitanism*, an inaugural lecture given at the University of Rhodesia (Salisbury: University of Rhodesia, 1971).

Burrell, David, *Analogy and Philosophical Language* (New Haven and London: Yale University Press, 1973).

Carpenter, Humphrey, *Jesus* (Oxford University Press, 1980).

Cassirer, Ernst, *Language and Myth*, trs by Susanne K. Langer (New York: Dover Publications, 1946).

Chomsky, Noam, *Cartesian Linguistics: a Chapter in the History of Rationalist Thought* (New York & London: Harper & Row, 1966).

——, *Language and Mind* (New York: Harcourt, Brace & World, Inc., 1968).

Cobb, John B. Jr., *The Structure of Christian Existence* (Philadelphia: The Westminster Press, 1967).

——, 'Explanation and Causation in History and the Social Sciences', in Cobb, John B. Jr and Schroeder, W. Widick. *Process Philosophy and Social Thought* (Chicago: Center for the Scientific Study of Religion, 1981) 3ff.

Cobb, John B. Jr., and Schroeder, W. Widick, *Process Philosophy and Social Thought* (Chicago: Center for the Scientific Study of Religion, 1981).

Conze, Edward, 'Buddhist Saviours', in S. G. F. Brandon (ed.), *The Saviour God: Comparative Studies in the Concept of Salvation Presented to Edwin Oliver James* (Manchester University Press, 1963) 67ff.

Cornford, F. M., *From Religion to Philosophy: a Study in the Origins of Western Speculation* (New York: Harper Torchbooks, 1957).

Cragg, Kenneth, *The Mind of the Qur'ān: Chapters in Reflection* (London: George Allen & Unwin., 1973).

Crosby, Donald A., *Interpretive Theories of Religion* (The Hague: Mouton, 1981).

Dampier, W. C., *A History of Science and Its Relations with Philosophy and Religion,* 4th edn (Cambridge University Press, 1977).

Dray, William H., *Laws and Explanation in History* (Oxford: Clarendon Press, 1957).

——, *Philosophy of History* (Englewood Cliffs: Prentice-Hall Inc, 1964).

Durkheim, Emile, *The Elementary Forms of the Religious Life*, trs. by Joseph Ward Swain (London: George Allen & Unwin, 1976).

Edgerton, Franklin, *The Bhagavad Gita: Translated and Interpreted* (Cambridge, Massachusetts: Harvard University Press, 1952).

Edwards, Paul (ed.), *The Encyclopaedia of Philosophy* (New York: The Macmillan Company and The Free Press; London: Collier-Macmillan Ltd, 1967).

Eliade, Mircea, *From Primitives to Zen: a Thematic Sourcebook of the History of Religions* (London: Collins Fount Paperbacks, 1977).

Encyclopaedia Judaica (Jerusalem, 1972).

Fairchild, Roy W., 'Delayed Gratification: a Psychological and Religious Analysis', in Strommen, Merton P. (ed.), *Research on Religious Development: a Comprehensive Handbook* (New York: Hawthorn Books Inc, 1978).

Feuerbach, Ludwig, *The Essence of Christianity*, trs by George Eliot (New York: Harper Torchbooks, 1957).

Feyerabend, Paul, *Against Method: Outline of an Anarchist Theory of Knowledge* (London: Verso, 1975 and 1978).

Flew, Antony, *God and Philosophy*, new edn (London: Hutchinson, 1974).

Frankfort, H. *et al.*, *Before Philosophy: the Intellectual Adventure of Ancient Man* (Baltimore: Penguin Books, 1971).

Franks, R. S., *The Work of Christ*, 2nd edn (London: Nelson, 1962).

Freud, Sigmund, *The Future of an Illusion*, trs by W. D. Rodson-Scott (London: Hogarth, 1943).

Friedrich, Gerhard (ed.), *Theological Dictionary of the New Testament*, vol. VII (Grand Rapids: Eerdmans, 1971).

Gallie, W. B., *Philosophy and the Historical Understanding* (London: Chatto & Windus, 1964).

Gardiner, Patrick, *The Nature of Historical Explanation* (London: Oxford University Press, 1952 and 1965).

Geering, Lloyd, *Faith's New Age: a Perspective on Contemporary Religious Change* (London: Collins, 1980).

Geertz, C., 'Religion as a Cultural System', in Banton, M. (ed.), *Anthropological Approaches to the Study of Religion* (London: Tavistock Publications, 1966) pp 1ff.

Glare, P. G. W. (ed.), *Oxford Latin Dictionary* (Oxford: Clarendon Press, 1982).

Goble, Frank G., *The Third Force: the Psychology of Abraham Maslow* (New York: Grossman Publishers, 1970).

Greeley, Andrew M., *Religion: a Secular Theory* (New York: The Free Press; London: Collier Macmillan, 1982).

Hall, Brian P., *The Development of Consciousness: a Confluent Theory of Values* (New York: Paulist Press, 1976).

Hallpike, C. R., *The Foundations of Primitive Thought* (Oxford: Clarendon Press, 1979).

Hammond-Tooke, W. D., 'Is There a Science of Religion?', in *Religion in Southern Africa*, vol. 3, no. 1, (1982) 3ff.

Hanson, N. R., *Perception and Discovery: an Introduction to Scientific Inquiry* (San Francisco: Freeman, Cooper & Co, 1969).

Hardy, Sir Alister, *The Divine Flame: an Essay Towards a Natural History of Religion* (London: Collins, 1966).

——, *The Biology of God: a Scientist's Study of Man the Religious Animal* (London: Jonathan Cape, 1975).

——, *The Spiritual Nature of Man: a Study of Contemporary Religious Experience* (Oxford: Clarendon Press, 1979).

Harré, R., *The Principles of Scientific Thinking* (London: Macmillan, 1970).

Harré, R. and Madden, E. H., *Causal Powers: a Theory of Natural Necessity* (Oxford. Blackwell: 1975).

Hastings, James (ed.)., *A Dictionary of the Bible* (Edinburgh: T & T. Clark, 1902).

Heidegger, Martin., *Being and Time* (London: SCM, 1962).

Hempel, Carl, 'The Function of General Laws in History, in *The Journal of Philosophy*, vol. 39 (1942).

——, 'The Logic of Functional Analysis', in May Brodbeck (ed.), *Readings in the Philosophy of the Social Sciences* (New York: Macmillan, 1968) 179–210.

——, 'Explanatory Incompleteness', in May Brodbeck (ed.), *Readings in the Philosophy of the Social Sciences* (New York: Macmillan, 1968) 398ff.

——, *Aspects of Scientific Explanation, and Other Essays in the Philosophy of Science* (New York: Free Press, 1965 and 1970).

Henslin, James M., *Introducing Sociology: Towards Understanding Life in Society* (New York: The Free Press; London: Collier Macmillan, 1975).

Hesse, Mary, 'Laws and Theories', in Paul Edwards (ed.), *The Encyclopedia of Philosophy*, vol. IV (New York: Macmillan & The Free Press; London: Collier-Macmillan, 1967) 404ff.

——, Revolutions and Reconstructions in the Philosophy of Science (Brighton: Harvester Press, 1980).

Hick, John (ed)., *Faith and the Philosophers* (London: Macmillan, 1964).

——, *Faith and Knowledge* (London: Collins Fontana Books, 1974).

——, 'Christology is an Age of Religious Pluralism', in *Journal of Theology for Southern Africa* no. 35 (June 1981) 4ff.

Hick, John, and Hebblethwaite, Brian (eds), *Christianity and Other Religions: Selected Readings* (London: Collins, 1980).

Hinchliff, P. and Young, D., *The Human Potential* (London: Darton, Longman and Todd, 1981).

Hinnells, John R., 'The Zoroastrian Doctrine of Salvation in the Roman World', in Eric J. Sharpe and John R. Hinnells (eds), *Man and His Salvation: Studies in Honour of S. G. F. Brandon* (Manchester University Press, 1973).

Hooper, Judith, 'Releasing the Mystic in Your Brain', *Science Digest*, May 1981, 79ff.

Hospers, John, *An Introduction to Philosophical Analysis*, 2nd edn (London: Routledge & Kegan Paul, 1967).

Hutchison, John A., *Paths of Faith*, 2nd edn (New York: McGraw-Hill Book Co., 1975).

Hutchison, John A., *Living Options in World Philosophy* (Honolulu: The University Press of Hawaii, 1977).

Interpreter's Dictionary of the Bible: an Illustrated Encyclopedia (Nashville and New York: Abingdon Press, 1962).

James, William, *The Varieties of Religious Experience: a Study in Human Nature* (London: Longmans, Green and Co, 1902).

Jaspers, Karl, *Vom Ursprung und Ziel der Geschichte* (Frankfurt & Hamburg: Fischer Bücherei, 1957).

——, *Philosophy*, 3 vols, trs. by E. B. Ashton (Chicago & London: The University of Chicago Press, 1970).

Kant, I., *Critique of Pure Reason*, trs. by Norman Kemp Smith (London: Macmillan, 1933).

Kaplan, Mordecai, *Judaism as a Civilization* (New York and London: Thomas Yoseloff, 1957).

Kenny, Anthony, *The Anatomy of the Soul: Historical Essays in the Philosophy of Mind* (Oxford: Basil Blackwell, 1973).

Kierkegaard, Søren, *The Concept of Anxiety: a Simple Psychologically*

Orienting Deliberation on the Dogmatic Issue of Hereditary Sin, trs by Reidar Thomte (Princeton University Press, 1980).

Kim, J., 'Explanation in Science', in Paul Edwards (ed.), *The Encyclopaedia of Philosophy*, vol. 3 (New York and London, 1967) 159ff.

Kramer, S. N., *Mythologies of the Ancient World* (New York: Doubleday, 1961).

Kuhn, Thomas S., *The Structure of Scientific Revolutions*, 2nd edn (Chicago University Press, 1970).

Küng, Hans, *Freud and the Problem of God*, trs. Edward Quinn (New Haven: Yale University Press, 1979).

Lacey, A. R., *A Dictionary of Philosophy* (London: Routledge & Kegan Paul, 1976).

Larouse Encyclopaedia of Mythology (London: Batchworth Press, 1959).

Laski, M., *Ecstacy: a Study of Some Secular and Religious Experiences* (London: Cresset Press, 1961).

Lewis, C. T. and Short, C., *A Latin Dictionary* (Oxford: Clarendon Press, 1962).

Lewis-Williams, J. D., 'Remarks on Southern San Religion and Art', in *Religion in Southern Africa*, vol. 1, no. 2 (July 1980), pp. 19ff.

——, *Believing and Seeing: Symbolic Meanings in Southern San Rock Paintings* (London: Academic Press, 1981).

Lin Yutang, *The Wisdom of China* (London: Michael Joseph, 1949).

Loder, James E., *The Transforming Moment: Understanding Convictional Experiences* (San Francisco: Harper, 1981).

Lucretius, *On the Nature of the Universe*, trs. R. E. Latham (Harmondsworth: Penguin Books, 1976).

McKeon, Richard (ed.), *Introduction to Aristotle* (New York: The Modern Library College Editions, 1947).

Mackie, J. L., *The Cement of the Universe: a Study of Causation* (Oxford: Clarendon Press, 1974).

Macquarrie, John, *An Existentialist Theology: a Comparison of Heidegger and Bultmann* (London: SCM Press, 1955).

Magee, Bryan, *Popper* (London: Fontana/Collins, 1973).

Malinowski, B., *A Scientific Theory of Culture, and Other Essays* (Chapel Hill: University of North Carolina Press, 1977).

Marx, Karl, *On Religion*, ed. by Saul K. Padover, The Karl Marx Library, vol. V (New York: McGraw-Hill Book Company, 1974).

Maslow, A. H., *Motivation and Personality* (New York: Harper, 1954).

——, *Towards a Psychology of Being* (Princeton: Van Nostrand, 1962).

——, *Religions, Values, and Peak Experiences*. New York: Penguin Books, 1976.

Miles, T. R., *Religious Experience* (London: Macmillan, 1972).

Milner, Peter M., *Physiological Psychology* (London & New York: Holt, Rinehart and Winston, 1971).

Moberg, David O. (ed), *Spiritual Well-Being: Sociological Perspectives* (Washington, DC: University Press of America, 1979).

Nagel, Ernest, *The Structure of Science: Problems in the Logic of Scientific Explanation* (London: Routledge & Kegan Paul, 1961).

Needham, Rodney, *Belief, Language, and Experience* (Oxford: Basil Blackwell, 1972).

Neil, William, *Concise Dictionary of Religious Quotations* (London & Oxford: Mowbrays, 1975).

Neill, Stephen, *Jesus Through Many Eyes: Introduction to the Theology of the New Testament* (Guildford and London: Lutterworth Press, 1976).

Nowell-Smith, P., 'Miracles – the Philosophical Approach, a reply to Mr Arnold Lunn', *Hibbert Journal*, vol. 48, July 1950, repr. in Rowe, W. L. and Wainwright, W. J. *Philosophy of Religion: Selected Readings* (New York: Harcourt Brace Jovanovich, Inc., 1973).

O'Hear, Anthony, *Karl Popper* (London: Routledge & Kegan Paul, 1980).

Otto, Rudolf, *The Idea of the Holy: an Inquiry into the Non-Rational Factor in the Idea of the Divine and Its Relation to the Rational* (London: Oxford University Press, 1931).

Owen, H. P., *Concepts of Deity* (London: Macmillan, 1971).

Oxtoby, Willard G., 'Reflections on the Idea of Salvation', in Eric J. Sharpe & John R. Hinnells (eds), *Man and His Salvation: Studies in Honour of S. G. F. Brandon* (Manchester University Press, 1973).

Palmer, Humphrey, *Analogy: a Study of Qualification and Argument in Theology* (London: Macmillan, 1973).

Parker, John William, *The Idea of Salvation in the World's Religions* (London: Macmillan, 1935).

Parrinder, E. G., 'An African Saviour God', in S. G. F. Brandon (eds), *The Saviour God: Comparative Studies in the Concept of Salvation Presented to Edwin Oliver James* (Manchester University Press, 1963) 117ff.

Parry, Thomas Alan, 'The Other Hemisphere and Wholeness', in *Pacific Theological Journal*, vol. VIII, no. 1 (1976) 5ff.

Penner, Hans H, 'The Poverty of Functionalism', in *History of Religions* vol. II (1971) 91ff.

Perrin, Norman, *Rediscovering the Teaching of Jesus* (London: SCM Press Ltd, 1967).

Phillips, D. Z., *Religion Without Explanation* (Oxford: Basil Blackwell, 1976).

Piaget, Jean, *The Construction of Reality in the Child* (New York: Basic Books, 1954).

——, *The Development of Thought: Equilibration of Cognitive Structures* (Oxford: Basil Blackwell, 1978).

Piattelli-Palmarini, M. (ed.), *Language and Learning: the Debate*

Between Jean Piaget and Noam Chomsky (London: Routledge & Kegan Paul, 1980).

Pokorny, Julius, *Indogermanisches Etymologisches Wörterbuch* (I. Band. Bern and München: Francke Verlag, 1959).

Polanyi, Michael, *Personal Knowledge: Towards a Post-Critical Philosophy* (London: Routledge & Kegan Paul, 1978).

Pope, Marvin H., *El in the Ugaritic Texts*, Supplements to *Vetus Testamentum*, vol. II (Leiden: E. J. Brill, 1955).

Popper, Karl, *The Poverty of Historicism* (London: Routledge & Kegan Paul, 1961).

——, *Conjectures and Refutations* (London: Routledge & Kegan Paul, 1963; 2nd ed, 1965).

——, *The Logic of Scientific Discovery* (London, Hutchinson, 1959; 3rd edition 1968).

——, *Objective Knowledge: an Evolutionary Approach* (Oxford: Clarendon Press, 1972).

Porter, Dale H., 'Explaining the Historical Process', in *Process Studies*, vol. 9 (1979) 73ff.

Prozesky, Martin, 'The Young Schleiermacher', in *Journal of Theology for Southern Africa*, no. 37 (December 1981), pp. 50ff.

Pye, Michael, *Skilful Means: a Concept in Mahayana Buddhism* (London: Duckworth, 1978).

Quine, W. V., *Ontological Relativity and Other Essays* (New York and London: Columbia University Press, 1969).

Quinton, Anthony, *The Nature of Things*, 2nd edn (London: Routledge & Kegan Paul, 1973).

Radhakrishnan, Sarvepalli and Moore, Charles A. (eds), *A Source Book in Indian Philosophy* (Princeton University Press, 1957 and 1967).

Richardson, Alan, 'Salvation, Savior', in *The Interpreter's Dictionary of the Bible*, vol. 4 (New York & Nashville: Abingdon Press, 1962) 168ff.

Rowe, W. L. and Wainwright, W. J., *Philosophy of Religion: Selected Readings* (New York: Harcourt Brace Jovanovitch, Inc., 1973).

Sage, George H., *Introduction to Motor Behavior: a Neurophysiological Approach*, 2nd edn (Reading, Massachusetts: Addison-Wesley Publishing Co, 1977).

Samuelson, P., *Foundations of Economic Analysis* (Cambridge: Harvard University Press, 1948).

——, *Economics: an Introductory Analysis* (New York: McGraw-Hill, 1967).

Sartre, Jean-Paul, *Being and Nothingness: an Eassy on Phenomeno-logical Ontology* (London: Methuen, 1957).

Schleiermacher, F. D. E., *Über die Religion: Reden an die gebildeten unter ihren verächtern* (2nd edn 1806; text given in the critical edition by B. Pünjer: Brunswick, 1879).

Sen, Amartya and Williams, Bernard (eds), *Utilitarianism and Beyond* (London: Cambridge University Press, 1982).

Sharpe, Eric J. and Hinnells, John R (eds), *Man and His Salvation: Studies in Honour of S. G. F. Brandon* (Manchester University Press, 1973).

Shaw, R. D. M., *Enlightenment and Salvation* (London, 1930).

Shutte, A., 'A Theory of Religion', in *International Philosophical Quarterly*, vol. XVI, no. 3 (Sept. 1976) 289ff.

Smart, N., *The Concept of Worship* (London: Macmillan, 1972).

——, *The Science of Religion and the Sociology of Knowledge: Some Methodological Questions* (Princeton University Press, 1973).

——, 'Beyond Eliade: the Future of Theory in Religion', in *Numen*, vol. XXV (1978) pp. 171–83.

——, *Beyond Ideology: Religion and the Future of Western Civilization* (London: Collins, 1981).

Smith, Wilfred Cantwell, *The Meaning and End of Religion* (London: SPCK, 1978).

——, *Faith and Belief* (Princeton University Press, 1979).

——, *Towards a World Theology*, Library of philosophy and religion (London: Macmillan, 1981).

Spiro, Melford, 'Religion: Problems of Definition and Explanation', in M. Banton (ed.), *Anthropological Approaches to the Study of Religion* (London: Tavistock, 1966).

Starbuck, Edwin D., *The Psychology of Religion: an Empirical Study of the Growth of Religious Consciousness*, 4th edn (London: The Walter Scott Publishing Co., 1914).

Strawson, P. F., *Individuals: an Essay in Descriptive Metaphysics* (London: Methuen, 1959).

Strommen, Merton P. (ed.)., *Research on Religious Development: a Comprehensive Handbook* (New York: Hawthorn Books, Inc., 1978).

Suzuki, D. T., *Manual of Zen* (London: Rider & Co., 1970).

Swinburne, Richard, *The Existence of God* (Oxford: Clarendon Press, 1979).

Tart, Charles T. (ed.)., *Transpersonal Psychologies* (New York etc: Harper & Row, 1975).

Taylor, Charles, *The Explanation of Behaviour* (London: Routledge & Regan Paul; and New York: The Humanities Press, 1964).

Taylor, Richard, 'Causation', in Paul Edwards (ed). *The Encyclopedia of Philosophy* (New York: Macmillan Co. & The Free Press; London: Collier-Macmillan, 1967, vol. II, 56ff).

Thakur, Shivesh Chandra, *Religion and Rational Choice*, Library of philosophy and religion (London: Macmillan, 1981).

Thomas, Lewis, *The Lives of a Cell: Notes of a Biology Watcher* (Toronto, New York & London: Bantam Books Inc., 1975).

Thomas, Owen C. (ed.), *Attitudes Towards Other Religions* (London:

SCM Press, 1969).

Thompson, Laurence G., *Chinese Religion: an Introduction*, 3rd edn, The religious life of man series (Belmont, California: Wadsworth, 1979).

Tillich, Paul, *Systematic Theology*, vol. I (University of Chicago Press, 1951).

——, *Biblical Religion and the Search for the Personal* (London: James Nisbet & Co. Ltd, 1955).

——, *The Courage to be* (London: The Fontana Library, 1965).

Toulmin, Stephen, *The Uses of Argument* (Cambridge University Press, 1964).

Trigg, Roger, *The Shaping of Man: Philosophical Aspects of Sociobiology* (Oxford: Basil Blackwell, 1982).

Tyler, E. B., *Primitive Culture: Researches into the Development of Mythology, Philosophy, Religion, Language, Art, and Custom* (London: 1871).

Underhill, Ruth M., *Red Man's Religion: Beliefs and Practices of the Indians North of Mexico* (Chicago & London: The University of Chicago Press, 1965).

Van der Leeuw, G., *Religion in Essence and Manifestation* (London: George Allen & Unwin Ltd, 1938).

Vermes, Geza., *Jesus the Jew: a Historian's Reading of the Gospels* (London: Fontana/Collins, 1973).

Verryn, Trevor. '"Coolness" and "Heat" among the Sotho Peoples', in *Religion in Southern Africa*, 1981, vol. 2, no. 1, 11ff.

Vidler, Alec R., *The Church in an Age of Revolution* (Harmondsworth: Penguin Books, 1968).

von Wright, Georg Henrik, *Explanation and Understanding* (Ithaca: Cornell University Press, 1971).

Waismann, Friedrich, *The Principles of Linguistic Philosophy*, ed. by R. Harré (London: Macmillan, 1965).

Waley, Arthur. (trs), *The Analects of Confucius* (New York: Vintage Books, 1938).

Walsh, W. H., 'The Intelligibility of History', in *Philosophy*, vol. 27, 1942.

Weingartner, Rudolf, 'The Quarrel About Historical Explanation', in Brodbeck, May (ed.), *Readings in the philosophy of the social sciences* (New York: The Macmillan Company, 1968).

Werblowsky, R. J. Zwi and Bleeker, C. Jouco (eds), *Types of Redemption*, Studies in the History of Religions, XVIII (Leiden: E. J. Brill, 1970).

Westermann, C., 'Salvation and Healing in the Community: the Old Testament Understanding', in *International Review of Mission*, vol. LXI (1972) 9–19.

——, *Creation* (London: SPCK, 1974).

——, *What Does the Old Testament Say About God?* (Atlanta: John Knox Press, 1979).

Whitehead, A. N., *Process and Reality: an Essay in Cosmology*, corrected edition (New York: The Free Press, 1978).

Widengren, Geo., 'Salvation in Iranian Religion', in Eric J. Sharpe & John R. Hinnells (eds), *Man and His Salvation: Studies in Honour of S. G. F. Brandon* (Manchester University Press, 1973).

Wieman, H. N., *Man's Ultimate Commitment* (Cardondale, Illinois: Southern Illinois University Press, 1958).

Wilson, Edward O., *Sociobiology: the New Synthesis* (Cambridge, Massachusetts, and London: The Belknap Press, 1975).

Winch, Peter, *The Idea of a Social Science and Its Relation to Philosophy* (London: Routledge & Kegan Paul, 1958).

Wittgenstein, Ludwig, *The Blue and Brown Books* (Oxford: Basil Blackwell, 1958).

——, *Value and Culture*, trs by Peter Winch (Oxford: Basil Blackwell, 1980).

Woods, G. F., *Theological Explanation* (Welwyn: James Nisbet and Co. Ltd., 1958).

Wright, Larry., *Teleological Explanations: an Etiological Analysis of Goals and Functions* (Berkeley: University of California Press, 1976).

Yang, C. K., *Religion in Chinese Society* (Berkeley and Los Angeles: University of California Press, 1967).

Young, J. Z., *Introduction to the Study of Man* (Oxford: Clarendon Press, 1971).

——, *Programs of the Brain* (London: Oxford University Press, 1978).

Yusuf Ali, Abdullah, *The Holy Qur-an: Text, Translation & Commentary*, 2 vols (Lahore, 1938).

Zaehner, R. C., *Hinduism* (London: Oxford University Press, 1962).

——, 'Salvation in the Mahabharata', in S. G. F. Brandon. (ed.), *The Saviour God: Comparative Studies in the Concept of Salvation Presented to Edwin Oliver James* (Manchester University Press, 1963) 218ff.

(All biblical quotations except the one on p.27 come from the New English Bible. The exception is from the Revised Standard Version.)

Index

187f, 215, 217, 230
Transcendent, the, 23, 41, 54ff, 56,
  58, 66, 157f, 187, 229, 231,
  233, 234
Trigg, Roger, 110
Trinity (in Christian doctrine), 18,
  50
Truth, 138f
Tycho Brahe, 212
Tylor, E.B., 159

Ultimate explanations, *see*
  Explanations, ultimate
Ultimate reality, *passim*, but see 62,
  163f, 188, 202, 205, 209, 230
Ultimate, the concept of the, 163f
Ultimate well-being, *passim*, but see
  9, 11, 21, 34, 153ff, 161ff, 185,
  186, 188, 205f, 209, 214, 227,
  230, 232, 234
Underhill, Ruth M., 44, 51, 52
Upanishads, 37, 50, 198, 199
Upaya, 211f
Utilitarian ethics, 109

Values, 49, 50, 116, 118, 149, 157,
  177, 180
Van der Leeuw, G., 46, 53, 161
Vedas, 53, 168, 173
Vermes, Geza, 30
Verryn, Trevor, 143
Vidler, Alec R., 216
Vishnu, 36, 150
Visionaries in religion, 206

Waley, Arthur, 42, 233
Walsh, W.H., 74
Weingartner, Rudolf, 71f
Well-being
  generally, *passim* but see 103f,
    115, 117, 158f, 180, 185, 196,
    197, 204
  drive to maximise, *see* Drive to
    maximise well-being

material or physical, 105ff, 210f
sense or experience of, *passim* but
  see 21, 48, 94, 171
Werblowsky, R.J. Zwi, 45
Westermann, Claus, 28, 171
Whitehead, A.N., 1, 226
Widengren, Geo, 35
Wieman, H.N., 47, 54
Wiener, Norbert, 111
Wiles, Maurice, xi
Williams, Bernard, 109
Will, will power, 133
Wilson, Edward O., 110, 161
Winch, Peter, 73
Winnebago Indians, 170
Wittgenstein, Ludwig, 101
Woods, G.F. 73, 79f
World-views
  characteristics of, 2, 123ff
  generally, *passim* but see 72f,
    159ff, 175, 188, 196, 198f,
    207, 214, 215, 230
  spiritual, *see* Spiritual world-view
Worship, 44, 54, 178f, 179, 186,
  202f, 204
Wright, Georg Henrik von, 75
Wright, Larry, 75
Writing, invention of, 200, 231

Yahweh, 24, 27, 50, 180, 216, 232
Yang, C.K. 41, 43, 48, 51
Young, David, 158
Young, J.Z., 114f, 116, 118, 127f,
  129, 173
Yusuf Ali, Abdullah, 32, 33, 34

Zaehner, R.C. 38
Zambia, 171
Zazen, 115
Zen Buddhism : *see* Buddhism, Zen
Zimbabwe, 45, 95
Zoroaster, 35
Zoroastrianism, 35
Zulus, 4, 99, 176

DATE DUE

14 Aug 86			

PRINTED IN U.S.A.